The European Community and the Management of International Cooperation

The European Community and the Management of International Cooperation

LEON HURWITZ

CONTRIBUTIONS IN POLITICAL SCIENCE, NUMBER 181

GREENWOOD PRESS
NEW YORK
WESTPORT, CONNECTICUT
LONDON

Library of Congress Cataloging-in-Publication Data

Hurwitz, Leon.
  The European Community and the management of
international cooperation.

  (Contributions in political science,
ISSN 0147-1066 ; no. 181)
  Bibliography: p.
  Includes index.
  1. European Economic Community.   2. Commission of
the European Communities.   3. European Parliament.
4. European federation.   I. Title.   II. Series.
HC241.2.H87   1987   337.1'4   87-229
ISBN 0-313-25030-8 (lib. bdg. : alk. paper)

British Library Cataloguing in Publication Data is available.

Library of Congress Catalog Card Number: 87-229
ISBN: 0-313-25030-8
ISSN: 0147-1066

First published in 1987

Greenwood Press, Inc.
88 Post Road West, Westport, Connecticut 06881

Printed in the United States of America

∞™

The paper used in this book complies with the
Permanent Paper Standard issued by the National
Information Standards Organization (Z39.48-1984).

10   9   8   7   6   5   4   3   2   1

TO

Irv, Barbara, Richard, Beverly, Shalom, and Ellen

Contents

Figures

Tables

Acknowledgments

The Department of Political Science at Cleveland State University, especially its chairperson Paul Dommel, has been most generous in terms of financial assistance and for providing an atmosphere conducive to research and writing. For efficient secretarial and support services, my thanks go to Carol Lattig and Ruth Ponikvar. I also want to thank the editorial and production staffs at Greenwood Press for their professional assistance, particularly Margaret Brezicki, Penny Sippel, and Mim Vasan. Jim Sabin deserves special mention since he helped define the nature of this book, and his continuous support is appreciated. In addition, Europa Publications, Ltd. (London), granted permission to print some previously copyrighted material. Finally, my wife Fran, and my children Elise and Jonathan, have been understanding of the demands of academic pursuits.

Abbreviations/Acronyms

ACP	African, Caribbean, and Pacific States
BENELUX	Belgium, the Netherlands, Luxembourg
BEU	BENELUX Economic Union
BLEU	Belgium-Luxembourg Economic Union
CAP	Common Agricultural Policy
CDU	Christian Democratic Union
CET	Common External Tariff
CMEA	Council of Mutual Economic Assistance
COMECON	Council of Mutual Economic Assistance
COMSAT	Communications Satellite Corporation
COPA	Committee of Professional Agricultural Organizations in the European Community
COPENUR	Standing Committee on Uranium Enrichment
COREPER	Committee of Permanent Representatives
CPR	Committee of Permanent Representatives
CREST	Scientific and Technical Research Committee
CSCE	Conference on Security and Cooperation in Europe
CSU	Christian Social Union
DG	Directorate-Général/Director General
EAD	Euro-Arab Dialogue
EAGGF	European Agricultural Guidance and Guarantee Fund
EC	European Community
ECHR	European Convention on Human Rights
ECJ	European Court of Justice

ECSC	European Coal and Steel Community
ECU	European Currency Unit
ED	European Democrats
EDC	European Defense Community
EDF	European Development Fund
EEC	European Economic Community
EFTA	European Free Trade Association
EIB	European Investment Bank
EMCF	European Monetary Cooperation Fund
EMS	European Monetary System
EP	European Parliament
EPC	European Political Cooperation
ERDF	European Regional Development Fund
ERP	European Recovery Program
ESC	Economic and Social Committee
ESF	European Social Fund
ETUC	European Trade Union Confederation
EUA	European Unit of Account
EURATOM	European Atomic Energy Community
FB	Belgian Franc
FDP	Free Democratic Party
FLUX	Luxembourg Franc
GATT	General Agreement on Tariffs and Trade
ICC	International Chamber of Commerce
IEPG	Independent European Program Group
IGO	Intergovernmental Organization
IRA	International Ruhr Authority
IVC	Index of Voting Cohesion
IVL	Index of Voting Likeness between Groups
JRC	Joint Research Center
MCA	Monetary Compensation Amount
MEP	Member, European Parliament
MFN	Most-Favored-Nation
MP	Member of Parliament
NATO	North Atlantic Treaty Organization
NCI	New Community Instrument for Borrowing and Lending
NGO	Nongovernmental Organization
OAPEC	Organization of Arab Petroleum Exporting Countries

OECD	Organization for Economic Cooperation and Development
OEEC	Organization for European Economic Cooperation
OPEC	Organization of Petroleum Exporting Countries
PD	Progressive Democrats
PPE	European Peoples Party
R & D	Research and Development
RA	Relative Acceptance
RI	Relative Intensity
SACEUR	Supreme Allied Commander, Europe
SACLANT	Supreme Allied Commander, Atlantic
SEPLIS	European Secretariat of the Liberal, Intellectual, and Social Professions
STABEX	Commodity Export Earnings Stabilization Scheme
SYSMIN	Mineral Accident Insurance System
TVA	Value-Added-Tax
UA	Unit of Account
UEMO	European Union of General Practitioners
UK	United Kingdom
UN	United Nations
UNICE	Union of Industries of the European Community
US	United States
USSR	Union of Soviet Socialist Republics
VAT	Value-Added-Tax
WCL	World Confederation of Labor
WEU	Western European Union
WHO	World Health Organization
WUDO	Western Union Defense Organization

The European Community and the Management of International Cooperation

Introduction: The Management of International Cooperation

The basis for the management of international cooperation, the harmonization of public policy across national frontiers, the formulation and coordination of regional responses to transnational challenges, and the existence of regional interdependence is the differential distribution of needs, aspirations, and capabilities of states and their peoples. These differences have played an important role in the establishment of intergorvernmental organizations (IGOs—organizations whose members are nation-states) and international nongovernmental organizations (NGOs—organizations comprised of nongovernmental entities). Some examples of IGOs are the United Nations (UN) and the European Community (EC); examples of NGOs are the International Chamber of Commerce (ICC) and the World Confederation of Labor (WCL). In some instances, mixed units have been formed—the members are nation-states and nongovernmental units; for example, large business corporations (COMSAT—Communications Satellite Corporation).

Showing a remarkable growth in the post–World War II era, both IGOs and NGOs have become increasingly significant factors in world politics. The total number of IGOs operating in 1986 was approximately 400, but this proliferation should not be surprising. The number of nation-states has more than tripled since the end of World War II, largely as a consequence of decolonization, and the number of nation-states who are members of the United Nations now exceeds 155.

THE NATURE OF INTERGOVERNMENTAL ORGANIZATIONS

Basically, IGOs are established by three or more states to fulfill common purposes or obtain common objectives.[1] In most instances, they constitute the framework for political and military alliances or economic cooperation schemes.

IGOs possess a number of particular features that are examined briefly here. The purposes and objectives of IGOs reflect common or converging national interests of the member-states and, therefore, are nominally long range in nature.

The achievement of IGO goals is theoretically carried out with the equal participation of all states although, in practice, this is often not the case. The process of achieving IGO goals is best described as a round-table operation. This is in contrast to normal one-on-one diplomacy under bilateral treaties through which two states may also pursue common purposes but for which the basis is trade-offs of advantages and disadvantages between the participating governments.

The most distinguishing feature of an IGO is its institutional framework. This framework may be very simple and consist of nothing more than a lightly staffed secretariat; or it may be complex and comprehensive, approximating the legislative, executive, and judicial branches of a national government. In most instances, however, the legislative functions are quite limited. Representatives of the member-states of the IGO normally meet in an annual plenary conference at which general policy is laid down. Decisions usually require a two-thirds majority and, in special circumstances, unanimity. A council (usually composed of the permanent representatives of the member-governments) is frequently entrusted with supervising the day-to-day executive functions of the IGO. It meets more frequently than the conference and almost always decides questions by unanimous vote. The performance of judicial functions is normally carried out by selected international tribunals, such as the International Court of Justice, which is a principal organ of the United Nations, but to which other IGOs may also assign jurisdictional competencies. Or a special court may be established, such as the European Community's Court of Justice.

IGOs are always established by a multilateral international treaty. This treaty is often called a convention, a charter, or a constitution. It stipulates the competencies of the intergovernmental or bureaucratic organs of the IGO, the interrelations among them, and sets up the basic norms and operational principles of the organization.

IGOs are considered to have "international legal personality," which means that, under international law, they can act in some ways similar to a state: some have standing to sue or may be sued in the appropriate judicial body. They can conclude international treaties in their own name, and diplomatic missions from their own member-states, as well as from other states or from NGOs, can be accredited to them.

THE REASON FOR INTERGOVERNMENTAL ORGANIZATION

As mentioned above, IGOs are established to attain the common objectives of the member-states. These objectives reflect common or converging national interests and thus are normally long range in nature, and the achievement of these objectives is theoretically carried out with the equal participation of all states, although this is often not the case in practice.

These common/converging interests can be varied, but the enhancement of a country's security and the hoped-for assurance that international peace can be maintained are major interests. Another set of interests may be advancing the level of economic development; raising the economic well-being of a country's citizens; managing economic interdependence in the world; and, in conjunction with national policy, participating in and perhaps controlling the exploration, marketing, and pricing of raw materials. Another important interest pursued through IGOs may be the strengthening of the political power of states. Finally, a major set of interests can be served by using IGOs to search for solutions arising from scientific and technological problems that emanate from worldwide communications and transportation as well as environmental problems, such as the transnational spread of pollution, and nuclear issues. Appropriate solutions may be increased border-crossing cooperation to enhance the technological capabilities of the individual states.

Although the above discussion of nation-states' interests reflects a variety of motivations for the establishment of IGOs, a determination must be made under what conditions a national government will resort to the instrument of intergovernmental organization to satisfy these and other interests. It is fair to assume that, under normal circumstances, a government will employ *national* means to meet its security, political, economic, scientific, and technological needs because, if it does decide to become involved in setting up an IGO for whatever purpose or to join an existing IGO, its independence and freedom of action will be impaired to some degree, even if the management authority conferred upon the IGO is very low. Moreover, relations with other member-countries of the IGO impose differing restraints on the actions and behavior of all participating governments.

INTERGOVERNMENTAL ORGANIZATION AND
INTERNATIONAL INTERDEPENDENCE

The governmental decision whether to organize multilaterally for the pursuit and satisfaction of particular interests depends to a large extent on a country's political, economic, security, and technological capabilities and resources. If these are perceived to be sufficient to ensure the successful implementation of appropriate domestic and foreign policies, then international organization through establishing or joining IGOs may not be desirable. If, on the other hand, national capabilities are not regarded as adequate—while IGOs appear to offer a more likely path to assuring the satisfaction of important national interests—then a state may be more inclined to encourage the performance of the necessary tasks multilaterally through the creation of appropriate IGOs. These are basically the circumstances forming the background for what John Ruggie calls a state's "propensity for international organization."[2]

Several propositions formulated by Ruggie seem to characterize the basic decision of governments to set up or join IGOs for the enhancement of national interests in various policy areas:

1. The propensity for international organization is determined by the interplay between the need to become dependent upon others for the performance of specific tasks and the general desire to keep such dependence to the minimum level necessary.

2. There exists an inverse relationship between the ratio of international to national task performance and the total level of national resources a state possesses. In other words, from the perspective of the state, the greater its resources, the lower the number and scope of tasks assigned to IGOs for performance and the more of its resources that can be assigned to national task performance.

3. The propensity for international organization decreases over time as national capabilities increase and become sufficient to perform a given task.

4. A process of encapsulation built into the international performance of any given task tends toward limiting further commitments to, or further increase in the scope or capacity of, the collective arrangements.[3]

The general loss of independence or the loss of control over a state's own activities resulting from the accumulation of collective restraints caused by the creation and behavior of IGOs is termed by Ruggie "interdependence" costs. There is a large amount of literature on this concept of "interdependence," and the following discussion presents a brief description of interdependence and its effects on national governments and IGOs.

William Coplin and Michael O'Leary describe "interdependence" as the existence of conditions in which the perceived needs of some individual groups in one state are satisfied by resources or capabilities that exist in at least one other state. The patterns of transnational interdependence thus are a product of the interface between needs and capabilities across national boundaries.[4] Such capabilities—military forces, economic and financial means, industrial and technological proficiency—can be translated into international power and influence while their absence may signal serious vulnerability. Small states are usually more modest in their policy goals than the big powers because of more limited resources although the skillful exploitation of a larger country's weaknesses may compensate for limitations in resources.

Another view of interdependence has been put forth by Oran Young, who defines it as "the extent to which events occurring in any given part or within any given component of a world system affect (either physically or perceptually) events taking place in each of the other parts or component units of the system."[5] Directed primarily to economics, Richard Cooper suggests that interdependence is present when there is an increased "sensitivity" to external economic developments.[6] Robert Keohane and Joseph Nye also emphasize sensitivity as a dimension of interdependence. According to them it "involves degrees of responsiveness within a policy framework—how quickly do changes in one country bring costly changes in another, and how great are the costly effects?''[7] A second dimension of interdependence stressed by Keohane and Nye is "vulnerability" that "rests on the relative availability and costliness of the alternatives that various actors face."[8] Vulnerability reflects a country's or IGO's or a private actor's varying inability to accept and cope with economic, political, and social costs imposed by external events even if policies have been or will be changed.

It is the inequality of capabilities within interdependence relationships that at times evokes fears of dependence in governments and nongovernmental entities. Instead of producing perceptions of *reciprocal* dependence that might induce governments to treat the acts of other governments or IGOs as though they were events within their own borders and might be seen within the context of converging—if not identical—interests, *unequal* capabilities among states are likely to lead to suspicion, envy, and tensions.[9] Hence, governmental leaders may feel called upon to resort to national means and solutions as a countervailing force against the real or imagined threat of dependence on other countries or private entities. Such actions harm the prospects of useful collaboration among states and are likely to undermine, if not destroy, the benefits that interdependence networks may produce. Perceptions of this dependence have aggravated all other problems that many leaders of developing countries have faced in their priority task of nation building and their consequent preoccupation with sovereignty and autonomy of choice.

During recent years, US foreign policy regarded growing interdependence as not only inevitable, but also desirable in producing consensus and restraining unacceptable international conduct. It was viewed as a positive value, and the State Department promoted the idea of purposefully pursuing a strategy of interdependence that included the deliberate support of larger entities such as the European Community.[10] These views are not shared in all quarters, however. Many Third World—as well as a number of Western—intellectuals look at interdependence as creating undesirable dependence, and some think it is a code word for economic bondage.[11] They see a widening economic gap between affluent and poor societies. For these observers, the process of interdependence escalates tensions over the restrictions of national or societal autonomy; threatens the achievement of national economic, social, and political objectives; and may produce violent nationalist and interstate conflict.

This brings the discussion back to IGO organizational tasks, which include the management of cooperation through coordination and harmonization measures, the achievement of compromise, the selection of appropriate goal-attaining strategies, and the resolution of conflicts. The effective execution of these tasks can produce or maintain beneficial interdependent relationships, accomplish a more adequate distribution of costs, resolve perceptions of dependency, and initiate new interdependent arrangements that maximally promote the interests of all participants.

THE EUROPEAN COMMUNITY AND INTERNATIONAL
INTERDEPENDENCE

It is in Western Europe that one finds the best examples of regional interde-
pendence-enhancement through the international management of cooperation and
the harmonization of certain public policies by various IGOs and NGOs. Although there have been many management failures, several European organizations have played an important role in the management of cooperation and
policy coordination-harmonization, and it is the European Community institutional framework that has enjoyed the most success in Europe.

This book discusses the European Community's experience in the international
management of cooperation. Part I presents a brief overview of the historical
background of the European Community and also presents some comments on
the organization's early years. Part II describes the Community's institutional
framework—a remarkable example of the transfer of certain national sovereign
powers and prerogatives to a supranational organization. Part III examines some
of the management tasks assigned to the European Community; some of these
have met with success, others have been outstanding failures. The chapter that
forms Part IV—the Conclusion—reviews the quality of the European
Community.

NOTES

The comments in this Introduction borrow from Werner J. Feld, Robert S. Jordan,
and Leon Hurwitz, *International Organizations: A Comparative Approach* (New York:
Praeger, 1983), esp. chapter 1, "Changing Conceptualizations" (pp. 9–42) and chapter
2, "The Creation of Intergovernmental Organizations" (pp. 43–84); and from Leon
Hurwitz, ed., *The Harmonization of European Public Policy: Regional Responses to
Transnational Challenges* (Westport, Conn: Greenwood, 1983), esp. chapter 1, "The
Harmonization of European Public Policy," pp. 3–23.

1. This is part of the conventional definition. Michael Wallace and J. David Singer
argue that bilaterally created IGOs should not be excluded; otherwise organizations such
as the Canadian-American North American Defense Command (NORAD) and the Saint
Lawrence Seaway Commission would be excluded. See their "Intergovernmental Organizations in the Global System, 1815–1964: A Quantitative Description," 24 *International Organization* (Spring 1970), 239–287.

2. John Ruggie, "Collective Goods and Future International Collaboration," 66
American Political Science Review (September 1972), 874–893.

3. Ibid., p. 882.

4. William D. Coplin and Michael K. O'Leary, "A Policy Analysis Framework for
Research, Education and Policy-Making in International Relations," paper delivered to
the 1974 International Studies Association Convention, St. Louis, Mo.

5. Oran Young, "Interdependence in World Politics," 24 *International Journal* (Au-
tumn 1969), 726.

6. Richard N. Cooper, *The Economics of Interdependence* (New York: McGraw-Hill, 1968), pp. 3–8.

7. Robert O. Keohane and Joseph S. Nye, *Power and Interdependence: World Politics in Transition* (Boston: Little, Brown, 1977), p. 12.

8. Ibid., p. 13.

9. An extensive literature on the issue of Third World dependency has evolved during the last few years. For example, the entire issue of 32 *International Organization* (Winter 1978) is devoted to dependency and dependence with five articles focusing on theoretical aspects and four dealing with regional problems. See also Richard B. Fagan, "Studying Latin American Politics: Some Implications of a Dependence Approach," 12 *Latin American Research Review* (1977): 3–26; Robert R. Kaufman, Harry I. Chermotsky, and Daniel S. Geller, "A Preliminary Test of the Theory of Dependence," 7 *Comparative Politics* (April 1975), 303–330; Benjamin Cohen, *The Question of Imperialism* (New York: Basic Books, 1973); and Thomas Moran, *Multinational Corporations and the Politics of Dependence* (Princeton, N.J.: Princeton University Press, 1974).

10. US Department of State, *Toward a Strategy of Interdependence* (Washington, D.C.: Bureau of Public Affairs, July 1975).

11. See Hayward A. Alker, Lincoln P. Bloomfield, and Nazli Choucri, *Analyzing Global Interdependence*, vol. 2 (Cambridge, Mass.: MIT Center for International Studies, 1974), p. 3.

PART I

Historical Background and the Early Years

The signing of the European Economic Community (EEC) Treaty in Rome on 25 March 1957 by France, West Germany, Italy, Belgium, the Netherlands, and Luxembourg represented a historic event. Six sovereign independent countries—each with its own separate history, culture, language, and traditions, and whose past relations were usually characterized more by suspicion and warfare than by cooperation and the resolution of conflict by peaceful means—willingly and voluntarily created a supranational organization. This historic transfer of sovereignty was based on the realization that the future of Western Europe could be secured only by greater international cooperation and integration.

The EEC (popularly called the "Common Market" but now generally referred to as the "European Community" [EC]) was not created in a vacuum. The present Community is the result of a long progression of events and attitude changes within Europe—a painful process at times—and the early years of the Community was a period characterized by strained relations within Western Europe. Part I discusses this historical background and the early years.

Chapter 1 discusses some events that can reasonably be interpreted as setting the stage for or leading toward the European Community. It is most probable that the individuals involved in these preparatory stages did not realize or foresee the eventual result but, since this chapter has the benefit of hindsight, we are able to make the linkages. Some of these attempts at international cooperation and integration were remarkably successful (e.g., the European Coal and Steel Community), while others (e.g., the European Defense Community) were abject failures. But even the failures contributed to the inexorable realization by Europeans that there was no viable alternative to political cooperation. In one sense, the failures might have contributed more to the process because they sensitized the policymakers and the population to the risks of unbridled nationalism and unlimited sovereignty. Chapter 2 discusses the period from the establishment of the EC in 1958 until the accession of Great Britain in 1973.

1

The Road to Rome

THE BELGIUM-LUXEMBOURG ECONOMIC UNION (1922)/
THE BENELUX ECONOMIC UNION (1960)

The Belgium-Luxembourg Economic Union (BLEU), a 50-year agreement on the elimination of most tariffs and customs duties between the two countries, was established in 1922. After World War II, the Netherlands entered into negotiations with BLEU, and on 1 January 1948, a customs union among the three countries was established.[1] This 1948 agreement was closely patterned after the 1922 BLEU arrangement, but no real *political* integration was envisaged in 1948, and even the economic coordination measures were slow to develop. Nevertheless, this 1948 agreement among the BENELUX countries—a remarkable experiment for three small countries whose total combined area is approximately 75,000 km^2 and whose combined population is roughly 25 million— eventually produced a microcosm of the future European Community. All duties, tariffs, and other artificial barriers to trade among the three countries were eliminated; a common external tariff was imposed on imports from third countries; capital and labor enjoyed free circulation throughout the area; and trade among the three expanded.

The 1922 and 1948 agreements subsequently led to the BENELUX Economic Union (BEU), established on 1 November 1960 by the Treaty of BENELUX Economic Union. This agreement was to strengthen the economic union of the three countries and was also patterned after the 1922 BLEU arrangement. But BEU also contained measures for increased social, political, and monetary cooperation as well as procedures for joint decision making and the peaceful resolution of disputes.

The BENELUX Economic Union, housed in Brussels, is a recognized intergovernmental organization with a separate and distinct legal existence from the

European Community. The main institutions of the BEU organization are as follows:[2]

Committee of Ministers. The Committee of Ministers supervises the BEU Treaty's application and usually consists of 15 people (five from each country): the ministers of foreign affairs, foreign trade, economic affairs, agriculture, and finance and social affairs. All decisions must be unanimous but, as usual, an abstention is not seen as a negative vote.

Council. This is an 11-person group, consisting of the chairs of the eight specialized committees and one additional person from each of the three countries. The Council coordinates the work of the committees; presents proposals to the Committee of Ministers; and is responsible for implementing the decisions/policies passed by the Committee of Ministers.

Committees. There are eight standing committees: foreign economic relations; monetary and financial; industrial and commercial; agriculture, food and fisheries; customs and taxation; transport; social affairs; and movement and establishment of persons.

Secretariat-General. The Secretariat-General provides the usual administrative and support service; it can also submit various proposals to the Committee of Ministers. The secretary-general of the BEU is specified by the treaty to be of Netherlands nationality, assisted by one Belgian and one Luxembourg deputy secretaries-general.

Court of Justice. The Court was not established until 1974, but it has the power to issue binding decisions in disputes arising out of the treaty or from the implementation/administration of various policies. The Court also has the power to issue advisory opinions if requested by any one of the three governments or by the BEU organization itself.

Consultative Inter-Parliamentary Council. This consultative council was established in 1956 as an advisory group within the BEU mechanism. It has no legislative power but is to be kept informed of all BEU activities. This Inter-Parliamentary Council has 49 members: the Belgian and Dutch parliaments each send 21, and there are seven from the Luxembourg Chamber of Deputies.

Economic and Social Advisory Council. This council represents the organized interest groups and functional organizations within the three countries. It provides its opinion on Committee of Ministers proposals, and it can also prepare studies on its own initiative. It has 27 members, each country providing an equal share.

The BENELUX Economic Union has served the three countries well. Border controls between Belgium and the Netherlands are almost nonexistent, and the Belgian-Luxembourg frontier no longer exists (except on maps). Belgium and Luxembourg (but not the Netherlands) have also created a quasi-monetary union: each country still maintains its own currency, but the exchange rate does not fluctuate (it is fixed at 1 FB = 1 FLUX), and Belgian currency is freely accepted in Luxembourg. Luxembourg currency, however, is accepted only in some Belgian towns near the border (i.e., Arlon and Bastogne). The BENELUX countries also engage in the coordination of their positions on external matters and within other IGOs. Although not totally unknown, it is very rare to see the three countries' representatives voting differently in IGOs such as the UN, the EC,

NATO, the Council of Europe, and the OECD. That there may be political differences among the countries is not disputed, but these differences are worked out into a common position by the caucus prior to voting.

The basic nature of the BEU—a common market with a common external tariff and the free circulation of persons—has largely been superceded by the European Community. Even the EC's institutions appear to mirror those of the BEU. But the Union allows these small countries a measure of influence within the EC (and other IGOs) that is greater than the sum of their individual influence.

CHURCHILL'S "UNITED STATES OF EUROPE" SPEECH (1946)

It is perhaps ironic, but one of the major intellectual origins of the postwar European unification process and the subsequent European Community can be found in a 1946 speech by Winston S. Churchill. It appeared that, at the time, the United Kingdom was encouraging the integrative process. In a speech given at Zurich University on 19 September 1946, Churchill offered the following comments:

I am now going to say something that will astonish you. The first step in the re-creation of the European family must be a partnership between France and Germany. In this way only can France recover the moral leadership of Europe. There can be no revival of Europe without a spiritually great France and a spiritually great Germany. The structure of the United States of Europe, if well and truly built, will be such as to make the material strength of a single state less important. Small nations will count as much as large ones and gain their honour by their contribution to the common cause. . . . I shall not try to make a detailed programme for hundreds of millions of people . . . but if this is their wish, they have only to say so, and means can certainly be found, and machinery erected, to carry that wish into full fruition.[3]

A careful reading of Churchill's speech, however, would have provided a hint of future British noninvolvement and, as events transpired, the British remained aloof for 27 years until 1973. It was "Europe" that must unite, but the United Kingdom was not part of this "Europe." The British would encourage the process, but it was limited to the countries of the Continent. In fact, the final paragraph of Churchill's speech made it quite clear that the United Kingdom thought that political integration was fine for the "Europeans," but not for the British:

In all this urgent work, France and Germany must take the lead together. Great Britain, the British Commonwealth of Nations, mighty America, and I trust Soviet Russia—for then indeed all would be well—must be the friends and sponsors of the new Europe and must champion its right to live and shine.[4]

This British self-perception—a "world power" with extensive ties to the Commonwealth countries, non-European, a country with its own special interests—turned full circle when French President Charles de Gaulle vetoed the UK's application for admission to EC membership in 1963. The French president, not known for his fondness of the British, categorized the United Kingdom as too "insular" and insufficiently "European" to be considered for EC membership. This insularity of the collective British psyche started to erode when the UK actually became an EC member on 1 January 1973; it probably disappeared forever in 1986 when it was announced that construction would begin for a railway tunnel under the English Channel to link Britain to the European continent.

THE EUROPEAN RECOVERY PROGRAM (1947)/THE ORGANIZATION FOR EUROPEAN ECONOMIC COOPERATION (1948)/THE ORGANIZATION FOR ECONOMIC COOPERATION AND DEVELOPMENT(1961)

The European Recovery Program (ERP), better known as the Marshall Plan, was first proposed by US Secretary of State George C. Marshall in a speech at Harvard University on 5 June 1947. The Marshall Plan envisaged, and eventually delivered, a massive economic assistance program for Western Europe.[5] The US Congress passed the Economic Cooperation Act of 1948 and a four-year economic aid program began to operate.

The ERP led to the establishment of the Organization for European Economic Cooperation (OEEC). The OEEC, established on 16 April 1948, had as its primary task the coordination of the distribution of Marshall Plan funds in Western Europe. But the OEEC went beyond just finding ways to spend the American funds: the countries involved recognized the interdependence of their economies, the need to maximize trade within the area, and the necessity of improving the international payment system.[6] The OEEC was transformed into the Organization for Economic Cooperation and Development (OECD) in 1961. The OECD has expanded beyond the original OEEC's European nature, and now it is an international forum where the representatives of most of the world's industrialized democracies attempt to coordinate economic and social policies.

Based in Paris, the OECD now has 24 members, and a representative from the EC Commission usually participates in OECD meetings.[7] The OECD has a council (each member country is represented) that sets general policy and adopts by mutual agreement various decisions and recommendations; an executive committee (a smaller group within the council) that prepares the work of the council; and a permanent secretariat that provides the usual administrative and organizational support services. But most of OECD's work, however, is done by specialized committees or expert working parties.[8] The meetings of these groups are usually not open to the public at large: they are restricted to the official representatives of the member-governments. But the results of these committee deliberations and studies are *not* restricted: the OECD maintains a large publishing service, and the documents are readily available at nominal charges. The

Organization for Economic Cooperation and Development is not a supranational organization that issues binding decisions on the member-governments but, beginning with the 1948 Organization for European Economic Cooperation, it is a mechanism for increased economic coordination and cooperation.

THE BRUSSELS TREATY (1948)/THE WESTERN EUROPEAN UNION (1955)

On 4 March 1947, France and the United Kingdom signed the Dunkirk Treaty, establishing a bilateral military alliance openly directed at any future possible German aggression. Events, however, soon thereafter overtook the rationale of the Dunkirk Treaty—Germany was no longer seen as the *main* threat to peace and security. The British foreign minister at the time, Ernest Bevin, wanted to replace the German-oriented France-UK alliance with a multilateral agreement based upon the Soviet threat. As a result, the Treaty of Brussels was signed on 17 March 1948 by Belgium, France, Luxembourg, the Netherlands, and the United Kingdom. The Brussels Treaty was much more than a limited military alliance; it was a defensive "partnership." The treaty called for "collective self-defense" and "economic, social and cultural collaboration." Although some nonmilitary collaboration was envisaged, the main context remained in the military sphere: any attack in Europe on one of the signatory states would obligate the other partners to render "all the military and other aid and assistance in their power."[9] Most of the treaty articles that called for greater economic, social, and cultural collaboration were not implemented.

The major task of military coordination (not integration) was performed by the Western Union Defense Organization (WUDO), established in September 1948 at Fontainebleu. The WUDO was rather haphazard in organizational efficiency and hierarchy—there were plenty of generals but not too many people for them to command—and no real military coordination took place. The Brussels Treaty and WUDO were soon overtaken by the North Atlantic Treaty and by the Western European Union.

When the Pleven Plan for a European Defense Community (discussed below) fell apart in 1954 after being proposed in 1950, a conference was held in London to salvage some sort of European military cooperation. A subsequent ministerial conference was then held in Paris (October 1954), and it was agreed to establish the Western European Union (WEU). The agreement included the strengthening of the Brussels Treaty; extended an invitation to Italy and Germany (no longer perceived as a possible military threat) to join the WEU; and invited Germany to join NATO. The agreement was ratified on 6 May 1955, and the seven-nation (Belgium, France, West Germany, Italy, Luxembourg, the Netherlands, and the United Kingdom) WEU thus was established.

Based in London and Paris, the WEU's major objectives are to coordinate (not integrate) defense policy and weapon procurement and cooperate in political, social, legal, and cultural matters. As is the BENELUX Economic Union, the

WEU is an IGO separate and distinct from the European Community. The WEU's main institutions are as follows:

Council. The WEU Council consists formally of the seven foreign ministers although it is usually the six ambassadors to the United Kingdom and an undersecretary of the British foreign ministry who participate in council meetings. The council is responsible for formulating general policy within the WEU structure.

Assembly. The Assembly of the WEU consists of the delegates from the seven national parliaments who are also the national delegates to the Parliamentary Assembly of the Council of Europe (18 from each of France, West Germany, Italy, and the United Kingdom; 7 each from Belgium and the Netherlands; and 3 from Luxembourg for a total of 89). The assembly meets twice a year in Paris and considers general defense policy in Western Europe. The assembly can issue (nonbinding) recommendations or opinions to the WEU Council, the member-governments, national parliaments and/or other IGOs. The assembly has six permanent standing committees: defense questions and armaments, general affairs, scientific questions, budgetary affairs and administration, rules of procedure and privileges, and relations with parliaments.

Some recent activities of the Western European Union have included the following: support of the United States in the latter's talks with the Soviet Union over arms control; the limitation of weapon-related technology exports to the Soviet Union; and activities directed at the prevention of the military use of space.[10]

THE NORTH ATLANTIC TREATY ORGANIZATION (1949)

The North Atlantic Treaty Organization (NATO) was created in 1949 by the North Atlantic Treaty.[11] The basic motivation for the creation of NATO was the enhancement of the security of the member-states because even the capabilities of the most powerful member—the United States—were perceived as insufficient to meet the threat of aggression in Europe by the Soviet Union.[12] NATO member-countries are expected to treat an armed attack on any one of them in Europe or in North America as an attack against them all. The treaty's crucial article reads as follows:

The Parties agree that an armed attack against one or more of them in Europe or North America shall be considered an attack against them all, and consequently they agree that, if such an armed attack occurs, each of them, in exercise of the right of individual or collective self-defense recognized by Article 51 of the Charter of the United Nations, will assist the Party or Parties so attacked by taking forthwith, individually and in concert with the other Parties, such action as it deems necessary, including the use of armed force, to restore and maintain the security of the North Atlantic area.[13]

A detailed organizational chart of the NATO structure is contained in Figure 1.1. The major body is the council, composed of the representatives of the

Figure 1.1
NATO Civil and Military Structures

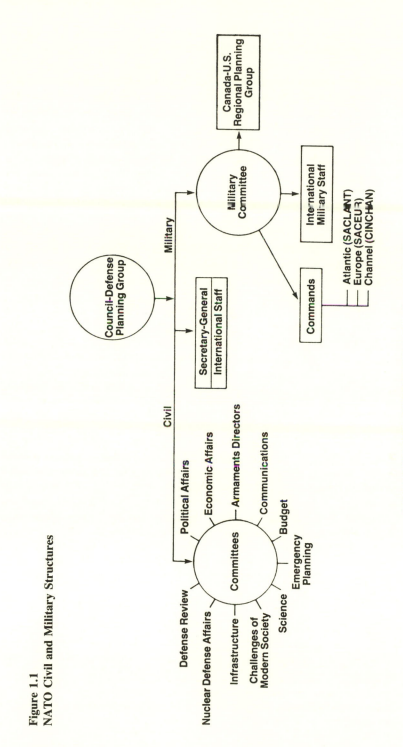

Source: *The NATO Handbook* (Brussels: NATO Information Service, 1978), p. 36

member-states, either the defense ministers or, in their (usual) absence, by the governments' permanent representatives to NATO headquarters in Brussels. Decisions in council have to be unanimous, and it is the forum for consultation among the member-states where general NATO policy is established.

Below the council level, NATO is divided into two principal areas: one deals with civil-political affairs and the second with military matters. The civil-political division has several major committees, each dealing with a specific area as illustrated in Figure 1.1. The military committee is composed of the member-governments' chiefs-of-staff (or their deputies) and is responsible for making recommendations to the council.

THE COUNCIL OF EUROPE (1949)

In May 1948, ten European countries established the Congress of Europe, a loose organization in which areas of common concern could be discussed. The congress received a report from the International Committee of the Movements for European Unity, and the report formed the basis of a very significant congress resolution.[14] The resolution reviewed the evils of nationalism and then called upon the European countries to transfer some sovereignty to an international organization. The following represents extracts of this 1948 Congress of Europe resolution:

The ravages wrought by six years of war and by the occupation, the diminution of world food production, the destruction of industrial capacity, the creation of huge debts, the maintenance of military expenditure all out of proportion to the resources of the people, the shifting of economic power, the rancours left by war, the progressive evils of nationalism and the absence . . . of an international authority sufficiently strong to provide law and order, constitute an unprecedented menace to the well-being and the security of the peoples of Europe and threaten them with ruin. . . .
The Congress:
    1. Recognizes that it is the urgent duty of the nations of Europe to create an economic and political union in order to assure security and social progress;
    2. Notes with approval the recent steps which have been taken by some European Governments in the direction of economic and political cooperation, but believes that in the present emergency the organizations created are by themselves insufficient to provide any lasting remedy;
    3. Declares that the time has come when the European nations must transfer and merge some portion of their sovereign rights so as to secure common political and economic action for the integration and proper development of their common resources;
    4. Demands the convening, as a matter of real urgency, of a European Assembly chosen by the Parliaments of the participating nations, from among their members and others, designed . . . to advise upon immediate practical measures designed progressively to bring about the necessary economic and political union of Europe; . . .
    11. Declares that the creation of a United Europe is an essential element in the creation of a united world.[15]

This resolution led, in May 1949, to the establishment of the Council of Europe. Based in Strasbourg, the Council has grown from the original ten members to a current 21.[16] The Council's major objectives are to achieve greater unity among its members, to increase economic and social progress, and to protect the principles of parliamentary democracy.

Organization

The Council of Europe has several similar bodies that also exist within the European Community, but the two organizations should not be confused with each other. Each is a separate IGO whose legal existence rests upon different treaties and texts, the 12 EC countries all belong to the Council of Europe but, obviously, the Council has an additional nine member-countries who are not within the EC framework. The organization of the Council of Europe is as follows:

Council of Ministers. The Council of Ministers consists of the foreign ministers from each of the 21 members. The Council is the formal decision-making unit within the framework and can make various recommendations to the governments; it also must approve any of the conventions passed before putting them before the member-governments for ratification. It meets about twice a year (usually in May and December) for a short period.

Committee of Permanent Representatives/Ministers' Deputies. This committee consists of 21 (one from each member-government) senior diplomats who are accredited to the Council of Europe. These diplomats deal with the routine matters at monthly meetings, prepare for the Council of Ministers' meetings, and any decision taken by this group has the same binding effect as decisions taken by the Council of Ministers.

Parliamentary Assembly. The assembly has 170 members, distributed as follows: France, West Germany, Italy, and the United Kingdom—18 each; Spain and Turkey—12 each; Belgium, Greece, the Netherlands, and Portugal—seven each; Austria, Sweden, and Switzerland—six each; Denmark and Norway—five each; Ireland—four; Cyprus, Iceland, Luxembourg, and Malta—three each; and two members from Liechtenstein. The members are appointed by and from their own national parliaments according to the strength of each political party; there are currently five major transnational party groupings represented in the Assembly: Socialist, Christian Democrat, European Democrat (Conservative), Liberal, and Communist. The assembly meets several times a year, and it is basically a consultative body without any real legislative powers. There are 14 standing committees: political; economic and development; social and health; legal; culture and education; science and technology; regional planning and local authorities; rules of procedure; agriculture; relations with nonmember European countries; parliamentary and public relations; migration; refugees and demography; and budget.

Activities

The Council of Europe's major success has not been in the area of political integration; rather, it is within the area of the harmonization across Europe of certain laws and standards and operating procedures. The Council has passed approximately 115 conventions or general agreements (some have yet to enter into force) on a wide range of issues. Some of these issues are social welfare, migrant workers, youth and sport, the environment, and monuments and historical sites.[17]

One of the best-known—and most effective—convention of the Council of Europe is perhaps the "Convention for the Protection of Human Rights and Fundamental Freedoms," popularly known as the European Convention on Human Rights (ECHR).[18] Passed on 4 November 1950 and entering into force on 3 September 1953, the ECHR describes certain activities that are prohibited to the governments (e.g., torture, inhuman treatment, discrimination, etc.). The convention established a commission to receive allegations from private individuals about mistreatment by their governments and, in the event the commission cannot resolve the problem, a court (the European Court of Human Rights) was also created to adjudicate the complaint.[19] The court is perceived to be a legitimate institution in Western Europe, and governments, even if found "guilty" of violating the convention, have invariably implemented the court's decision. The European Community itself does not have its own human rights charter, but the EC's Court of Justice has issued a ruling that the EC institutions are, in fact, bound by the Council of Europe's Convention requirements.[20]

THE EUROPEAN COAL AND STEEL COMMUNITY (1950–1952)

The European Coal and Steel Community (ECSC) represented a milestone in the European integrative process and, as events subsequently transpired, the ECSC was seen to be a pilot project for the larger and more ambitious EEC/EC.[21] Briefly stated, the ECSC established a common market—a free-trade zone with the elimination of artificial barriers to trade—for the coal and steel sectors of the economy. It also transferred several areas of decision making away from the sovereign national governments to a supranational High Authority. The ECSC approached the integrative process from the functionalist point of view: if governments could learn to cooperate in certain, limited "nonpolitical" areas, then perhaps spillover effects would lead to additional coordination, cooperation, and integration. This spillover effect did indeed take place: the ECSC was basically an economic solution to a political problem, but, as the economic benefits mounted for the participating governments, it was all but inevitable that the functional areas would be expanded.

The ECSC was conceived by Jean Monnet, a well-known French economic planner and tireless supporter of greater European cooperation and integration.[22] Monnet's central conviction was that the 19th-century European model of the sovereign nation-state had become an anachronism and was quite inadequate to deal with the challenges of the 20th century. He perceived that the problems in Europe were simply incapable of being resolved within the structure of competing sovereignties, and thus the very structure of the state system had to be altered. The ECSC was to be Monnet's functionalist first step toward greater European cooperation. He was able to persuade his colleague, French Foreign Minister Robert Schuman, of the benefits of the plan, and Schuman, in turn, approached Konrad Adenauer, West Germany's chancellor and foreign minister. The idea was readily accepted by Adenauer, and then Italy, Belgium, the Netherlands, and Luxembourg joined the negotiations. The ECSC Treaty (the Paris Treaty) was signed by the six countries on 18 April 1951 and the High Authority, with Jean Monnet as its first president, began operations on 10 August 1952 in Luxembourg Ville.

The Proposal

When on 9 May 1950, Robert Schuman announced Monnet's now-famous plan for the European Coal and Steel Community (it was immediately called the "Schuman Plan" but Schuman always gave full credit to Monnet), he proposed not only an experiment in economic cooperation and integration, he also conceived this community to be the beginning of the political unification of Western Europe. He stated that the pooling of coal and steel production would immediately "assure the establishment of common bases for economic development, which is the first stage for the European federation, and will change the destiny of these regions which have long been devoted to the production of arms to which they themselves were the first to fall constantly victim."[23]

It is instructive to cite Schuman's statement at some length because it illustrates both the functional approach to international integration and the European realization that such integration was an absolute political necessity. Schuman's statement continues:

The peace of the world can only be preserved if creative efforts are made which are commensurate, in their scope, with the dangers which threaten peace. The contribution which an organized and active Europe can make to civilization is indispensable for the maintenance of peaceful relations. France, by championing during more than 20 years the idea of a United Europe, has always regarded it as an essential objective to serve the purposes of peace. Because Europe was not united, we have had war. A United Europe will not be achieved all at once, nor in a single framework: it will be formed by concrete measures which first of all create a solidarity in fact. The uniting of the European nations requires that the age-old opposition between France and Germany be eliminated: the action to be taken must first of all concern France and Germany. To that end, the French Government proposes that immediate action be concentrated on one limited, but decisive point. The French Government proposes that the entire French-German production of coal and steel be placed under a joint high authority, within an organization open to the participation of other European nations. . . .

The community of production, which will in this manner be created, will clearly show that any war between France and Germany becomes not only unthinkable but in actual fact impossible. The establishment of this powerful production unit, open to all countries who wish to participate in it, will give a real foundation to their economic development, by furnishing on equal terms to all countries thus united the fundamental elements of industrial production.[24]

As mentioned above, the French proposal was readily accepted in principle and the treaty followed soon thereafter. But before discussing the organization and operation of the ECSC, it is essential to look in greater detail at the economic and political motivations of the two main powers (France and West Germany) involved in this experiment in international integration and the transfer of some sovereignty to a supranational authority. Why did France offer such a plan and why did the other countries—especially West Germany—accept?

Economic and Political Motivations

In West Germany, the direct economic benefits that might flow from a common market in the coal and steel sectors were not seen as persuasive as the indirect advantages of the proposed ECSC.[25] First, with the establishment of the ECSC institutions, controls upon the West German economy were lifted, especially those of the International Ruhr Authority that, under the direction of the French, limited the economic resurgence of the vital Ruhr industrial region.[26] Second, the ECSC provided domestic benefits clearly in the West German national interest, since it marked an end to export controls on West Germany's redeveloping steel industry and an end to tariff barriers against the export of West German coal. A third reason for the West German willingness to accept the ECSC concerned the Saar. The ECSC solution removed the Saar, which France had claimed as war reparations, from French administrative control and placed it in the hands of the ECSC's High Authority in which West Germany would have an equal amount of input as the French concerning the administration of the Saar. West Germany, through the ECSC, thus could entertain a reasonable hope for the Saar's eventual repatriation.

The Saar was, up to this point, under the nominal administration of the International Ruhr Authority (IRA), established in December 1948. The authority, composed of the United States, Great Britain, France, and the BENELUX countries, was an obvious attempt to control any future German military aggression. The authority had a two-fold purpose: "1. To avoid the misuse of the resources of the Ruhr for aggression in the future; and 2. To assure the countries cooperating [i.e., the six countries who ran the IRA] equitable access to the coal, coke, and steel of the Ruhr."[27]

The solution to the Saar and other French-administered West German territory was obtained by a compromise, with the ECSC being an intermediate step. The ECSC did *not* return the Saar to West Germany, but it set the stage for its return. This intermediate step was accomplished in an exchange of letters between Konrad Adenauer and Robert Schuman on 18 April 1951, the day the ECSC

Treaty was signed. Adenauer's letter to Schuman contained the following sentence:

I . . . would ask you to confirm that the French Government agrees with the Federal Government that the status of the Saar can finally be settled only by the Peace Treaty or a similar Treaty and that the French Government does not view the Federal Government's signature of the European Coal and Steel Community Treaty as recognition by the Federal Government of the present status of the Saar.[28]

Schuman and the French government accepted this construction in the reply letter, but it was not until 1959 that the Saar was fully integrated back into West Germany. Under a French–West German agreement of October 1954, the Saar was to have "European" status within the framework of the Western European Union and the Council of Europe, subject to acceptance by the Saar's population. The Saarlanders, however, did not approve the referendum in October 1955, but, instead, expressed the wish for a return to the Federal Republic of Germany. Political incorporation of the Saar into West Germany was attained in January 1957, and full economic incorporation in July 1959.

In terms of West German foreign policy objectives, the creation of the ECSC was also useful. Generally, it acknowledged West Germany's presence as a minimally sovereign state within Europe, equipped with the power to negotiate and conclude treaties. Additionally, the ECSC gave West Germany the opportunity to participate within regional cooperative institutions as an equal to France and a superior to other Western European states. Thus, two important major goals of West German foreign policy were met by the ECSC.

For France, the direct economic benefits of the ECSC were also less important than certain political considerations. French foreign-policy planners were cognizant of the fact that West Germany could not be kept under Allied control forever. This seemed especially true in the heavy industry sector, where the Korean War had placed emphasis on the renewed production of European steel.

In fact, security planning dominated the French decision to propose the Schuman Plan. In April 1950, a memorandum had been submitted to Prime Minister Georges Bidault that outlined the ECSC as a means of controlling West German industrial revitalization and of eliminating the possibility of renewed French–West German hostilities on a long-range basis.[29] As Derek Bok notes, the ECSC presented France with the solution to a serious security dilemma:

Without an expanding industry, and with the growing demand for steel production occasioned by the Korean War, France could not expect the controls upon German production to be continued indefinitely. At the same time, however, the French were fearful of an unbridled development of the Ruhr into a powerful arsenal which might once more become linked with the aggressive policies of a German government. Under these circumstances, the Schuman Plan was conceived by France as a compromise whereby she would give up part of her sovereign power to secure a degree of international control over German coal and steel.[30]

The motivations of the other prospective ECSC members, Italy and the BEN-ELUX countries, to support the ECSC were less complex. They perceived that their prospects for domestic economic rehabilitation were enhanced and that political advantages were to be gained on the national as well as international level. The United Kingdom was also invited to become a charter member of the ECSC, but turned down the invitation primarily on the grounds that it would not be beneficial either to its economic or political interests. At that time, Britain's relations with the Commonwealth countries were seen as the first priority and, in addition, the United Kingdom was apprehensive about the supranational powers that were to be transferred to the ECSC institutions.

Goals and Objectives

The preamble to the European Coal and Steel Community Treaty is a lofty statement, identifying the reasons why six European nations decided to establish a supranational organization with effective, independent, and binding decision-making powers:

CONSIDERING that world peace can be safeguarded only by creative efforts commensurate with the dangers that threaten it,
CONVINCED that the contribution which an organized and vital Europe can make to civilization is indispensable to the maintenance of peaceful relations,
RECOGNIZING that Europe can be built only through practical achievements which will first of all create real solidarity, and through the establishment of common bases for economic development,
ANXIOUS to help, by expanding their basic production, to raise the standard of living and further the works of peace,
RESOLVED to substitute for age-old rivalries the merging of their essential interests; to create, by establishing an economic community, the basis for a broader and deeper community among peoples long divided by bloody conflicts; and to lay the foundations for institutions which will give direction to a destiny henceforward shared,
HAVE DECIDED to create a European Coal and Steel Community.

As mentioned above, the ECSC established a common market for coal, steel, coke, iron ore, and scrap; it also harmonized certain freight rates. Articles 2 and 3 of the ECSC Treaty specifies the Community's tasks: ensure an orderly supply, equal access, aim for lowest prices, encourage research and development, promote improved working conditions, promote the growth of international trade, and to prohibit "improper" national protectionist measures.

Institutions

In the negotiations for the institutional framework, agreement was reached by the prospective ECSC member-states to set up a comprehensive structure for the management and performance of the tasks assigned to the organization. These institutions were eventually incorporated into the larger European Community institutional framework (discussed in greater detail below in Part II).

The most important organ was the High Authority, conceived to be the major executive and administrative agency and endowed with supranational powers to issue binding decisions affecting coal and steel enterprises and individuals in the member-states (Article 14). Other major organs were the Council, consisting of ministers of the member-states representing both the interests of these states and those of the ECSC (Articles 26–30); an Assembly composed of delegates appointed by the parliaments of the member-states and possessing only very limited powers (Articles 20–25); a Consultative Committee to represent the functional–interest groups within the six countries (Articles 18–19); and a very powerful Court of Justice with extensive jurisdictional competencies (Articles 31–45).

The voting procedures in the High Authority and the Council were based generally on majority rule, but in a number of cases the treaty required unanimity of the Council. The High Authority was given limited taxing powers, but its decisions to impose financial obligations were enforceable only through the use of the legal procedures of the member-states. National enterprises and member-governments were given the right to appeal decisions or recommendations of the High Authority before the Court of Justice.

Impact

The European Coal and Steel Community had an almost immediate impact in the economic field—the elimination of the artificial barriers to trade led to a revitalization of the coal and steel sectors within the six countries. Although many less efficient enterprises, previously insulated by national protectionist measures, found themselves unable to compete, many more firms were able to compete and expand. Much of the High Authority's expenditures (the funds being derived mostly from a tax levied on freight charges) dealt with the social problems of unemployment and economic dislocation attributable to the ECSC.

A large number of workers and their families were affected by this free-trade experiment, and the ECSC had an extensive program to deal with the individual and human costs of political integration. Administered by the national governmental authorities but eventually reimbursed by the ECSC, a vast program was undertaken to deal with the human problems—early pensions, vocational retraining, relocation assistance—but there were still countless individuals who fell between the cracks. The overall economic impact, however, was seen as extremely beneficial for all six countries, and this helped to prepare the way for the subsequent EEC Treaty a few years later. It was soon recognized that there were too many other sectors of the economy that were related to coal and steel but with which the ECSC structure had no competence to deal. The development of the ECSC revealed the need to enlarge the common market.

The ECSC also had a significant political impact. Coordination and international cooperation, albeit in some limited economic areas, were seen to actually work. Countries were at the first stage of the very slow—and yet to be completed—change from national identity and parochial national interests to approaching certain problems within a "European" mind-set. The traditional barriers were being eroded very slowly, and the European Coal and Steel Community thus had a direct link to the subsequent European Community.

THE EUROPEAN DEFENSE COMMUNITY (1950)

The ill-fated European Defense Community (EDC), proposed by the French in 1950 but eventually rejected by the French parliament in 1954, was Europe's collective reaction to the Korean War and the perceived Soviet military threat to Western Europe.[31] The EDC proposal was also based on the realization that West Germany had to be rearmed, but that a unilateral rearmament was also perceived as a threat. In addition, the EDC was a proposal to create a "European" army with a full integration (not just coordination) of the defense-military sectors.

The idea was first broached by Winston S. Churchill in a speech to the Consultative Assembly of the Council of Europe on 11 August 1950:

I beg to move that: The Assembly, in order to express its devotion to the maintenance of peace and its resolve to sustain the action of the Security Council of the United Nations in defence of peaceful peoples against aggression, calls for the immediate creation of a unified European Army subject to proper European democratic control and acting in full cooperation with the United States and Canada.[32]

Some two months later, on 24 October 1950, the idea was advanced with much more precision and detail by René Pleven, the French prime minister, in a speech to the National Assembly. Popularly known as the Pleven Plan, the European Defense Community was based on two perceptions: (1) the general European wariness of the Soviet threat, and (2) specific French fears of a rearmed and militaristic German nation. Pleven called for much more than the usual military alliance—he proposed a fully integrated European army under the command of a single European political and military authority (a "European" defense minister).

Pleven's comments are presented in some detail because they illustrate the motivations behind the EDC proposal:

The French Government thought that the realization of the coal and steel plan would enable people to grow accustomed to the idea of a European community before the delicate question of a common system of defense was embarked upon. World events have removed this breathing space. Accordingly, confident of Europe's pacific destiny and conscious of the need to inculcate in all the peoples of Europe a feeling of collective security, the French Government proposes to deal with this question by the same methods and in the same spirit. But the pressure of events alone will not make possible a constructive solution. Any system that would lead, immediately or in due course, directly or indirectly, subject to conditions or not, to the creation of a German army, would cause mistrust and suspicion to be reborn. The creation of German divisions, of a German Ministry of Defense, would inevitably lead, sooner or later, to the reconstitution of a national army and, thereby, to the resurrection of German militarism. . . .

The French Government will ask for a solution to be given to the problem of the German contribution to the creation of a European force that takes account of the cruel lessons of the past and of the direction which so many Europeans in all countries would like to see Europe take. It proposes the creation, for our common defense, of a European army tied to political institutions of a united Europe. . . .

The setting up of a European army cannot result from a mere grouping together of national military units, which would in reality only mask a coalition of the old sort. For tasks which are inevitably common ones, only common institutions will do. The army of a united Europe, composed of men coming from different European countries, must, so far as is possible, achieve a complete fusion of the human and material elements which make it up under a single European political and military authority.[33]

Prime Minister Pleven then filled in the gaps with a detailed description of how such a defense community might be organized.[34] The participating countries would jointly appoint a European "minister of defense" who would be responsible to those appointing him and, perhaps, also responsible to the Parliamentary Assembly of the Council of Europe in Strasbourg. This defense minister's powers over the European army would be identical to those of a national minister of defense over the national military forces of his own country. Pleven also envisaged that the actual integration of defense forces would be at the lowest possible level. Some critics exaggerated this, believing a six-man squad would be comprised of six different nationalities, each soldier speaking a language that the others could not understand. Finally, the European minister of defense would have the authority to release a part of a country's contingent in the European army back to the government for purposes other than those of the common defense of Europe.

Pleven's proposal found preliminary acceptance in principle and, after the United States and the United Kingdom announced their support (but nonparticipation), negotiations among France, West Germany, Italy, and the BENELUX countries began in February 1951. The European Defense Community Treaty was signed on 27 May 1952 but still had to be ratified by the governments of the signatory states. The story of the defeat of the EDC by the French parliament need not be repeated here, but on 30 August 1954, the National Assembly refused to ratify the EDC.[35] The French had some basic concerns: the lack of British participation; the French were not yet quite ready to transfer sovereign decision-making power to an international actor in the military sphere; and, what was perhaps the most crucial argument, the supporters of the EDC in France just were unable to convince their colleagues that if German rearmament were such a danger—the rationale of the EDC—how could it be dealt with by limiting the freedom of the French army?[36]

The European Defense Community thus failed, and, even to this day, there is very little integration—distinguished from coordination or cooperation—in the military defense area in Western Europe. The EC does *not* have competence in the military defense sectors, and each country continues to maintain its own national prerogatives.

THE BENELUX CHALLENGE (1955)

Encouraged by the success of the European Coal and Steel Community and realizing that the development of the activities of the ECSC revealed the need to enlarge the common market into other areas and, more significantly, recognizing the fact that international integration was an absolute necessity to guarantee the future of Western Europe, the governments of Belgium, the Netherlands, and Luxembourg issued a joint call for action to the other members of the ECSC. Submitted on 18 May 1955, the Joint Memorandum must be considered as the immediate catalyst of the subsequent EEC and EURATOM Treaties. The BENELUX statement called for a conference among the ECSC states, as well as any other "interested" party (a not-too-subtle reference to the United Kingdom), to prepare a program for a general and enlarged integration of the region's economy. Such integration was envisaged to go far beyond the important but limited functional areas (coal and steel) of the ECSC.

The first two paragraphs of the Joint Memorandum presented the main thrust of the BENELUX position:

1. The Governments of Belgium, Luxembourg and the Netherlands believe that the time has come to take a new step on the road towards European integration. They are of the opinion that such integration must be achieved in the first place in the economic field. They consider that the establishment of a united Europe must be sought through the development of common institutions, the progressive fusion of national economies, the creation of a large common market and the progressive harmonization of social policies. Such a policy seems to them indispensable for maintaining Europe's position in the world, for restoring its influence and prestige and for securing a constantly rising standard of living for its people.
2. The development of the activities of the ECSC has revealed the need to enlarge the common market into domains bordering upon that organization's field of activity. The Benelux countries consider, however, that such an enlargement can only succeed if a general economic integration is undertaken.[37]

The memorandum concluded with the suggestion of holding a conference to draft treaties that would accomplish the above-cited objectives. The BENELUX Memorandum, or challenge, was accepted by France, Italy, and West Germany, and this acceptance then led to the Messina and Venice Conferences.

THE MESSINA CONFERENCE (1955)/THE VENICE CONFERENCE (1956)

In response to the 18 May 1955 BENELUX Joint Memorandum, the foreign ministers of the six ECSC member-states held a conference at Messina on 1–2

June 1955. The Messina Conference was not a treaty-drafting conference; rather, it was a preparatory stage at which the BENELUX proposal was formally accepted. The Final Joint Resolution of the Messina Conference opened with the following paragraph:

The Governments of the German Federal Republic, Belgium, France, Italy, Luxembourg and the Netherlands believe that the time has come to make a fresh advance towards the building of Europe. They are of the opinion that this must be achieved, first of all, in the economic field. They consider that it is necessary to work for the establishment of a united Europe by the development of common institutions, the progressive fusion of national economies, the creation of a common market and the progressive harmonization of their social policies. Such a policy seems to them indispensable if Europe is to maintain her position in the world, regain her influence and prestige and achieve a continuing increase in the standard of living of her population.[38]

The six foreign ministers then issued a formal declaration to the effect that each of the six governments would begin to "study" the questions under consideration and that an international Committee of Governmental Representatives, assisted by experts, would participate in this preparatory stage. This international committee was instructed to report its findings and recommendations back to the foreign ministers by 1 October 1955. The foreign ministers also declared at Messina that the United Kingdom, although not a member of the ECSC (the UK had "associative" status), would be issued a formal invitation to participate in the deliberations of the special committee. The invitation to the United Kingdom was based on the realization that it was indeed a major European power and, in addition, was a founding member of the Western European Union. The invitation was duly extended and the United Kingdom duly declined, saying that it was still not yet quite ready to forego the Commonwealth in order to join the European integrative process.

The report of the international Committee of Governmental Representatives was eventually completed and delivered to the six national governments by way of the foreign ministers. A second conference was then held in Venice (29–30 May 1956) by the six foreign affairs ministers under the chair of Christian Pineau, then the French foreign minister. The other participants in the Venice Conference were those individuals who must receive the credit for the establishment of the European Community: Walter Hallstein (West Germany), Paul-Henri Spaak (Belgium), Maurice Faure (France), Gaetano Martino (Italy), Joseph Bech (Luxembourg), and J. W. Beyen (the Netherlands). These individuals had intimate knowledge of a past tragic history as well as the foresight of a future united Europe; they also were able to translate their beliefs and ideals into a practical political reality.

The Venice Conference accepted the final report of the Committee of Governmental Representatives and the Conference's Final Communiqué called for a treaty-drafting conference:

The Ministers have expounded the views of their respective governments on the proposals put forward in the report of the heads of delegations of the Committee of governmental representatives created by the Messina conference and which has met in Brussels under the chairmanship of M. Spaak. The Ministers noted that the six Governments agreed to take the proposals contained in this report as a basis for negotiations, to be pursued with a view to drafting a treaty establishing a Common Market as well as a treaty setting up a European organization for nuclear energy (Euratom). They decided to convene for this purpose a conference which will open in Brussels on 26 June 1956 under the chairmanship of M. Spaak. At the request of his colleagues, M. Spaak has agreed to continue in his task of coordinator.[39]

THE BRUSSELS CONFERENCE (1956)

The BENELUX challenge was thus accepted and the treaty-drafting conference did, in fact, begin its deliberations in Brussels on 26 June 1956 under the guidance of Paul-Henri Spaak of Belgium. The conference lasted several months, and it was here that the actual drafting of the EEC and EURATOM Treaties took place. Several iterations of the texts were necessary, and the drafts were subject to a very close scrutiny by the national governments, but, eventually, the treaties were completed. The United Kingdom did not participate in the deliberations of the Brussels Conference; there is more than ample evidence that it was the UK who declined to participate rather than being shut out deliberately from the process. A treaty-signing ceremony was then scheduled for Rome (thus the "Rome" Treaties rather than the "Brussels" Treaties) on 25 March 1957.

NOTES

The literature on the development of the European integrative process is enormous. For a good historical overview, see the following: René Albrecht-Carrie, *One Europe: The Historical Background of European Unity* (New York: Doubleday, 1965); Stuart de la Mahotière, *Towards One Europe* (New York: Penguin, 1970); Amitai Etzioni, *Political Unification* (New York: Holt, Rinehart & Winston, 1965); Jacques Freymond, *Western Europe Since the War* (New York: Praeger, 1964); Ernst B. Haas, *The Uniting of Europe: Political, Social and Economic Forces, 1950–1957* (Stanford, Calif.: Stanford University Press, 1958); Walter Hallstein, *United Europe: Challenge and Opportunity* (Cambridge, Mass.: Harvard University Press, 1962); Richard J. Mayne, *The Community of Europe* (London: Gollancz, 1963); Roger Morgan, *The Shaping of the European Community: West European Politics Since 1945* (London: Batsford, 1972); and Hans Schmitt, *The Path to European Union: From the Marshall Plan to the Common Market* (Baton Rouge, La.: Louisiana State University Press, 1962).

1. Alan Valentine, "BENELUX: Pilot Plan of Economic Union," 44 *The Yale Review* (September 1954), 23–32.
2. *BENELUX Textes de Base* (Brussels: BENELUX Economic Union, n.d.).
3. Speech by Winston S. Churchill at Zurich University (19 September 1946). Randolph S. Churchill, ed., *The Sinews of Peace: Post-War Speeches by Winston S. Churchill* (London: Cassel & Co., 1948), pp. 198–202.

4. Ibid., p. 202.

5. See Thomas A. Bailey, *The Marshall Plan Summer* (Stanford, Calif.: Hoover Institution, 1977); John Gimbel, *The Origins of the Marshall Plan* (Stanford, Calif.: Stanford University Press, 1976); Seymour E. Harris, *The European Recovery Program* (Cambridge, Mass.: Harvard University Press, 1948); Harry B. Price, *The Marshall Plan and Its Meaning* (Ithaca, N.Y.: Cornell University Press, 1955); and Imanuel Wexler, *The Marshall Plan Revisited* (Westport, Conn.: Greenwood Press, 1983).

6. *The Organization for European Economic Cooperation: History and Structure* (Paris: OEEC, 1953).

7. The members of the OECD are: Australia, Austria, Belgium, Canada, Denmark, Finland, France, West Germany, Greece, Iceland, Ireland, Italy, Japan, Luxembourg, the Netherlands, New Zealand, Norway, Portugal, Spain, Sweden, Switzerland, Turkey, the United Kingdom, and the United States. Yugoslavia has observer status.

8. The OECD has committees/expert working groups in the following areas: economic policy, economic development review, environment, urban affairs, development assistance, technical cooperation, trade, payments, capital movements and invisible transactions, international investment and multinational enterprises, financial markets, fiscal affairs, restrictive business practices, tourism, maritime transport, consumer policies, agriculture, fisheries, scientific and technological policy, information and communications, education, industry, steel, energy, manpower and social affairs, road research, and North-South economic issues.

9. Article 4, Treaty of Brussels. *European Yearbook* (Strasbourg: Council of Europe, 1955), I, pp. 208–209.

10. *Annual Report* of the Council (Paris: Western European Union, 1985); *Texts Adopted and Brief Account of the Session* (Paris: Assembly of the Western European Union, 1985).

11. See Edwin H. Fedder, *NATO: The Dynamics of Alliance in the Postwar World* (New York: Dodd, Mead, 1973); Robert S. Jordan, *Political Leadership in NATO: A Study in Multinational Diplomacy* (Boulder: Westview Press, 1979); NATO Information Service, *The NATO Handbook* (Brussels: 1978); and Robert Strausz-Hupé et al., *Building the Atlantic World* (New York: Harper and Row, 1963).

12. The current members of NATO are: Belgium, Canada, Denmark, West Germany, Greece, Iceland, Italy, Luxembourg, the Netherlands, Norway, Portugal, Spain, Turkey, the United Kingdom, and the United States. France withdrew from NATO's integrated military structure in 1966 although it still is a member of the Atlantic Alliance and sends observers to NATO's Military Committee.

13. Article 5, North Atlantic Treaty.

14. Resolution of the Political Commission of the Congress of Europe, The Hague (May 1948). Reprinted in S. Patijn, ed., *Landmarks in European Unity: 22 Texts on European Integration* (Leyden: Sijthoff, 1970), pp. 36–41.

15. Ibid.

16. The following countries are members of the Council of Europe: Austria, Belgium, Cyprus, Denmark, France, Germany, Greece, Iceland, Ireland, Italy, Liechtenstein, Luxembourg, Malta, the Netherlands, Norway, Portugal, Spain, Sweden, Switzerland, Turkey, and the United Kingdom.

17. The following are just a few examples of the more than 100 conventions passed by the Council of Europe: European Social Charter, European Code of Social Security, Convention on the Elaboration of a European Pharmacopaeia, Convention on the Legal

Status of Migrants, and Convention on the Conservation of European Wildlife and Natural Habitats.

18. For a discussion of the European Convention on Human Rights mechanism, see Leon Hurwitz, *The State as Defendant: Governmental Accountability and the Redress of Individual Grievances* (Westport, Conn.: Greenwood Press, 1981), esp. chapter 6, "Public Supranational Institutions: The European Convention on Human Rights," pp. 135–164.

19. The Strasbourg-based, Council of Europe-created European Court of Human Rights, dealing solely with the European Convention on Human Rights, should not be confused with the Luxembourg-based European Community–created European Court of Justice, dealing with the three EC treaties.

20. For an analysis of the relations among the Council of Europe's Convention on Human Rights and the European Court on Human Rights, on the one hand, and the European Community's institutions and the European Court of Justice, on the other hand, see Jonathan Miller, "A European Bill of Rights?" chapter 10 of Leon Hurwitz, ed., *The Harmonization of European Public Policy* (Westport, Conn.: Greenwood Press, 1983), pp. 219–235.

21. See Derek C. Bok, *The First Three Years of the Schuman Plan* (Princeton, N.J.: Princeton University Press, 1955); William Diebold, *The Schuman Plan: A Study in Economic Cooperation, 1950–1959* (New York: Praeger, 1959); Louis Lister, *Europe's Coal and Steel Community* (New York: Twentieth Century Fund, 1960); and Arnold J. Zurcher, *The Struggle to Unite Europe, 1940–1958* (New York: New York University Press, 1958).

22. Richard J. Mayne, "The Role of Jean Monnet," 2 *Government and Opposition* (April–July 1967), 349–371.

23. Statement by Robert Schuman, minister of foreign affairs of France (9 May 1950). *U.S. Department of State Bulletin* (12 June 1950), p. 936.

24. Ibid., p. 937.

25. This section is based on Werner J. Feld, Robert S. Jordan, and Leon Hurwitz, *International Organizations: A Comparative Approach* (New York: Praeger, 1983), pp. 63–65.

26. See F. Roy Willis, *France, Germany, and the New Europe, 1945–1967* (New York: Oxford University Press, 1968), p. 105.

27. See Georges Kaekenbeek, "The International Authority for the Ruhr and the Schuman Plan," 37 *Transactions of the Grotius Society* (1952), 4–8.

28. Exchange of Letters Between the Government of the Federal Republic of Germany and the Government of the French Republic Concerning the Saar, Paris (18 April 1951). Reprinted in Sweet & Maxwell's Legal Editorial Staff, eds., *European Community Treaties*, 2nd ed. (London: Sweet & Maxwell, 1975), p. 46.

29. Richard J. Mayne, *The Recovery of Europe* (New York: Harper and Row, 1970), pp. 177–178.

30. Derek C. Bok, *The First Three Years of the Schuman Plan*, p. 3.

31. See Hamilton F. Armstrong, "Postscript to the EDC," 33 *Foreign Affairs* (October 1954), 17–27; Raymond Aron and Daniel Lerner, *France Defeats the EDC* (New York: Praeger, 1957); and Clarence C. Walton, "Background for the European Defense Community," 68 *Political Science Quarterly* (March 1953), 42–69.

32. Statement by Winston S. Churchill at the Consultative Assembly of the Council

of Europe on the Creation of a European Army (11 August 1950). Council of Europe, Consultative Assembly, 2nd Session (7–28 August 1950), *Reports*, p. 229.

33. Statement by the French Prime Minister, René Pleven, at the National Assembly on the Creation of a European Army (24 October 1950). *Journal Officiel*, Débats, no. 104 (25 October 1950), pp. 7118–7119.

34. Ibid.

35. For a detailed discussion of the ratification debates and the eventual vote, see Hans Schmitt, *The Path to European Union*, pp. 206–229.

36. Ibid., p. 215.

37. "Joint Memorandum from the BENELUX Countries to the Member States of the ECSC, 18 May 1955." *Annuaire du Ministère des Affaires Etrangères des Pay-Bas*, 1954/1955, Annexe 4 (The Hague: 1955), pp. 210–211.

38. "Final Joint Resolution adopted by the Foreign Ministers of the Member States of the ECSC at the Messina Conference, 1–2 June 1955." La documentation française, *Articles et Documents*, no. 0216 (7 June 1955), pp. 1–2.

39. "Final Joint Communiqué of the Ministers of Foreign Affairs of the Signatory States of the Resolution of Messina," Venice (29–30 May, 1956). *Keesing's Contemporary Archives* (13–20 October 1956), p. 15,137.

2

The United Kingdom and the European Community

The period between the establishment of the EEC and EURATOM in 1958 and the eventual accession to the European Community by Denmark, Ireland, and the United Kingdom in 1973—a full 15 years—was a period characterized by strained relations within Western Europe. The United Kingdom was the focal point, especially in its dealings with French President Charles de Gaulle, and this chapter discusses the UK's relationship with the European Community: the establishment of the European Free Trade Association as a rival to the EC; the long (1960–1972) and painful negotiation process between the UK and the EC (that included two vetoes by the French); the eventual accession on 1 January 1973; the June 1975 British referendum to decide whether the country should remain in or leave the EC; and, finally, some comments on Britain's continuing tenuous relations with the European Community.

THE EUROPEAN FREE TRADE ASSOCIATION

Although not a formal participant at the Brussels Conference, where the EEC and EURATOM Treaties were drafted, the United Kingdom did initiate some very tentative discussions at the time with the governments of the Six. These discussions soon reached an impasse because the British were asking too much from the EC and giving far too little in return: the UK wanted to be within the EC framework only for trade in industrial products where, presumably, the UK could compete effectively, but at the same time keeping British agriculture outside the EC mechanism. Such a proposal was something that the six EC countries could afford to pass up—some (read "French President Charles de Gaulle") even interpreted it as a British attempt to sabotage the entire process— and these early talks were short lived. Apparently, the United Kingdom did not believe in the reality of the EC nor in the resolve of the six governments, and thus the country remained on the sidelines.

In the course of these negotiations, and once the EEC began operating in 1958, the United Kingdom became the unofficial leader and spokesman for a number of European countries who, at the time and for various reasons (some of these were "neutrals," others were not), did not want to be associated with the European integrative process but who were also concerned about the possible effects the formation of the EEC would have on their trade flows and balance of payments. The EEC, as a unit, had some discussions with this group of countries with the objective of achieving some sort of a European-wide free-trade zone but no agreement could be reached (especially after Charles de Gaulle became president of the Fifth Republic in November 1958). Western Europe was then seen to be split into two rival and competing economic camps: the "Inner Six" of the EEC (France, West Germany, Italy, and the BENELUX countries) and the "Outer Seven" (Austria, Denmark, Norway, Portugal, Sweden, Switzerland, and the United Kingdom). This "Outer Seven" group, led by the United Kingdom, felt the need to take some sort of action to counter the EEC.[1]

The Stockholm Convention

These seven "outsiders," acting on a Swedish proposal in May 1959, decided to patch together some sort of rival free-trade area organization both to protect their own interests and to compete with the EEC. Negotiations took place in June and July 1959 and, on 20 November, a convention was signed in Stockholm by the seven countries that established the European Free Trade Association (EFTA). Compared to the long negotiation and treaty-drafting process by the EEC countries and the rather detailed provisions of the Rome Treaties, the Stockholm Convention was rushed through and had very little resemblance to the EEC framework. Stripped of the accompanying political rhetoric, EFTA was an attempt to have free trade (in limited sectors) among the seven countries. The EFTA mechanism did not contain any measures aimed at integration, the harmonization of public policy, the free movement of persons, or the establishment of a common external tariff. The EFTA also allowed the United Kingdom to maintain its preferential trading agreements with the Commonwealth countries.

The Communiqué issued by the seven governments in Stockholm described the objectives of the European Free Trade Association:

The purposes of the Association are economic expansion, full employment, the rational use of resources, financial stability and a higher standard of living. The Convention will establish a free market between the members of the Association. This will be achieved by the abolition of tariffs and other obstacles to trade in the industrial products of members over a period of ten years, or earlier if so decided. Each country will be free to decide its own external tariffs. Freer trade between the participating countries will stimulate competition and economic expansion. There are provisions to ensure that the effects of the removal of the barriers to trade are not nullified by means of subsidies, practices of state undertakings, restrictive business practices, and limitations to the establishment of enterprises. The Convention also covers agricultural goods, for which special provisions are made and agreements concluded so as to promote expansion of trade and ensure a sufficient degree of reciprocity to the countries whose major exports are agricultural. To the same end there are also special rules for trade in non-processed fish and marine products. . . .

The Convention reaffirms the determination of the seven member countries to facilitate the early establishment of a multilateral association for the removal of trade barriers and the promotion of closer economic cooperation between the members of the Organization for European Economic Cooperation, including the six members of the European Economic Community. As world trading nations, the countries of the European Free Trade Association are particularly conscious of Europe's links with the rest of the world. They have therefore chosen a form of economic cooperation which, while strengthening Europe, enables them to take full account of the interests of other trading countries throughout the world, including those facing special problems of development. The Association is a further expression of the postwar drive towards lower trade barriers, and reflects the principles which have been established by the General Agreement on Tariffs and Trade (GATT). The individual freedom of action of EFTA members in their external tariffs will allow each of them to participate actively in GATT negotiations for tariff reductions.[2]

An accompanying resolution recognized in quite explicit terms that EFTA was a rival organization to the EEC and that EFTA presented a risk to the continued integrative process within Western Europe. At the very moment that the other seven countries were creating the rival organization, the resolution stated that "new" divisions should be avoided:

The existence of two groups, the European Free Trade Association and the European Economic Community, inspired by different but not incompatible principles, implies the risk that further progress . . . be hampered, if such a danger could not be avoided by an agreement to which all countries interested in European economic cooperation could subscribe. Such an agreement, based on the principle of reciprocity, should not cause any damage to the measures taken by the European Free Trade Association and the European Economic Community. Moreover, it should allow member States of either organization to eliminate in common the obstacles to trade between them, and more generally, to seek to solve the problems they share. Among these, there is the problem of aiding the less developed countries in Europe and in other continents, which is one of the foremost tasks of the more advanced countries. . . .

Common action in these fields would strengthen the already existing bonds between the European countries as well as the solidarity arising from their common destiny, even if their views on the way in which European integration should be achieved are not always identical. For these reasons, the seven Governments who will sign the Convention establishing the European Free Trade Association, declare their determination to do all in their power to avoid a new division in Europe. They regard their Association as a step toward an agreement between all member countries of OEEC.[3]

The very last sentence of this seven-country resolution underlined the extent to which EFTA was a British-led and British-inspired riposte to the European Community: "the seven Governments are ready to initiate negotiations with the members of the EEC as soon as *they* [emphasis supplied] are prepared to do so.'' The United Kingdom, through the EFTA mechanism, thus informed the European Community that it was now EFTA that was at the center of the universe—with Great Britain at the center of EFTA—and that EFTA expected the EC to make the first move at reconciliation; the EC declined the British offer.

The Current Status of EFTA

The European Free Trade Association never amounted to very much when compared to the much more ambitious and integrated European Community. Most of the free trade was between Great Britain and each of the others separately—the UK was the hub of the wheel and there was very little interaction among the spokes. EFTA, which began operations on 1 April 1960, is still in existence but with a vastly altered membership. The United Kingdom and Denmark left EFTA on 1 January 1973, and Portugal left on 1 January 1986; Iceland and Finland joined subsequently to 1960. EFTA's present membership is thus six countries: Austria, Finland, Iceland, Norway, Sweden, and Switzerland.

The EFTA countries' economies and foreign trade are extremely oriented toward the EC rather than within EFTA itself. The European Community has signed trading agreements with each individual EFTA member—the agreement was *not* with EFTA as an IGO—and, since 1 January 1984, all restrictions on industrial trade between the EFTA countries and the EC were removed. Table 2.1 contains the figures for each EFTA members' imports and exports. It is obvious that the EC is many more times important to the EFTA countries than is EFTA itself. As Table 2.1 indicates, the EFTA countries as a group, in 1984, had some 54 percent of their total imports coming from the EC; only 13 percent originated in the EFTA group. Also, approximately 52 percent of all EFTA exports went to the EC while only 14 percent was directed to the EFTA countries.

But EFTA does offer some tangible benefits for the six countries. Four (Austria, Finland, Sweden, and Switzerland) of the six are "neutrals" whose accession to the EC would be quite difficult under current political conditions. Along with Iceland and Norway, these six are small states with many similar interests and problems that can be dealt with as a group. The EFTA countries do attempt to present a common position on international trade matters in the larger international organizations (OECD, GATT), and the EFTA mechanism is employed by the countries to coordinate the free-trade agreements (the agreements are almost identical) with the European Community.

In 1960, the British-led European Free Trade Association was perceived as a direct challenge to—and a veiled attempt at sabotage of—the European Community; EFTA is now a welcomed partner within Western Europe. EC-EFTA cooperation has developed very rapidly in the 1980s, especially in R & D activities. Several agreements have been signed between the two groups that have enabled firms and research institutions in the EFTA countries to participate in EC-sponsored high-technology programs, especially in information storage-and-retrieval systems and telecommunications.

THE NEGOTIATION PROCESS, 1960–1972

Although the United Kingdom was the major proponent and organizer of the 1960 European Free Trade Association, it was obvious to all concerned that EFTA could never have possibly become a competitor or a viable alternative to the much more coherent and integrated EEC. Also, even with its strange sense of insularity, the United Kingdom had no illusions about its ability to effectively compete with the economies of the EC countries if it remained an outsider. And, finally, even with its traditional and extensive ties with the Commonwealth countries and its perception of having a "special relationship" with the United States, the United Kingdom realized that it was indeed a "European" country and that its future was with the Continent. It could not wait for the EC to take the initiative.

The United Kingdom thus began the slow—and dreadfully painful—process of negotiating entry into the EC. The first talks began in October 1960, only six months after EFTA entered into force and just a little more than two and one-half years after the Rome Treaties. This negotiation process lasted from October 1960 until the UK's eventual accession on 1 January 1973.

The First French Veto (1963)

In October 1960, the United Kingdom began informal talks and discussions—they were not characterized as formal *negotiations*—with the governments of the six EC member-states and with the EC Commission. In July 1961, it was decided to make a formal application to begin serious negotiations over the terms and conditions of British entry. The informal discussions obviously dealt only with generalities, and the British wanted more specific and concrete terms put on the table. The decision to make a formal application to begin negotiations over entry was announced on 31 July 1961 in a statement in the House of Commons by Harold Macmillan, the British prime minister:

The future relations between the European Economic Community, the United Kingdom, the Commonwealth and the rest of Europe are clearly matters of capital importance in the life of our country and, indeed, of all the countries of the free world. This is a political as well as an economic issue. Although the Treaty of Rome is concerned with economic matters it has an important political objective, namely, to promote unity and stability in Europe which is so essential a factor in the struggle for freedom and progress throughout the world. In this modern world the tendency towards large groups of nations acting together in the common interest leads to greater unity and thus adds to our strength in the struggle for freedom. I believe that it is both our duty and our interest to contribute towards that strength by securing the closest possible unity within Europe. . . .

On the economic side, a community comprising, as members or in association, the

Table 2.1
EFTA Trade, 1984 ($US Million)

IMPORTS FROM

Importing Country	EFTA		EC		Rest of World	
	Amount	Percent	Amount	Percent	Amount	Percent
Austria	1,552.8	7.92	11,840.7	60.43	6,201.4	31.65
Finland	2,234.2	17.96	4,426.9	35.58	5,781.3	46.46
Iceland	179.2	21.24	399.3	47.32	265.3	31.44
Norway	3,524.6	25.38	6,334.4	45.60	4,030.9	29.02
Portugal(a)	405.4	5.22	2,791.7	35.93	4,573.6	58.85
Sweden	4,732.2	17.97	13,906.9	52.80	7,700.4	29.23
Switzerland	1,980.6	6.65	20,039.2	67.29	7,759.6	26.06
Total	14,609.0	13.20	59,739.1	53.98	36,312.5	32.82

EXPORTS TO

Exporting Country	EFTA		EC		Rest of World	
	Amount	Percent	Amount	Percent	Amount	Percent
Austria	1,698.3	10.81	8,383.7	53.34	5,635.4	35.85
Finland	2,574.3	19.06	5,047.0	37.36	5,886.0	43.58
Iceland	96.4	12.86	289.2	38.58	364.1	48.56
Norway	2,485.5	13.14	13,239.7	69.98	3,194.7	16.88
Portugal(a)	543.9	10.24	3,003.2	56.55	1,763.7	33.21
Sweden	5,370.4	18.31	14,049.7	47.91	9,905.8	33.78
Switzerland	2,107.0	8.12	13,061.9	50.32	10,788.9	41.56
Total	14,875.8	13.59	57,074.4	52.13	37,535.6	34.28

a. Portugal is included in this table since the country did not leave EFTA until 31 December 1985.

Source: Calculated from figures in The Europe Year Book: A World Survey, Volume I, Part One, "International Organizations" (London: Europe Publications, Ltd., 1986), pp. 154-155.

countries of free Europe, could have a very rapidly expanding economy supplying, as eventually it would, a single market of approaching 300 million people. This rapidly expanding economy could, in turn, lead to an increased demand for products from other parts of the world and so help to expand world trade and improve the prospects of the less developed areas of the world. . . .

During the past nine months, we have had useful and frank discussions with the European Economic Community Governments. We have now reached the stage where we cannot make further progress without entering into formal negotiations. I believe that the great majority in the House and in the country will feel that they cannot fairly judge whether it is possible for the United Kingdom to join the European Economic Community until there is a clearer picture before them of the conditions on which we could join and the extent to which these could meet our special needs.[4]

But Macmillan's statement was not simply an announcement that the United Kingdom was prepared to negotiate; it also contained some British preconditions for such negotiations. The prime minister put the EC on notice that the UK would not negotiate away the Commonwealth or EFTA countries nor would it abandon its agricultural workers to the maw of the common agricultural policy. The British position was quite straightforward:

If a closer relationship between the United Kingdom and the countries of the European Economic Community were to disrupt the long-standing and historic ties between the United Kingdom and the other nations of the Commonwealth the loss would be greater than the gain. The Commonwealth is a great source of stability and strength both to Western Europe and to the world as a whole, and I am sure that its value is fully appreciated by the member Governments of the European Economic Community. I do not think that Britain's contribution to the Commonwealth will be reduced if Europe unites. On the contrary, I think that its value will be enhanced. . . .

Secondly, there is the European Free Trade Association. We have treaty and other obligations to our partners in this Association and . . . we agree that we should work closely together throughout any negotiations. Finally, we are determined to continue to protect the standard of living of our agricultural community.[5]

Macmillan must have been able to see the future when he cautioned the House of Commons that the negotiations would probably be difficult, protracted, and without any guarantee of success—an excellent description of what eventually transpired! The formal negotiations soon began, but immediately bogged down over the British insistence that it simply would not accept the common agricultural policy and its refusal to sever its trading arrangements with the Commonwealth countries (the Commonwealth Preference is discussed below).

The procedure for admission into the EC is that the applicant country negotiates the terms of accession with the Commission; the Commission makes a recommendation to the Council of Ministers; the Council—by a *unanimous* vote—accepts the applicant and calls for a treaty of accession to be drawn up (usually already agreed upon); the treaty is then ratified by all governments concerned (the original members and the new members). The EC Commission, however, never had the opportunity to reach a decision on Britain's first application. French President Charles de Gaulle, in a 14 January 1963 press conference, announced that the French member of the Council of Ministers would vote against any British application if it ever reached the Council stage. This promised veto put an abrupt end to the negotiation process. The British were wounded by de Gaulle's comments—he described them as "insular" with "original" (read "strange") habits and traditions and strongly implied that the UK's insistence on preconditions represented political chutzpah in its most extreme form.

Several observers have commented that de Gaulle's veto stemmed from personal animosity toward the British, formed by his perceived mistreatment by the British during World War II and the condescending attitude displayed by Churchill. Personality may have—or may not have—been relevant; what was certainly relevant was de Gaulle's emphatic refusal to allow Great Britain, as an outsider, to determine the rules of an already existing game. De Gaulle flayed Great Britain for her political hypocrisy, her insularity, her non-European attitudes, and her extensive ties with the United States and the Commonwealth countries.

It is instructive to cite at some length some excerpts from de Gaulle's press conference because they illustrate the total rejection by France of the British demands, preconditions, and the British claim that the European Community needed Great Britain more than Great Britain needed the Community:

Great Britain posed her candidature to the Common Market. She did it after having earlier refused to participate in the communities we are now building, as well as after creating a free trade area with six other States, and, finally, after having—I may as well say it, the negotiations held at such length on this subject will be recalled—after having put some pressure on the Six to prevent a real beginning being made in the application of the Common Market. If England asks in turn to enter, but on her own conditions, this poses without doubt to each of the six States, and poses to England, problems of a very great dimension. England in effect is insular, she is maritime, she is linked through her exchanges, her markets, her supply lines to the most diverse and often the most distant countries; she pursues essentially industrial and commercial activities, and only slight agricultural ones. She has in all her doings very marked and very original habits and traditions. . . .

One might sometimes have believed that our English friends, in posing their candidature to the Common Market, were agreeing to transform themselves to the point of applying all the conditions which are accepted and practiced by the Six. But the question, to know whether Great Britain can now place herself like the Continent and with it inside a tariff which is genuinely common, to renounce all Commonwealth preferences, to cease any pretense that her agriculture will be privileged, and, more than that, to treat her engagements with other countries of the free trade area as null and void—that question is the whole question. . . .

Yet it is possible that one day England might manage to transform herself sufficiently to become part of the European community, without restriction, without reserve and preference for anything whatsoever; and in this case the Six would open the door to her and France would raise no obstacle, although obviously England's simple participation in the Community would considerably change its nature and its volume. . . .

Lastly, it is very possible that Britain's own evolution, and the evolution of the universe, might bring the English little by little towards the Continent, whatever the delays the achievement might demand. And for my part . . . it will in any case have been a great honor for the British Prime Minister . . . to have discerned in good time, to have had enough political courage to have proclaimed it, and to have led their country the first steps down the path which one day, perhaps, will lead it to moor alongside the Continent.[6]

President de Gaulle's comments about Great Britain being an "outsider" and his petulant remark about their "marked and very original habits" most likely stemmed from his dislike of the British; similarly, his fears that the UK was only a stalking horse for an American attempt to dominate Europe most likely stemmed from his dislike of the Americans. But de Gaulle's comments on the British preconditions—preconditions on the Commonwealth Preference, the EC's common external tariff (CET), and the common agricultural policy (CAP)—were much more rational and concerned the very essence of the European Community. It is this author's perception that de Gaulle, however strident his tone, reached the correct decision when he vetoed Britain's first application in 1963.

The Commonwealth Preference, the Common External Tariff, and the Common Agricultural Policy

The EC of the Six expanded the concept of the ECSC and established a customs union—a common market—that had as its objective the eventual elimination of artificial barriers to trade (tariffs, duties, quotas) among the countries. Linked to this open internal market was the creation of a common external tariff (CET), applicable to goods coming into the EC from third countries. Both the customs union and the CET were slowly phased in by stages, but the basic mechanisms were already in place at the time of Britain's first application. Many goods that do not compete with EC-produced goods face no tariff at all; others may not face a tariff but be subject to country-of-origin national quotas (e.g., exports of bananas under the Lomé Convention to the EC had national quotas applied—there were simply too many bananas chasing too few Europeans); other goods face a very high tariff, making the EC-produced product far less expensive than the import (e.g., there are very few Japanese automobiles on the European roads); and, finally, some goods are simply denied entry (e.g., frozen chickens from the United States).

But whatever the specific nature of the CET, it is the same regardless of what EC country is doing the importing. The CET may vary from (third) country to country, season to season, and/or product to product, but for the same product from the same third country, the terms of entry will be identical across the entire EC. For example, a very high tariff is levied on California and Florida oranges throughout the year; Israeli oranges also face a high tariff during the summer months. But in winter, oranges from Haifa are given a preferential rate. The "common" part of the CET means that the tariff rate on the Israeli oranges will be identical, whether the oranges are shipped to Paris, Rome, Brussels, or to any other EC location. The imposition of a CET is an absolute necessary corollary to the internal customs union. In the absence of the CET, a third-country exporter would seek out the EC member with the most favorable entry terms and then—once within the EC's internal market—would have free access to the other countries. Obviously, the common external tariff is intended to prevent such a situation.

The British preconditions denied the very essence of this process. The UK's negotiating position held that the internal market and CET would apply only to industrial goods but *not* to raw materials or agricultural commodities and, therefore, most of the common agricultural policy's mechanisms would not apply to the United Kingdom. If met, this demand would have given the United Kingdom the best of both worlds (reaping the benefits of the EC without having to pay any costs): British industrial products would have free entry into the EC's internal market and probably would have been able to compete very effectively; at the same time, Britain could continue to place a high tariff on EC raw materials and agricultural commodities to maintain its very advantageous trading relations with the Commonwealth (the Commonwealth Preference) and the other EFTA members.

The Commonwealth Preference had evolved very slowly over the years, and it provided enormous economic benefits for Great Britain.[7] Basically, the Commonwealth Preference was a series of bilateral trading agreements between the United Kingdom and many Commonwealth countries—the UK would give "preference" to Commonwealth products if, in turn, this preference was reciprocal. For example, the UK would place a high tariff on, say, French wheat, and give preference to Canadian wheat. There is, in theory, nothing strange about such agreements, but the specific content of the Commonwealth Preference ran counter to the European Community's basic objectives.

Being a very heavily industrialized and urbanized country with a very small number of people engaged in agriculture, Great Britain has to import the raw materials for its factories and food for its population. In return, Great Britain exports the finished products (e.g., the UK would import New Zealand butter and export the milking machines; Canadian wheat would be traded for the tractors; wool from Australia to fuel the textile mills would be traded for the finished blankets and sweaters).

There are two conflicting interpretations to such an arrangement: (1) such international specialization brings economic benefits to both sides; or (2) it is simply another form of capitalist oppression and exploitation of the nonindustrialized countries. The argument employed by Great Britain—and accepted for a time by the Commonwealth countries—was that such specialization in production brought economic benefits to all concerned. For example, Canada is ideally suited to deliver wheat at a very competitive price to London—why should Canada attempt to build tractors when they were available from the United

Kingdom? Or, perhaps, Australia could specialize in the production of wool, but the mills would be in Great Britain. Each partner would produce what it was suited to produce and such efficiency would mean lower prices all around.

The above rationale may be true, but there are two counterarguments to the position. First, any country who relies on raw materials and/or agricultural commodities as the major economic sectors and sources of foreign exchange constantly runs the risk of being devastated by a crop failure (disease, weather conditions) and/or by drastically falling prices in the world market for its one export. Examples of this situation are numerous: Mexico and its reliance on oil exports; Brazil and its (former) reliance on the coffee crop; Malaysia and its rubber exports. The second counterargument to the presumed benefits of such arrangements is that the economic benefits always accrue to the industrial exporter (the United Kingdom). The changes in the terms of trade over the years have always favored the industrial exporter and have worked to the raw materials/ commodities exporter's disadvantage. That is to say, the "price" of the industrial goods have always risen faster than the price of the raw materials. Canada might have been able to exchange one ton of wheat for one tractor; the next year the tractor's price would be two tons; then three tons. . . . In the absence of international price-fixing cartels such as OPEC (Organization of Petroleum Exporting Countries)—something the Commonwealth countries wouldn't dream of organizing in their relationship with Great Britain—the raw materials/agricultural commodities producers would find themselves having to pay more and more for the same industrial product.

The second interpretation of the Commonwealth Preference—an interpretation never accepted by the British but eventually recognized by some of the Commonwealth countries—is that such an arrangement was only a subterfuge by Great Britain to prevent the Commonwealth countries from developing their industrial capacity. It is simply another situation of the capitalist countries maintaining their economic dominance over the developing countries and maintaining the latter's total dependence on either the good will of the industrial country or upon the vagaries of the weather.

But whatever the interpretation, Great Britain felt the need to protect the interests of the Commonwealth countries. At the time of the negotiations leading up to the establishment of EFTA (1959), several Commonwealth countries had a much larger volume of trade with the United Kingdom than with the EC countries. Table 2.2 shows the extent to which the countries depended upon Great Britain rather than the European Community countries for their imports. As Table 2.2 indicates, Canada imported some 10.6 percent of its products from the United Kingdom and only 5.3 percent from the EC countries; South Africa's figures are 31.1 percent compared to 18.3 percent; Australia was at 36.3 percent to 11.4 percent; and New Zealand showed the largest difference—32.2 percent of New Zealand's imports came from the United Kingdom and only 6.3 percent came from the EC. In addition, the Commonwealth Preference provided real economic benefits to Great Britain, particularly in relation to the price of food-

Table 2.2
UK, US, and EEC Shares of Selected Commonwealth Import Markets, 1959 (percent of total imports)

Importing Country	From the EEC	From the US	From the UK	Rest of World
Canada	5.3	67.7	10.6	16.4
South Africa	18.3	17.0	31.1	33.6
New Zealand	6.3	8.3	32.2	53.2
Australia	11.4	14.6	36.3	37.7

Source: Emile Benoît, Europe at Sixes and Sevens: The Common Market, The Free Trade Association, and the United States (New York: Columbia University Press, 1961), Table 4, p. 107.

Figure 2.1
Cost of Wheat in the United Kingdom (Hypothetical)

	Under Commonwealth Preference	Under the CET-CAP
Canadian Wheat	$1.00	$1.50
French Wheat	$2.00	$1.25

stuffs. The phasing out of the Commonwealth Preference—and the concurrent phasing in of the EC's CET and CAP—would have raised the cost of foodstuffs for the British consumer. A hypothetical example of this relationship is contained in Figure 2.1. Under the Commonwealth Preference, Canadian wheat would sell at, say, $1/bushel in London while French wheat, facing the high British tariff, would be at $2/bushel. Without the Preference but with the CET and CAP applied, Canadian wheat would now be at $1.50/bushel (Canadian wheat would be subject to the EC's tariff on wheat), and French wheat would be at $1.25/bushel. Even without the British tariff against the French, French wheat is more expensive than Canadian Preference wheat—this is due to the workings of the CAP and the less efficient French wheat production compared to Canadian wheat production.

The problem for the British economy and consumers is *not* that they decide that $1.25 French wheat is cheaper than $1.50 Canadian wheat and thus conclude it is a good buy; on the contrary, this $1.25 French wheat is 25 percent higher than what they were used to in the old days before the imposition of the CET and CAP and when the Commonwealth Preference was still in effect. The British (correctly) saw that food prices would skyrocket if the Commonwealth Preference were traded in for the common external tariff and the common agricultural policy; thus the preconditions. Maintaining the Preference without the CET and CAP would ensure the continuation of low-cost food in the United Kingdom and, as some observers commented, might have even allowed the Commonwealth products into the EC's internal markets without being subject to the CET. This would have totally devastated the EC's common agricultural policy.

President de Gaulle (rightly) perceived that such a situation would not have been in the long-term best interest of the European Community and thus vetoed the British application for membership in 1963. The British went off in a huff and sulked until 1966.

The Second French Veto (1967)

On 10 November 1966, Harold Wilson, then the British prime minister, announced that a second round of discussions about Britain's possible accession to the EC would begin. These discussions—they were not characterized as formal *negotiations*—took place from January to March 1967 between the British and the heads of the governments of the six EC countries and the Commission. The decision to make a formal application to begin serious negotiations over the terms of entry was announced on 2 May 1967 in a statement in the House of Commons by Harold Wilson:

Her Majesty's Government have today decided to make an application under Article 237 of the Treaty of Rome for membership of the European Economic Community and parallel applications for membership of the European Coal and Steel Community and Euratom. . . .

All of us are aware of the long-term potential for Europe, and, therefore, for Britain, of the creation of a single market of approaching 300 million people, with all the scope and incentive which this will provide for British industry, and of the enormous possibilities which an integrated strategy for technology, on a truly Continental scale, can create. . . .

We do not see European unity as something narrow or inward-looking. Britain has her own vital links through the Commonwealth, and in other ways, with other continents. So have other European countries. Together, we can ensure that Europe plays in world affairs the part which the Europe of today is not at present playing. For a Europe that fails to put forward its full economic strength will never have the political influence which I believe it could and should exert within the United Nations, within the Western Alliance, and as a means for effecting a lasting detente between East and West; and equally contributing in ever fuller measure to the solution of the world's North-South problem, to the needs of the developing world. It is for all these reasons that we intend to pursue our application for membership with all the vigour and determination at our command.[8]

But Wilson's Labor government made the same fatal mistake as did Macmillan's Conservative government in 1961—Wilson's statement also listed preconditions to the negotiations and eventual terms of entry. These preconditions, not surprisingly, dealt with the Commonwealth, the application of the common agricultural policy to the UK, capital movements, and the EC's regional policy. Prime Minister Wilson laid out the issues:

As I have already made clear publicly, we must be realistic and recognize that the Community's agricultural policy is an integral part of the Community; we must come to terms with it. But the Government recognizes that this policy would involve far-reaching changes in the structure of British agriculture. This will require suitable arrangements, including an adequate transitional period, to enable the necessary adjustments to be made. It is also the Government's view that the financial arrangements which have been devised to meet the requirements of the Community's agricultural policy as it exists today would, if applied to Britain as they now stand, involve an inequitable sharing of the financial cost and impose on our balance of payments an additional burden which we should not in fairness be asked to carry. There are also highly important Commonwealth interests, mainly in the field of agriculture, for which it is our duty to seek safeguards in the negotiations. These include, in particular, the special problems of New Zealand and of Commonwealth sugar-producing countries, whose needs are at present safeguarded by the Commonwealth Sugar Agreement. We have . . . been in touch with all our Commonwealth partners, and will make special arrangements to keep in close consultation with them, as with our EFTA partners, throughout the negotiations.[9]

Great Britain, joined this time by Denmark, Ireland, and Norway, then made formal application, and negotiations with the EC Commission began—Charles de Gaulle of France was only biding his time. On 29 September 1967, the Commission recommended to the Council of Ministers that the four countries' applications be accepted in principle with additional negotiations to make the details more precise; the British, to say the least, were quite pleased. But on 27 November 1967, Charles de Gaulle, in another press conference, simply announced that the British were not "ready" for EC membership. De Gaulle's 1967 statement was much less petulant than his 1963 broadside, but the effect was the same.

At the 19 December 1967 Council of Ministers' meeting, the French minister—obviously acting upon instructions from de Gaulle—vetoed the application. The statement issued by the Council of Ministers contained the following comments:

1. . . . the Council . . . noted that no Member State has raised any fundamental objection to the enlargement of the Communities. When noting this fact, the Council assumed that the new member states would fully accept the Treaties and the decisions adopted by the Community. One Member State, however, expressed the opinion that this enlargement would profoundly alter the nature of the Communities, and the methods of administering them . . .
5. Five Member States agreed with the Commission's point of view. They expressed their desire for the immediate opening of negotiations for the accession of Great Britain, Denmark, Ireland and Norway, so that these negotiations might be undertaken in parallel with the re-establishment of Great Britain's economic situation. One Member State considered that the re-establishment of the British economy must be completed before Great Britain's request can be considered.
6. For this reason, there was no agreement in the Council at this stage on the next step to be taken.
7. The requests for accession presented by the United Kingdom, Ireland, Denmark, and Norway remain on the Council's agenda.[10]

The British, joined by Denmark, Ireland, and Norway, again went off in a snit and sulked some more until 1970.

The Third Attempt (1970–1972)

The British did not have very long to wait after the second French veto in 1967. French President Charles de Gaulle resigned on 28 April 1969—he was succeeded by Georges Pompidou in July—and the entire political environment was changed overnight. President Pompidou may not have been enamored of the British but, at least, he did not harbor any personal animosities, and the British finally realized that setting preconditions to any negotiations would only invite a third veto. In this changed political atmosphere, the British (and Denmark, Ireland, and Norway) fully expected progress to ensue.

On 1–2 December 1969, the European Council (the heads of state or government of the six EC countries) met at The Hague. This particular European Council meeting was held because President Pompidou took the initiative—a very significant (and symbolic) gesture on the part of the French. The Hague Summit reviewed the past 12 years of the EC's existence—the transitional period was about to expire—and pledged further efforts within the integrative process. One of the most important paragraphs of the Summit's Final Communiqué was a *direct* invitation to Great Britain and the three other countries to return to the negotiating table, with the obvious objective of joining the EC. This invitation was worded as follows:

The European Communities remain the original nucleus from which European unity has been developed and intensified. The entry of other countries of this continent to the Communities—in accordance with the provisions of the Treaties of Rome—would undoubtedly help the Communities to grow to dimensions more in conformity with the present state of world economy and technology. The creation of a special relationship with other European states which have expressed a desire to that effect would also contribute to this end. A development such as this would enable Europe to remain faithful to its traditions of being open to the world and increase its efforts in behalf of developing countries.

Formal negotiations thus began for the third time in 1970, but with two vital differences: Charles de Gaulle was no longer available to protect the Continent from the "very original" British and, probably more significant, the British did not insist on the "what is mine is mine and what is yours is negotiable" principle. On 19 January 1972, the EC Commission, chaired by Franco Malfatti, delivered a unanimous favorable recommendation to the Council of Ministers regarding the accession of the four applicants to the European Community. Sections of the Commission's opinion are presented below, and they should be compared to de Gaulle's intemperate 1963 comments:

THE COMMISSION OF THE EUROPEAN COMMUNITIES....
—whereas the terms for the admission of these States and the adjustments necessitated by their accession have been negotiated in a Conference between the Communities and the applicant States; and whereas singleness of Community representation was ensured with due regard for the institutional dialogue provided for by the Treaties;
—whereas, on the completion of these negotiations, it is apparent that the provisions so agreed are fair and proper; and whereas, this being so, the Community's enlargement, while preserving its internal cohesion and dynamism, will enable it to take a fuller part in the development of international relations;

—whereas in joining the Communities the applicant States accept without reserve the Treaties and their political objectives, all decisions taken since their entry into force, and the action that has been agreed in respect of the development and reinforcement of the Communities;

—whereas it is an essential feature of the legal system set up by the Treaties establishing the Communities that certain of their provisions and certain acts of the Community institutions are directly applicable, that Community law takes precedence over any national provisions conflicting with it, and that procedures exist for ensuring the uniform interpretation of this law; and whereas accession to the Communities entails recognition of the binding force of these rules, observance of which is indispensable to guarantee the effectiveness and unity of Community law,

HEREBY DELIVERS A FAVORABLE OPINION.[11]

The EC Council of Ministers, on 22 January 1972, unanimously accepted the Commission's opinion that the four applications for accession be accepted in a very short statement: "The conditions of admission and the adjustments to the Treaties necessitated thereby are to be the subject of an agreement between the Member States and the Applicant States."[12] The conditions of admission and the adjustments to the treaties were, obviously, already agreed to, and, on 22 January 1972, in Brussels, the Treaty of Accession was signed by each of the four applicant states (Denmark, Ireland, Norway, and the United Kingdom) and by each of the six original EC members. The Treaty of Accession had to be ratified by each of the ten countries, following their own national constitutional procedures.

The treaty was ratified in all but one of the states (Norway). But the Community's enlargement was accepted by large margins in the other nine countries— 67.7 percent of the French electorate approved—and on 1 January 1973, the European Community's membership increased from six to nine members, with the entry of Denmark, Ireland, and the United Kingdom.

THE 1972 NORWEGIAN REFERENDUM

On 24–25 September 1972, the Norwegian population went to the polls to vote on accession to the EC; membership was rejected by a vote of 46 percent for and 54 percent against. The referendum was a nonbinding advisory to the Norwegian parliament, but the Storting soon thereafter, in a formal vote, declined membership. Norwegian Prime Minister Trygve Bratteli, who strongly supported entry, subsequently resigned after his position was rejected. Several reasons have been advanced to explain the Norwegian opposition:[13]

1. The "pro-Europe" political parties and interest groups mounted a rather low-key and ineffectual campaign, started only after the Treaty of Accession was negotiated. Prime Minister Bratteli waited until every last detail was ironed out before the campaign was put into operation, but the opposition "anti-Europe" forces started some two

years earlier, during the negotiation process itself. This two-year head start placed EC supporters on the defensive, and they just couldn't overcome the lead of the anti-Europe forces.

2. The Danish Prime Minister, Jens Otto Krag, did not help matters by scheduling the Danish referendum to take place *after* the Norwegian vote. Support for the pro-EC position had always been much stronger in Denmark than in Norway, and if the Danes had voted first, perhaps many Norwegians might have been swayed to change their minds.

3. The EC itself contributed to the rejection by a very untimely and callous decision. Just a short time before the referendum, the Council of Ministers (without, obviously, the Norwegian minister) issued some regulations on fishing rights in coastal areas. These regulations—opening up Norwegian coastal areas to other EC countries—were perceived by many people in Norway as a direct threat to a vital national interest. The action by the Council of Ministers was perceived as a symbolic gesture of the EC's ill will to Norway. The fishing-rights question was a decisive factor for the very large (up to 93 percent) no vote in many coastal and northern areas.

4. Opponents of entry were able to convince many Norwegians that the EC—rightly or wrongly—stressed industrial growth and sterile economic development at the expense of individual happiness and fulfillment, social concerns, and environmental quality. These arguments—some true, some false—reinforced an emotional nationalism among farmers and created real doubts about the future of Norway as a member of the European Community.

THE 1973 ENLARGEMENT

An important milestone was reached in the European integrative process when Denmark, Ireland, and the United Kingdom formally entered the European Community on 1 January 1973. It was an obviously significant event for the three new countries—transferring some sovereign decision-making powers to Brussels, Great Britain renouncing her insularity by becoming a "European" country, and Denmark and the UK leaving EFTA—but the 1973 enlargement also represented a significant event for the original EC countries. The six original European Community countries—15 years after the EEC began operating and 20 years after the ECSC—perceived the intracommunity consensus and integration levels to have been of sufficient strength and stability to deal with the problems inherent in the expansion by 50 percent in the number of participants in the decision-making process and in the marked increase in the group's heterogeneity. Decisions that previously had to synthesize six separate (and often quite diverse) views now, in the post–1973 period, had to reconcile nine national interests and positions.

Not unexpectedly, the short-term results of this increase in numbers and cultural heterogeneity were less decisions from the EC framework and, for these, what was able to be coordinated among the Nine was more limited in scope and applicability. With nine participants, a decision-making process that used either the lowest common denominator or splitting the difference obviously resulted in a lower level of productivity than the same process in a group of six. It was really not until the end of the 1970s that the EC was able to return to the upgrading of a common-interests decision-making process.

Be that as it may, the Treaty of Accession and the accompanying protocols were concluded, and it appears there was a compromise reached between the United Kingdom and the original EC members (the Danes and the Irish might have been joined with the British application, but they did not subscribe to all of the British demands).[14] Specifically, arrangements were made concerning the Commonwealth Preference, the common external tariff, and the common agricultural policy. A five-year transitional period—lasting until 31 December 1977—was established to allow the three new countries to phase in by annual steps the EC mechanisms.

This five-year transitional period was most relevant for the United Kingdom. The dismantlement of her tariffs–import duties against EC members coincided with the gradual imposition of the CET against third countries (including the importation of raw materials and agricultural commodities from the Commonwealth). In addition, during this transitional period, any product imported into the UK under the (slowly disappearing) Commonwealth Preference, if then reexported to another EC member, would *not* be considered in free circulation within the internal market and thus would be subject to 100 percent of the relevant CET.

This transitional period recognized the situation of the Commonwealth countries (Great Britain was most concerned about New Zealand). The Commonwealth countries would now have five years to seek out new markets for their exports and/or diversify their economies so that they would no longer be dependent on a single crop with a single customer. Canada was not affected to any great extent since, even before the UK's accession to the EC, the dominant part of Canada's trade was with the United States. But for other Commonwealth countries (Australia, South Africa [South Africa in 1973 was not yet quite the international pariah that it became in the 1980s], and especially New Zealand), the five-year transitional period afforded the time to accommodate themselves to UK membership in the EC.

The European Community itself recognized the problems of the Commonwealth, most of whom were not modern westernized countries such as Australia, Canada, and New Zealand, but, rather, were those who belonged to the impoverished Third World underdeveloped areas (India, Pakistan, the African members of the Commonwealth). In a classic political deal between the British and the French, the EC at the time signed an association agreement (economic development, cooperation, and trade) with 46 African, Caribbean, and Pacific (ACP) countries—Lomé I—that offered preferential access to the EC market. Of these 46, 22 belonged to the British Commonwealth; most of the others belonged to the French Community of Nations.

The British felt relieved: they had five years to adjust to the EC mechanisms; they believed the Commonwealth was protected; and, even though food prices might eventually increase, British industry now had free access to the large EC market. All was well until one year later, in February 1974, when the British had a general parliamentary election.

THE 1975 REFERENDUM

For most of the 1960s and 1970s, the British relationship to the European Community was a political football, with the party out of power adopting the opposite position to the one supported by the government; consistency was not necessarily a virtue. It was all very similar to the late 1940s–early 1950s, with the constant flip-flop by the two major parties concerning the nationalization of the steel industry: each new government would undo whatever decisions its predecessor made. The European Community was perceived as a partisan political issue, with both the Conservative and Labor parties constantly changing their position depending upon what they thought would appeal to the voters and, no less important, to distinguish themselves from the other party.

It was a Conservative government under Harold Macmillan that suffered Charles de Gaulle's first veto in 1963; Harold Wilson and the Labor party lost the second round in 1967; the Conservatives under Edward Heath successfully negotiated Britain's entry in 1973. But the Labor party, in opposition in 1973, was against the terms of entry and promised (threatened) to make Great Britain's membership in the EC an issue in the next general parliamentary election.

The United Kingdom had a general parliamentary election in February 1974 and, as promised, the Labor opposition, led by Harold Wilson, made EC membership a salient issue during the campaign. The Labor party's election manifesto made it quite clear that the party *rejected* the Conservative-negotiated terms under which the country joined the EC. Wilson made a campaign pledge to the effect that, if returned to power, the Labor party would set out to get "better" terms by renegotiating. If "better" terms could not be won, Wilson added, the United Kingdom would leave the European Community forthwith. Finally, Wilson promised the electorate that after the renegotiations were completed, his government would then hold a referendum to allow the British population to decide for themselves whether or not to remain in the EC under the hoped-for new terms and conditions.

The election was held in February 1974, and the Labor party unseated Edward Heath and the Conservatives. Returned as prime minister, Harold Wilson now had to honor his election pledges. The renegotiation process started all over again in April 1974 and lasted until March 1975.

The Reasons for the Referendum

The British decision to renegotiate "better" terms or leave the EC was a result of their reaction to factors that occurred within a very short time. Some were totally outside the EC framework and would have had an impact upon the United

Kingdom to the same extent (or even more) had Great Britain *not* been in the EC or even if the EC had not existed. The EC countries themselves were affected by some of these same events. Other factors were attributable to Great Britain's membership in the Community.

Thus, only one year after Britain's accession, a large number of people wanted out! Most did not bother to distinguish between EC-relevant factors and the factors not attributable to the EC—the European Community (particularly the French) was blamed for everything. Prior to 1 January 1973, the British economic environment was reasonably stable; by February 1974 it had deteriorated to a serious degree. With an almost childlike thinking process that looked for simple explanations, people in the United Kingdom blamed the EC (read "the French") for the economic downturn. Great Britain suffered a severe case of "stagflation"—inflation and unemployment and interest rates all were increasing at staggering rates—and, obviously, it could only have been the result of the country's ill-advised association with all those foreigners on the Continent. In reality, however, only about half of Britain's economic problems were attributable to the EC; the other half had nothing to do with the European Community. The following sections discuss some of the reasons for Britain's problems which, in turn, led to the renegotiations and the referendum.

The Political Environment

The political environment, obviously, did not increase the price of a loaf of bread to an unemployed person in London, but the political rhetoric fueled an already heated atmosphere. Wilson and the Labor party deliberately made EC membership a political issue in the 1974 campaign. But the exposition of subtle arguments do not sit well in political campaigns—politicians and the people prefer one-liners rather than lengthy discussions—and the entire issue of continued EC membership was thus reduced to political slogans. The Conservatives brought the country into the EC and, therefore, by political definition, Labor had to oppose it and constantly tell the population what an unfair deal had been achieved. There was no question that the EC contributed to Britain's economic problems, but the partisan political environment magnified the situation and raised it to a matter of high-state politics and the defense of the national interest.

Wilson spent so much time telling people how bad it was for the United Kingdom to be in the EC under the terms negotiated by the Conservatives that quite a few people began to believe the political rhetoric. If Wilson had not pursued this course of action with so much resolve, the EC would have been seen in its proper framework. But Wilson the candidate had to engage in Tory-bashing; the problem was that there was a lot of EC-bashing as well.

The Energy Crisis

On 6 October 1973, the Yom Kippur War between Egypt and Israel broke out. Shortly thereafter, the Arab oil producers (OAPEC—Organization of Arab Petroleum Exporting Countries) began a boycott on the export of oil to Western

Europe, the United States, and Japan to pressure these countries to change their policies vis-à-vis Israel and make them bring pressure on Israel. This "crisis of supply" soon gave way, however, to the "crisis of price"—OAPEC by January 1974 increased the price of oil by some 400 percent compared to pre–October 1973 levels. The energy-dependent, industrialized West thus faced a severe economic problem.[15]

The energy crisis—and its effects upon Great Britain—could *not* be attributable to the EC or to the French by any stretch of the imagination. Some Community countries, especially the Netherlands, were affected much more than Great Britain. But the 1974 energy crisis had a direct relationship to the increased cost of a loaf of bread because the price of oil and energy was relevant in almost every stage of the production process: fertilizer to grow the wheat; fuel to harvest and store the grain; the milling and baking process consumed energy; the plastic wrap around the bread was a petroleum derivative; gasoline to fuel the trucks that delivered the bread to the retailer; even the supermarket had to pay more for heat and electricity. All these factors combined on the grocery shelves, and when a London shopper, facing unemployment, high interest rates, *and* higher energy costs, had to pay more for a loaf of bread, there had to be a simple reason for it or there had to be someone to blame. The blame was usually leveled at the EC (read "the French") because, most likely, the loaf of bread was now baked from French wheat rather than Canadian wheat.

The energy crisis affected all segments of the British economy. This was in 1974–1975, well before North Sea oil was being produced in large quantities (it was not until 1980 that North Sea oil made Great Britain self-sufficient in oil supplies, and it was not until 1981 that Great Britain became a net exporter). Prices were increasing rapidly, interest rates were soaring, unemployment was at record levels, and the cost of the weekly grocery cart skyrocketed—OAPEC had all the pleasure and the EC received the blame.

The Currency Conversion

Another factor that contributed to increased prices was the lingering effects of the 15 February 1971 conversion of the British currency to the decimal system. Although instituted well before Britain's entry into the EC, it occurred close enough so that many people thought that, somehow, the currency conversion was linked to Britain's EC membership. The currency conversion and its effects, similar to the energy crisis, were not attributable to the European Community, but this did not matter. More often than not, the part of the loaf of bread's price increase that could be attributable to the currency conversion was not perceived as such—as usual, it was all the fault of those French.

The British retired its rather quaint but totally incomprehensible (except, of course, to the British) system of shillings, pence, and half-pence and instituted the extremely more rational decimal system. The value of the currency did not alter, but a new coinage system was introduced. Rather than having two one-half pence = one pence and 12 pence = one shilling and 20 shillings = one pound (480 half-pence or 240 pence to the pound), the new system had 100 pence = one pound with coins of various amounts (a five "new pence" piece, being one-twentieth of a pound, was equal to the old shilling in value, but the coins were changed).

This conversion had costs associated with it, and, as usual, it was the British taxpayer/consumer who paid. With new coins and the retirement of the shilling piece, extensive conversions were necessary: new cash registers, new vending machines, new price-marking tools, new coin boxes for telephones, new automatic toll baskets, etc. Thus, when the London consumer bought the loaf of bread, in addition to the increased price caused by the energy crisis, most often a few extra pence were added on by the retailer to cover the costs of the new cash registers and the price markers.

When the consumer complained about the price rise, the stock answer was *not* that OAPEC raised the price of energy some 400 percent and/or that the consumer had to pay for the new cash register; rather, the response was that since Great Britain was now in the European Community, the bread was made from French wheat and it was the French-led EC that was at fault. Such an argument had its own inner logic and was fueled by the Labor government. Some even went so far as to believe that the EC made the currency conversion a prior condition before the country could enter the EC and that this was a direct attack on the country's national sovereignty. In addition, more than a few people even believed that the French were about to force the British to eat Euro-bread and drink Euro-beer and, in what was perhaps the height of this paranoia, the French were about to force the British to switch from driving on the left!

The EC Contribution

The energy crisis and the lingering effects of the currency conversion accounted for approximately 50 percent of the increase in our loaf of bread; the remaining 50 percent was directly attributable to the EC mechanisms. As a result of the combined effects of the gradual elimination of the Commonwealth Preference, together with the gradual imposition of the common external tariff for agricultural commodities (Canadian wheat and New Zealand butter were becoming more expensive), along with the gradual elimination of British tariffs against EC foodstuffs (the internal customs union), French wheat and French butter were less expensive than Commonwealth products.

But due to the high support prices within the EC's common agricultural policy (the CAP is discussed in Chapter 7) and, in addition, due to the imposition of the value-added-tax (the VAT is discussed in Chapter 3), French wheat and butter were *more* expensive than were Preference Canadian wheat or New Zealand butter before Great Britain entered the EC.

People in the United Kingdom most definitely had to pay more for foodstuffs, and the entire increase was seen to flow from the CET, the CAP, the VAT, and the phasing out of the Commonwealth Preference. What was conveniently overlooked, however, were the gains made by the British industrial sector by its increased exports to the large EC market. Be that as it may, the French were seen to be "doing in" the British, and thus Wilson's demand for renegotiations or else.

The Renegotiations

As mentioned above, the renegotiations lasted from April 1974 until March 1975. On 18 March 1975, Prime Minister Wilson made the following announcement: "I believe that our renegotiation objectives have been substantially though not completely achieved." The main objectives Wilson referred to concerned food, money, and jobs (all with obvious political overtones). In a pamphlet issued by the Labor government prior to the June referendum, the new terms of EC membership were explained to the British population in very simple language:

Britain had to ensure that shoppers could get secure supplies of food at fair prices. As a result of these negotiations the Common Market's agricultural policy (known as CAP) now works more flexibly to the benefit of both housewives and farmers in Britain. The special arrangements made for sugar and beef are a good example. At the same time many food prices in the rest of the world have shot up, our food prices are now no higher because Britain is in the Market than if we were outside. The Government also won a better deal on food imports from countries outside the Common Market, particularly for Commonwealth sugar and for New Zealand dairy products. These will continue to be on sale in our shops. This is not the end of improvements in the Market's food policy. There will be further reviews. Britain, as a member, will be able to seek further changes to our advantage. And we shall be more sure of our supplies when food is scarce in the world.
. . .

Under the previous terms, Britain's contribution to the Common Market budget imposed too heavy a burden on us. The new terms ensure that Britain will pay a fairer share. We now stand . . . to get back from Market funds up to £125 million a year. There was a threat to employment in Britain from the movement in the Common Market towards an Economic and Monetary Union. This could have forced us to accept fixed exchange rates for the pound, restricting industrial growth and so putting jobs at risk. This threat has been removed. Britain will not have to put VAT on necessities like food. We have also maintained our freedom to pursue our own policies on taxation and on industry, and to develop Scotland and Wales and the Regions where unemployment is high.[16]

The 1975 Referendum

The Labor government under Harold Wilson recommended to the British people to vote for staying in the European Community under the renegotiated terms. The government's pamphlet not only listed the advantages of staying in—more funds from the European Investment Bank and the Regional and Social Funds, for example—but warned the British population about the effects on the country if it gave up community membership:

What would be the effect on Britain if we gave up membership of the Common Market? In the Government's view, the effect could only be damaging. Inevitably, there would be a period of uncertainty. Businessmen who had made plans for investment and development on the basis of membership would have to start afresh. Foreign firms might hesitate to continue investment in Britain. Foreign loans to help finance our trade deficit might be harder to get. We would have to try to negotiate some special free trade arrangement, a new Treaty. We would be bound by that Treaty. Its conditions might be harsh. But unless and until it was in force, Britain's exports to the Common Market would be seriously handicapped. We would no longer be inside the Common Market tariff wall—but outside. For a time at least, there would be a risk of making unemployment and inflation worse. Other countries have made these special arrangements with the Community. They might find Community decisions irksome, even an interference with their affairs. But they have no part in making those decisions. The Common Market will not go away if we say "No." The countries of the Common Market would still be our nearest neighbours and our largest customers. Their policies would still be important to us. But Britain would no longer have a close and direct influence on those policies. More than that, decisions taken in Brussels—in which Britain would have no voice—would affect British trade and therefore British jobs. Britain would no longer have any say in the future economic and political development of the Common Market. Nor on its relations with the rest of the world—particularly on the help to be given to the poorer nations of the world. We would just be outsiders looking in. Whether we are in the Market or not, Common Market policies are going to affect the lives of every family in the country. Inside the Market, we can play a major part in deciding these policies. Outside, we are on our own.[17]

On 9 April 1975, the British House of Commons, in a vote of conscience, voted by 396 to 170 in favor of staying in the European Community under the renegotiated terms. The referendum was scheduled for 5 June 1975 and, following past traditions, since the Labor party was recommending a yes vote, the opposition Conservative party recommended a no vote. The referendum was duly held, and approximately 64 percent of the electorate voted; two-thirds of those voting opted for the United Kingdom to remain in the Community.[18] Although Britain thus remained within the European Community, the referendum showed that there was serious opposition to the EC: only 42 percent of all eligible voters supported continued membership, 22 percent were against, and a full 36 percent didn't even bother to vote. This "anti-Europe" sentiment was based on the widespread belief that the UK had received very little in tangible benefits since accession, and such views continue to be quite strong in Great Britain.

SOME RECENT DEVELOPMENTS

The British relationship to the European Community has continued to be tenuous. As discussed in Chapter 3, the British attempted to employ a de facto veto based on the then-discredited national interest defense within the Council of Ministers. Several major decisions were taken over the strong objections of the British representative, and the incident showed that the United Kingdom was still not totally committed to the collective decision-making process of the Community. Also (as discussed in Chapter 7), the British (with some justification, however) continue to oppose the operation of the common agricultural policy. The British perceive the CAP as a vast entitlement program only for the benefit of the French agricultural sector paid for by the British consumer. In her eight years as prime minister, Margaret Thatcher has frequently been criticized by many for making the UK Europe's "odd man out" and for resisting closer political and economic cooperation; the prime minister has graciously returned the compliment by referring to her critics as "Euroloons" or "Eurofanatics." The British still remain outside the European Monetary System (discussed in Chapter 3), and the political rhetoric continues, with the opposition Labor party calling during the last parliamentary elections for a British withdrawal. The British are no longer threatening to leave the Community—some 45 percent of its total trade is with the EC—but it should be obvious that its level of commitment is far less than, say, the Dutch or the Belgian.

NOTES

The literature on the United Kingdom's relationship with the European Community—both for the pre–1973 period and then as a member—is quite extensive. For a representative overview of the various positions and arguments, see: Richard Bailey, *The European Connection: Britain's Relationship with the European Community* (Elmsford, N.Y.: Pergamon, 1983); Miriam Camps, *Britain and the European Community, 1955–1963* (Princeton, N.J.: Princeton University Press, 1964); Paul Einzig, *The Case Against Joining the Common Market* (New York: St. Martin's, 1971); F. E. C. Gregory, *Dilemmas of Government: Britain and the European Community* (London: Martin Robinson, 1983); John Lambert, *Britain in a Federal Europe* (London: Chatto and Windus, 1968); A. Lamfallusy, *The United Kingdom and the Six* (Homewood, Ill.: Richard Irwin, 1963); and S. Z. Young, *Terms of Entry: Britain's Negotiations with the European Community, 1970–1972* (London: Heinemann, 1973).

1. For a most detailed discussion of this period, see Emile Benoit, *Europe at Sixes and Sevens: The Common Market, The Free Trade Association, and the United States* (New York: Columbia University Press, 1961).

2. Communiqué and Resolution regarding the establishment of the European Free Trade Association, Stockholm (20 November 1959). *Her Majesty's Command Papers*, no. 106 (London: Her Majesty's Stationery Office, 1959), pp. 5–6.

3. Ibid.

4. Statement by the British Prime Minister, Harold Macmillan, on the British Application for Membership in the European Economic Community; House of Commons, 31 July 1961. *Parliamentary Debates* (London: Hansard), Fifth Series, Vol. 645, pp. 928–931.

5. Ibid.

6. Press Conference of General Charles de Gaulle, President of France, at the Elysée Palace, Paris (14 January 1963). Direction des services d'information et de presse du Ministère des Affaires Etrangères, *Textes et Notes*, no. 39/IP (23 January 1963).

7. For some analysis of the Commonwealth Preference, see: Dennis Austin, *Britain, Commonwealth Africa and the EEC* (New York: Penguin, 1968); S. J. Rogers and B. H. Davey, *The Common Agricultural Policy and Britain* (Lexington, Mass.: D. C. Heath,

1973); and Pierre Uri, ed., *From Commonwealth to Common Market* (New York: St. Martin's Press, 1976).

8. Statement by the British Prime Minister, Harold Wilson, on the British Application for Membership in the European Economic Community; House of Commons, 2 May 1967. *Parliamentary Debates* (London: Hansard), Fifth Series, Vol. 746, pp. 310–314.

9. Ibid.

10. Communiqué of the Council of Ministers of the EC on the Application for Membership of the United Kingdom, 19 December 1967. *Bulletin of the European Communities*, no. 1 (January 1968), 8–9.

11. Commission Opinion on the Applications for Accession to the European Communities by the Kingdom of Denmark, Ireland, the Kingdom of Norway, and the United Kingdom of Great Britain and Northern Ireland (19 January 1972). Sweet & Maxwell's Legal Editorial Staff, eds., *European Community Treaties*, 2nd ed. (London: Sweet & Maxwell, 1975), p. 245.

12. Decision of the Council of the European Communities on the Accession of the Kingdom of Denmark, Ireland, the Kingdom of Norway, and the United Kingdom of Great Britain and Northern Ireland to the European Economic Community and to the European Atomic Energy Community (22 January 1972). Sweet & Maxwell's Legal and Editorial Staff, eds., *European Community Treaties*, 2nd ed. (London: Sweet & Maxwell, 1975), p. 247.

13. Frederik Bolin, "Why Norway Bolted," 161 *Europe* (December 1972), 13.

14. The texts of the Treaty of Accession, the Act Concerning the Conditions of Accession and the Adjustments to the Treaties, and some of the more than two dozen protocols, declarations, and annexes are reproduced in Sweet & Maxwell's Legal Editorial Staff, eds., *European Community Treaties*, 2nd ed. (London: Sweet & Maxwell, 1975), pp. 248–310.

15. For a comprehensive analysis of the impact of the energy crisis on the European Community, see Robert J. Lieber, *Oil and the Middle East War: Europe in the Energy Crisis* (Cambridge, Mass.: Harvard Center for International Affairs, 1976).

16. "Britain's New Deal In Europe" (London, Her Majesty's Stationery Office, 1975), pp. 8–9.

17. Ibid., pp. 13–14.

18. The Welsh voted 64.8 percent yes; the Scots 58.4 percent yes; the English 68.3 percent yes; but in Northern Ireland, only 52.1 percent voted to remain in the EC. Stephen L. Bristow, "Partisanship, Participation and Legitimacy in Britain's EEC Referendum," 14 *Journal of Common Market Studies* (June 1976), 297–310.

PART II

The Institutional Framework

Each of the three treaties (ECSC, EEC, and EURATOM), separately and independently from one another, provided the legal basis for very similar institutions:

1. A Council of Ministers;
2. A Commission (called the High Authority in the ECSC Treaty);
3. An Assembly (or Parliament);
4. A Court of Justice; and
5. An Economic and Social Committee (under the EEC and EURATOM Treaties) and a Consultative Committee (under the ECSC Treaty).

In order to avoid the highly illogical situation of having three *separate* assemblies and three *separate* courts, however, the Six also signed a convention in Rome that provided for only one Assembly and only one Court of Justice for all three Communities. Thus, from 1 January 1958, there were, in legal existence, three Councils of Ministers, two Commissions and one High Authority, one Assembly, one Court of Justice, one Economic and Social Committee, and one Consultative Committee. But since the composition of the Councils of Ministers were identical under all three treaties, a strange ritual had to be observed. The Council of Ministers would convene and conduct business under the authority of, say, the ECSC Treaty, but, before dealing with EEC matters, the Council would have to adjourn formally and then reconvene immediately under the authority of the second treaty. This charade lasted for almost ten years.

On 8 April 1965, the Six signed the Merger Treaty, consolidating the three Communities' executive institutions into a single, unified framework. The Merger

Treaty became effective on 1 July 1967, and, since that date, each of the major executive institutions have had the ability to deal with questions arising from any one of the three treaties. The major institutions now existing within the European Community framework are as follows:

1. A Council of Ministers, assisted by the Committee of Permanent Representatives (CPR or, following the more frequently used French title, COREPER);
2. A Commission;
3. A Parliament;
4. A Court of Justice; and
5. An Economic and Social Committee (for EEC and EURATOM matters) and a Consultative Committee (for ECSC matters).

The Council of Ministers (usually the foreign ministers but often other ministers, depending upon the subject matter being discussed) dominates the Community decision-making process and it is expected to protect and represent the interests of the national governments. The European Commission initiates most policy proposals and then implements whatever particular policy the Council approves; the Commission is expected to protect, represent, and further the "European" interest or the Community's interest to counter the member-governments' more narrow national self-interests. The European Parliament, originally chosen by and from each member's national parliament but now elected directly by the Community's voters, is expected to represent the European peoples' interest. The Court of Justice is expected to represent the interests of law, justice, and equity in adjudicating disputes arising from the three treaties. Finally, the Economic and Social Committee (and the Consultative Committee) represent the organized economic, social, and functional groups across the Community. Figure II.1 contains the restructured (post–1967) bureaucratic-institutional framework. The following chapters present a discussion of these major institutions.

Figure II.1
The Institutions of the European Community

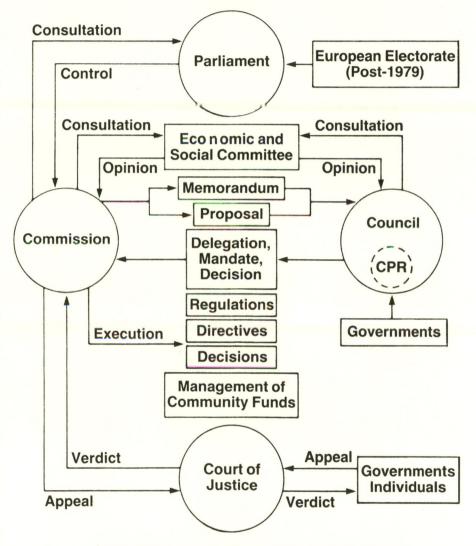

Source: Commission of the European Community, *The Courrier:
European Community - Africa - Caribbean - Pacific*, no. 48 (March-
April 1978), p. 36.

3

The Council of Ministers, the European Commission and the Bureaucracy, and Financial Mechanisms

The major decision-making unit within the European Community is the Council of Ministers, assisted by the Committee of Permanent Representatives. Although having the explicit power to act on its own initiative, most of Council's decisions are based upon proposals from the European Commission—the Commission proposes and the Council disposes—and then the implementation and administration of the specific policy is left to the Commission and the EC's bureaucratic structures. This chapter discusses the Council, the Commission and the bureaucracy, and concludes with some brief comments on several financial mechanisms within the European Community.

THE COUNCIL OF MINISTERS

The European Community's Council of Ministers is the primary decision-making unit within the EC institutional framework.[1] The other bodies, including the Commission and the European Parliament (but *not* the Court of Justice), are adjuncts or peripheral satellites to the Council. It is the implicit—but recognized by anyone who has even the barest knowledge about the Community—mandate of the Council of Ministers to represent and protect the "national" interest of the member-states. These national interests are often conflicting, and they are also quite frequently at odds with what other actors in the process perceive to be the "European" interest.

The Council is a collective body of 12 individuals; usually, but not always, the foreign ministers of the 12 EC member-states. The relevant treaties do not mandate that the Council *must* be the foreign ministers, and other national ministers, with different portfolios, may legally constitute a particular Council session depending upon the substance of the agenda. If, for example, the topic under discussion dealt solely with agricultural or financial matters, most likely the 12 agricultural ministers or finance ministers (or their deputies) would attend in place of the foreign ministers. But each Council session—regardless of agenda or composition—has the identical legal status and the treaty-specified authority to issue binding decisions, and there is no hint whatsoever that a Council meeting of ministers other than the foreign ministers is in any way "inferior" to a foreign ministers' Council meeting. Nevertheless, the more important and significant "political" issues are always reserved for the foreign ministers, and the other national ministers deal with more limited or technical issues.

The Council of Ministers, both as a collective body and as individual members, is not "responsible" to any other entity within the European Community framework. They cannot be forced out of office en masse as can the Commission by Parliament (an unlikely scenario) or be censured. The members of the Council are the foreign ministers of the 12 EC members, and their place on the Council automatically comes with the position—the domestic political environment controls the membership of the Council. There is obviously frequent turnover within the Council—the majority party or coalition is voted out of office or the individual minister resigns—but such turnover is due to domestic political factors. The Council is a permanent body composed of whoever happens to be a country's foreign minister at the time. It is rare that two successive Council sessions have the identical individuals in attendance.

The Council is housed in Brussels at Schuman Place, adjacent to the much larger and imposing Commission building. Most of the sessions are held in Brussels although it frequently goes on the road to other EC cities (Greece, and now Spain and Portugal, are favored sites in the winter months). The presidency of the Council—much more an administrative chore than a position with additional prerogatives—is a rotating position, each country holding it for a six-month period. Council meetings total about 100 working days a year (not including travel time), and each foreign minister (or his deputy) spends approximately 25 to 30 working days at Council sessions. Agricultural ministers are usually in Brussels (or the Greek islands) about 25 days a year, and the finance ministers, concerned with the EC budget, about 20 days. The remaining 25 days or so are spread out among other ministries (health, education, transport, etc.).[2]

Council decisions are usually based on Commission proposals which, in turn, are usually the result of the Commission being instructed by the Council to prepare various studies, recommendations, or policy alternatives. The Commission is then charged with the implementation and administration of Council decisions, and this latter process is subject to Council review at any stage. It has been relatively infrequent, however, that the Council has intervened with the Commission's implementation of a particular Council decision.

There are five types of Council decisions, each having a different impact within the Community: regulations, directives, decisions, recommendations, and opinions. *Regulations* are of general application, binding in every respect, and have direct force of law in every member-state. *Directives* are binding on the member-states to which they are addressed regarding the results to be achieved, but leave the specific means of implementation to the discretion of the national authorities. *Decisions* are specific, addressed to a government and/or a business enterprise and/or a private individual, and they are binding in every respect on the party or parties named. *Recommendations* and *opinions* are not binding; these only give the sense of Council's thinking.[3]

Voting Procedures

The relevant treaties (ECSC, EEC, EURATOM, Merger, Accession) specify three voting procedures for Council decisions: a unanimous vote ("common accord"), a "qualified" majority, or a simple majority. There are not that many types of decisions for which a unanimous vote is *required*—the admission of new members, the amendment (but not the approval or disapproval) of a Commission proposal, the appointment of high-level Community officials (the Commission and the judges of the Court of Justice, for example). The term "veto" does not appear anywhere in any of the treaties, but by employing the words "common accord," each country can exercise a de facto veto when unanimity is required. This de facto veto has been exercised several times by various countries, the most publicized occasions being the French (read "Charles de Gaulle") refusal to agree to the United Kingdom's applications for EC membership in 1963 and 1967. An absence or an abstention, however, does not count as a negative vote, and unanimous decisions can be achieved even if one or more Council members are not present or cast an abstention.

A "qualified" majority voting procedure is more frequent than a required unanimous vote. This was a process originally instituted to expressly prevent the four larger countries (France, West Germany, Italy, and the United Kingdom) from dominating the decision-making process and the resulting public policy. With this "qualified" majority, the vote of each Council member was weighted as follows: France, West Germany, Italy, and the United Kingdom each had a weight of ten; Belgium, Greece, and the Netherlands each of 5; Denmark and Ireland each of 3; and Luxembourg's vote (far in excess of its size) was valued at 2—a total of 63. To adopt any measure under this process, the winning side required 43 votes from at least six countries.[4]

Under this "qualified" majority, the four larger countries (or the six smaller countries) couldn't dominate the process; neither side had the required 43 votes from at least six countries. This process was more of a safeguard measure, however, since most issues within the Council were not seen as split between large against small countries. But if it were split large versus small, the four large countries (40 votes) needed the support of at least two small countries (one to reach the required 43—although Luxembourg would have brought it only to 42—and one to reach the required six countries). Alternatively, the small countries needed the support of at least two large countries to have reached the required 43 votes. But since the three BENELUX countries usually voted the same way, most "qualified" majority votes turned out to be unanimous or "common accord" decisions.

The entry of Spain and Portugal has altered this "qualified" majority process. Spain has eight votes and Portugal five; the new total is 76. A "qualified majority" is now 54 and a "blocking minority" is thus 23. This new array might lead to deadlocks in the future, especially in budgetary matters. On the one side are the budget "disciplinarians" (Britain, the Netherlands, West Germany), having 25 weighted votes and committed to fiscal restraint; on the other side are those (Italy, Greece, Denmark, Spain, and Portugal) who have an interest in increasing the budget because they gain a net advantage. This group has 34 total votes. Although neither side can muster the required 54, each has enough strength to prevent a "qualified majority," and the prospects for deadlock are very real. Although not required for most decisions, the Council of Ministers for the first decade or so of the EC acted on the principle of unanimity. In retrospect, most observers agree that this was a very advantageous political strategy. The breadth and impact of these earlier decisions might have been low level—the lowest common denominator with which all the governments could agree—but at least no government was compelled to implement policies that it opposed. These low-level common policies were then locked in and, in turn, were expanded in later years. The lowest common denominator base of decision making evolved into a process of splitting the difference between the various positions (compromise) which, in turn, has evolved into the process of upgrading the common interests. The European Community might have had a far different evolution if, at the very beginning, the simple majority voting procedure alienated too many governments too many times.

This reliance on the unanimous vote slowly gave way to the simple majority but with a significant twist. Any country who declared that the particular agenda item dealt with a subject "in the national interest" had a de facto veto. That is to say, only a simple majority was required, but the "national interest" Council member had to be on the positive side; if not, the proposal would not pass. This "national interest" defense was not employed too frequently: some agenda items were (are) not that central to a country's interest (e.g., Luxembourg could not claim "national interest" on questions dealing with fisheries since there are no commercial fishermen in the Grand Duchy; or Ireland and Denmark, in relation to wine, since these two countries have no domestic wine industry). In addition, even in situations in which a country could have claimed a legitimate "national interest," quite frequently the country abstained from the voting or declined to invoke the argument, thus allowing itself to be outvoted. This de facto veto based on claimed "national interest" led, however, to a severe crisis in 1965.

The 1965 Crisis and the Luxembourg Agreement of 1966

In June 1965, the French member of the Council of Ministers invoked the "national interest" position about agricultural pricing regulations within the common agricultural policy. Unfortunately (at least from the French point of view), the other five ministers refused to accept the long-standing but implicit practice and passed several decisions over the strong objections of the French minister. The French then boycotted the Council of Ministers for six months.[5] Although the treaties expressly stated that a Council member's abstention or absence (the French situation) could not prevent a vote even where unanimity was required—the vote depends on those present and voting yes or no—the Council and the entire EC structure were at an impasse for those six months.

The impasse was finally "resolved" by what has been called the "Luxembourg Agreement" (or Compromise) of 29 January 1966, and the French minister returned to the Council of Ministers. The Luxembourg Agreement, however, really didn't "solve" anything—all it did was to recognize that a problem existed with the de facto veto based upon "national interest," but that the failure to resolve the problem was not a sufficient cause to discontinue the entire EC process. The Council's Luxembourg Agreement—saying that unanimous agreement should be reached but also saying that it didn't know what to do if unanimity couldn't be achieved (a classic political statement)—contained the following comments:

1. Where, in the case of decisions which may be taken by majority vote on a proposal of the Commission, very important interests of one or more partners are at stake, the Members of the Council will endeavour, within a reasonable time, to reach solutions which can be adopted by all the Members of the Council while respecting their mutual interests and those of the Community. . . .
2. With regard to the preceding paragraph, the French delegation considers that where very important interests are at stake the discussion must be continued until unanimous agreement is reached.
3. The six delegations note that there is a divergence of views on what should be done in the event of a failure to reach complete agreement.
4. The six delegations nevertheless consider that this divergence does not prevent the Community's work being resumed in accordance with the normal procedure.[6]

There was most certainly a "divergence of views" on what should be done in the event of a failure to reach complete agreement, but the issue, while not totally resolved, became less pronounced. For some time after the 1965–1966 crisis, the de facto veto based on the "national interest" argument was limited to "political" matters and was not applicable to administrative or budgetary questions. Then, in December 1974, the European Council (the heads of state or government) agreed to discontinue the practice even for "political" matters. The only decisions that had to be unanimous ("common accord") were those expressly mandated by the treaties. Since 1974, many relatively important issues had been settled by majority vote (usually unanimous), with an abstention from the member-state who was in disagreement.

The issue appeared to be resolved until the early 1980s when, at a Council session again dealing with CAP-pricing mechanisms, the British minister invoked the moribund "national interest" position and demanded the de facto veto. The British claim was simply ignored by the Council—especially by the French—

and the decisions were made over strenuous British objections. The United Kingdom did a lot of grumbling about how they were being mistreated, and the British press correctly pointed out that the high agricultural support prices were most definitely *not* in the British national interest, but the United Kingdom did not boycott the Council as did the French in 1965. It now appears that the EC is on a firm enough foundation to weather some split votes, and the affected governments eventually work within the parameters of the final decision.

The Committee of Permanent Representatives and the Committee of Jurists-Linguists

The Council of Ministers is assisted by the Committee of Permanent Representatives (CPR or, following the more frequently used French term, COREPER), the real workhorse of the Council mechanism. Housed in Brussels at the Council building, COREPER is a 12-member committee, composed of the ambassadors of the member-states to the European Community. These people are *not* EC employees—they are high-level (ambassadorial rank) diplomatic personnel, belonging to the home country's foreign service, whose posting is to the EC (not to the Belgian government; each country sends another ambassador to Brussels who is accredited to the Belgian government).

The COREPER prepares the Council meetings and it is within COREPER that most of the bargaining, consensus-formation, and political compromises take place. These people represent the national interest and are responsible to the home governments. More often than not, the actual Council of Ministers meeting is a rather dull affair—each minister has at his side his country's COREPER member who "instructs" the minister on how to vote on the agenda items or who points out the various technical arguments and the possible policy alternatives.

The policy-formulation and coordination function of COREPER has so increased in recent years that now there are two committees: COREPER I and COREPER II. The COREPER I is composed of the Deputy Permanent Representatives (diplomatic personnel also), and it generally deals with low-level technical and administrative matters. The COREPER II is at the full ambassadorial level and deals with the "political" issues. The positions of president/chair of both COREPERs, the various internal committees, and the working parties are rotating, held by the representative of the member-state who currently holds the office of president of the Council of Ministers.

The Council is also assisted by a very specialized group called the Committee of Jurists-Linguists. These people are lawyers specializing in legal administrative drafting and who have excellent language capabilities. They are seen as high-level officials—not as ordinary translators—and their task is to review the various decisions and regulations passed by the Council before the texts are published. This specialized committee must make certain that the texts mean exactly the same thing—or are as equally vague—in all nine Community languages.

THE EUROPEAN COMMISSION AND THE BUREAUCRACY

The European Commission

The European Commission is a collegiate body composed of 17 members (two each from France, West Germany, Italy, Spain, and the United Kingdom, and one each from the other seven EC members).[7] The national governments nominate the members, and the Council of Ministers, by common accord, appoints them to a renewable four-year term. The Council also appoints the Commission's president and four vice-presidents to a two-year renewable term. The Commission, as a collective body but not individually, can be forced to resign by a vote of censure by the European Parliament (not a very effective tool, as is discussed in Chapter 4). The Commission is housed in Brussels; as a collegiate body, decisions must be taken by the group as a whole, and power cannot be delegated to individual commissioners; all decisions are by a simple majority vote of its members.

The Commission's major duties are as follows:

1. To present the Council of Ministers with policy proposals;
2. To supervise the execution of the various treaties and call member-countries and companies to task if they fail to observe relevant Community legislation;
3. To administer the operation of the Community; and
4. To act as a conciliator of national viewpoints and secure acceptance of measures that appear to it to be in the Community's interest.

The current Commission took office on 6 January 1985, and unless removed en masse by the European Parliament (not a very likely probability), will serve its four-year term until January 1989. The presidency of the Commission was assumed by Jacques Delors, a former French finance minister. The distribution of the portfolios among the commissioners appears to have contained a diplomatic gesture to the smaller EC members in that some of the more important portfolios were assumed by the representatives from some of the smaller countries: Agriculture (the Netherlands); External Relations and Commercial Policy (Belgium); Energy and EURATOM (Luxembourg); and Budget, Financial Control, and Administration (Denmark). The composition of the present Commission, including the two new Spanish and one Portuguese commissioners, and the portfolios assigned to each, are as follows:

1. Jacques Delors (France): President of the Commission, Monetary Affairs, Coordination of Community Funds;
2. Franciscus Andriessen (the Netherlands): Agriculture;
3. Antonio Cardoso e Cunha (Portugal): Fisheries;
4. Claude Cheysson (France): Mediterranean Policy, North-South Relations;

5. H. Christothersen (Denmark): Budget, Financial Control, Administration;

6. Stanley Clinton-Davis (United Kingdom): Environment, Consumer Protection, Nuclear Safety, Forests, Transport;

7. Lord Cockfield (United Kingdom): Internal Market, Customs Union;

8. Willy de Clercq (Belgium): External Relations, Commercial Policy;

9. Manuel Marin Gonzalez (Spain): Social Affairs, Employment, Education and Vocational Training;

10. Abel Matutes (Spain): Credit, Investments, Financial Instruments, Small- and Medium-Sized Businesses;

11. Nicolas Mosar (Luxembourg): Energy, EURATOM;

12. Lorenzo Natali (Italy): Cooperation and Development, Enlargement;

13. Karl-Heinz Narjes (West Germany): Industrial Affairs, Information, Science and Research;

14. Alois Pfeiffer (West Germany): Economic Affairs, Statistical Office;

15. Carlo Ripa di Meana (Italy): Institutional Affairs, Culture, Tourism;

16. Peter Sutherland (Ireland): Competition Policy; and

17. Grigoris Varfis (Greece): Regional Policy, Relations with the European Parliament.

The commissioners, singly as individuals and as a collective group, are prohibited by the various treaties from seeking or accepting any instructions or mandate from any national government. This does not mean, however, that the Commission operates in a vacuum; quite the contrary. The commissioners are in frequent contact with their home governments to be kept informed of the political realities and practicalities of Commission-inspired proposals. The commissioners themselves are men (there has yet to be a woman named to the Commission) with previous—and future—national political experience. The perception exists that a revolving door operates between the Commission and the national governments. Many well-known national politicians have become Commission members, and many former commissioners have returned to the home country's domestic political wars.[8]

The Bureaucracy

The European Community employs some 18,000 people, usually referred to in the literature (but not by the European population) as "Eurocrats."[9] As a recognized IGO, the EC institutions are alone responsible for its personnel policies—the bureaucrats or European civil-service employees are hired by the EC institutions by competitive examination (for the higher entry-level positions), work for and are paid by the EC (i.e., the European taxpayer), and are professionally responsible to the EC. The civil servants are *not* responsible to any national government, and the relevant treaties forbid them from seeking or accepting instructions or mandates from any national government, especially their own. In addition, the Eurocrats are accorded a quasi-diplomatic status—they are immune from legal proceedings directed at their official actions, immigration restrictions or formalities, and most import-export regulations. These privileges and immunities extend to spouses and dependent family members and, not least, their salaries are not subject to national income taxes.[10]

The EC Commission is by far the largest employer within the Community framework, with approximately 12,500 of the 18,000 or so civil servants. Of these 12,500 Commission employees, about 3,100 are classified as "administrative-grade" officials (those people who are directly responsible for the formulation and execution of European-wide public policies); 1,200 or so are employed as interpreters/translators (an expanding industry within the EC, especially for the less popular languages of Danish, Dutch, Greek, and Portuguese); 2,500 are research scientists and staff, most of whom are at one of the four EC-directed Joint Research Centers;[11] and the remainder are mostly clerical-service grade (secretaries, typists, receptionists, chauffeurs, and security and maintenance personnel). The Council of Ministers employs about 1,800 persons; the European Parliament about 2,700; the Economic and Social Committee and the Consultative Committee of the ECSC around 500; the European Court of Justice has a permanent staff of 500; and the Court of Auditors employs about 300 persons.[12]

The Bureaucratic Organization

Since the EC Commission employs most of the personnel (approximately two-thirds), this discussion of the Eurocrats and the EC bureaucratic structure concentrates on the Commission. Figure 3.1 presents the bureaucratic and organizational chart of the Commission.

The office of each commissioner is patterned after the French bureaucratic model. Each commissioner brings with him to Brussels a personal staff. This staff is paid by the EC, but the individuals are not seen as "civil servants." They work directly for the commissioner; are invariably (but not legally required) of the same nationality of the commissioner; their employment ends when the commissioner's term of office expires or if the commissioner resigns. The highest ranking member of this personal staff is the chief of staff (*chef du cabinet*)—the immediate personal deputy of the commissioner—and there are about half a dozen or so staff members. Appointed at the discretion of the commissioner, the staff aids in the bureaucratic functions of the office: drafting regulations, memorandums, and speeches; dealing with the permanent civil service within the portfolio; and providing the usual support services.

The next level in the bureaucratic hierarchy is the Directorate-Général (DG), headed by a semipermanent official called a Director-General (DG). These DGs are semipermanent in the sense that tradition (and politics) dictate that a DG should not be of the same nationality as the commissioner responsible for the portfolio that includes that specific Directorate-Général. Thus, when a new Commission takes office—and the portfolios are distributed—many DGs may have

Figure 3.1
The Bureaucratic Structure of the EC Commission

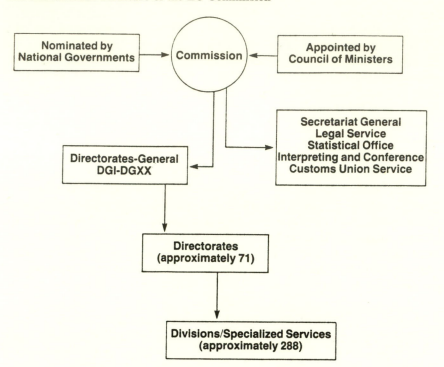

to be switched around in a shuffle. The DGs do not lose employment (as does the personal staff) when the Commission is reconstituted, but there is frequent lateral movement among the DGs.

There are currently 20 Directorates-Général. Some are large (Agriculture, for example); others are relatively small (Transport, Regional Policy). Some commissioners may have only one or two DGs within the portfolio(s); others may have several. The 20 Directorates-Général are as follows:

I.   External Relations;

II.   Economic and Financial Affairs;

III.   Internal Market and Industrial Affairs;

IV.   Competition;

V.   Employment, Social Affairs, Education;

VI.   Agriculture;

VII.   Transport;

VIII.   Development;

IX.   Personnel and Administration;

X.   Information;

XI.   Environment, Consumer Protection, Nuclear Safety;

XII.   Science, Research and Development;

XIII.   Information Market and Innovation;

XIV.   Fisheries;

XV.   Financial Institutions and Taxation;

XVI.   Regional Policy;

XVII.   Energy;

XVIII.   Credit and Investments;

XIX.   Budgets;

XX.   Financial Control.

In addition to the 20 cited above, there are five specialized services attached to the Commission. These services are not part of any of the DGs above nor are they classified as a Directorate-Général; but the head of each service has the rank and title of Director-General. These five are Legal Service, Interpreting and Conference Service, Statistical Office, Customs Union Service, and the Commission's Secretariat.

As mentioned above, some of these DGs are quite large while others are relatively small. The largest is DG VI (Agriculture), responsible for approximately 60 to 70 percent of the EC's budget. The CAP is discussed in greater detail in Chapter 7, but DG VI administers the European Agricultural Guidance and Guarantee Fund (EAGGF), import levies on agricultural products, the Monetary Compensation Amounts (border levies/subsidies), and export subsidies. Most of the policy decisions regarding agriculture are made at the EC level, and this explains why DG VI is so large. Another large DG is DG IX (Personnel and Administration), but here size only refers to number of employees and *not* to scope of responsibility and/or decision-making power. DG IX is a service DG that makes no policy but only provides the support and housekeeping services to the rest of the Commission. It is here, for example, where the translators, security personnel, and maintenance staff are managed. Two of the smallest are DG VII (Transport) and DG XVI (Regional Policy). These are no larger than some of the component parts (the directorates) of the Agriculture DG. These two are small because their work is primarily the coordination of activities performed by the national governments and local and regional authorities.[13]

Each DG is then divided into a number of directorates, and the directorates, in turn, are organized by divisions. There are approximately 70 directorates and about 290 divisions across the entire Commission. These levels of organization can be best illustrated by reference again to DG VI (Agriculture). DG VI alone accounts for eight of the 70 directorates and 91 of the 290 divisions. The eight directorates in DG VI, each headed by a director, are as follows:

1. General matters, relations with nongovernmental organizations, statistical studies and documentation;

2. Agricultural legislation;

3. Organization of markets in crop products;

4. Organization of markets in livestock products;

5. Organization of markets in specialized crops;

6. Agricultural structures and forestry;

7. European Agricultural Guidance and Guarantee Fund; and

8. International affairs relating to agriculture.

These eight directorates are, in turn, organized into 91 separate divisions, each division led by the head of the division. For example, directorate 4 above (livestock products) has three divisions: (1) milk products; (2) beef, veal, and sheep meat; and (3) animal feed, pig meat, and poultry. And there are dozens of management committees within each of the divisions.

Recruitment Patterns, Nationality, and Institutional Problems

The civil service of the Community is broken down into four general categories, with several levels within each group.[14] The categories are A, B, C, and D. Category A is reserved for the administrative elite (the Directors-General [A–1], directors [A–2], division heads [A–3]); category-B personnel do not have to meet the same stringent educational requirements as do those in A, and these people work under the supervision of the A officials; the C category includes the secretaries and skilled workers; and D personnel are the chauffeurs and other service workers. Our discussion is concerned mainly with those in the A category.

Several studies have indicated that the higher the level within the A category, the more probable a vacant position will be filled by a lateral entry from one of the national bureaucracies and *not* filled by promotion from within. This reliance on the national administrations, especially for the A–1 and A–2 levels, presents a severe morale problem for those in levels A–3 through A–7. Promotion to the highest levels is difficult—the A–1s and A–2s are in a revolving door between Brussels and the national capitals, but the A–3s through A–7s appear to be locked in place.

Another severe problem is nationality. The EC, as an IGO, attempts to hire and promote the civil service in terms of professional competence *and* an equitable geographical distribution (read "national quota system"). The implications of the quota system are far reaching: every country is entitled to its fair share of the positions, and quite frequently a vacancy has to be filled by someone of the same nationality of the departing official to maintain the balance. This practice does not necessarily engender pleasant feelings or cordial relationships from those passed over because they have the "wrong" nationality. It has also been mentioned—not infrequently—that sometimes it is difficult to remove someone unless the superior can find a qualified replacement of the same nationality; if not, this too could unbalance the geographical distribution.

The quotas are not hard and fast, but they exist nonetheless. They are very relevant in the A category, less so in B, and almost nonexistent in category D. The D personnel—service workers—are overwhelmingly Belgian since the Commission is located in Brussels. But even within this group, the logic of a quota system applies: there is a conscious effort to balance French and Flemish speakers. Someone at the A–1 or A–2 level has no real problems in relocating to Brussels for several years; a person who cleans the rest rooms in the Commission building is a local person. But even though specific quotas are not mandated— the various treaties and documents talk about geographical distribution—a brief review of the A category demonstrates clearly that a national quota system operates. Table 3.1 contains the nationality breakdown of the Commission's senior staff. The figures relate to 1982, but other studies have found a very similar situation.

As Table 3.1 indicates, although some countries are a bit "overrepresented" and some are a bit "underrepresented," the percentages of each nationality corresponds roughly to the country's population size. Belgium is highly overrepresented, but this is probably due to the simple fact that most of the Commission's activities are housed in Brussels. The obvious antagonistic demands of a multinational civil service, on the one hand, and the need for appointment and promotion to be based on professional competence, on the other hand, is well evidenced within the European civil service. Unfortunately, it also appears that the situation will continue well into the future, exacerbated by the need to give Spain and Portugal their "fair share" of the available positions.

The European civil service, as a bureaucratic organization, exhibits (or is afflicted with) the same problems that beset similar structures, both in Europe as well as in the United States. One such problem is the *almost* nonexistent ability to dismiss incompetent civil servants after the probationary period. The following comments are by Sir Roy Denham, a former British director-general: "There can be somebody working here . . . who can spend most of the day drunk under the table, can lie, steal, and engage in whatever immorality takes his fancy; quite apart from the fact that he will be doing no work we cannot sack him. . . . This is a state of affairs which in any organization paid for by the Community taxpayer strikes me as quite indefensible."[15]

The above statement *might* be an exaggeration and, if not, could probably apply to many other bureaucratic organizations (universities included). However, survey research has shown that national civil servants in the member-states do not have the highest regard for the qualifications and working habits of the Eurocrats in Brussels.[16] This perception may be based on the view that the national civil servants simply believe that their colleagues in Brussels are less competent—the Eurocrats couldn't succeed in the national environment and thus "retired" to the Brussels refuge. This may also be true, but it has not yet been demonstrated by any empirical means that the Eurocrats, not as individuals but

Table 3.1
General Service of the Commission

Country	A1-A7	Percent	A-1	Percent	A-2	Percent
France	494	19.3	7	15.9	25	19.7
West Germany	476	18.6	8	18.2	23	18.1
Italy	449	17.5	7	15.9	21	16.5
United Kingdom	345	13.5	8	18.2	19	15.0
Belgium	338	13.2	5	11.3	13	10.2
Netherlands	151	5.9	3	6.8	10	7.9
Greece	90	3.5	1	2.3	1	0.9
Denmark	72	2.8	3	6.8	4	3.1
Ireland	71	2.8	1	2.3	6	4.7
Luxembourg	67	2.6	1	2.3	5	3.9
Non-EC	11	0.3	0	-	0	-
Total	2,564	100	44	100	127	100

Source: Answer by EC Commissioner Burke (Ireland) to Parliamentary Question 1080-82 by Mr. Alan Tyrrell (ED-UK). Cited by Anthony J.C. Kerr, The Common Market and How It Works (Elmsford, N.Y.: Pergamon, 1983), p. 58.

as a group, are any less (or more) qualified and/or industrious than those who work in the national administrations. Rather, as Werner J. Feld argues, much of this negative perception may rest upon envy of the Eurocrats' much higher salaries and other benefits:

In the middle and junior grades they are paid two to three times as much as they would receive if they were employed by their national governments. For example, an EC chauffeur has a take-home pay equal to the salary of a minister in the Belgian government. On higher levels Eurocrats earn roughly twice the salary of comparable civil servants in the EC member states, often up to and over $100,000. The German deputy foreign minister, Claus von Dohnanyi, complained to his counterparts from the other EC countries that it was "scandalous for middle-level Community officials to receive a larger salary than the German Chancellor." In addition, EC civil servants benefit from special privileges. They can buy subsidized liquor in the Commission's own supermarket and they receive discounts on gasoline purchases. They can also send their children to free, special "European" schools. [And there are very attractive tax advantages.][17]

The European Community's Commission defends this situation with two counterarguments: (1) the need for multilingual people with particular qualifications and specialized skills necessitates the high salaries and benefits; and (2) the salaries and benefits only rightly compensate the civil service for the tremendous costs—economic, cultural, social—of having to uproot one's family from the comfortable home country and reside in a foreign country with an alien culture (Belgium). The Commission's arguments have an inner logic, but the argument about the hardship of living in Brussels is a bit tenuous.

FINANCING THE EUROPEAN COMMUNITY

The absolute amount of EC revenues and expenditures may appear to be quite large (approximately $US 36.5 billion in 1986), but this sum pales in comparison to the national budgets of the member-states.[18] This section presents a brief discussion of the European Community's financial framework: the European Currency Unit, "own resources" revenue, and areas of expenditures. Some comments are also offered on European economic and monetary cooperation.

The European Currency Unit

The European Currency Unit (ECU) came into existence on 1 March 1979. It replaced the European Unit of Account (EUA), which had previously replaced the Unit of Account (UA). The old UA officially represented the value of 0.88867088 grams of gold, and it roughly corresponded to the value of one US dollar before its 1971 devaluation. The EUA was a composite unit, corresponding to the value of a "basket" of the member-states' national currencies. The ECU is also a composite unit of a basket of national currencies.

The ECU is *not* a currency that people use to purchase goods and services; it is not locked away in vaults as is a nation's gold reserves; it has no physical existence; and the ECU should not be confused with a common EC currency or with frozen exchange rates (the European Community does *not* have a common currency nor are the exchange rates frozen).[19] Rather, the ECU is an abstract accounting unit employed within the EC for financial and monetary purposes. It is a logical result of a system in which 12 different national currencies with different values exist. The ECU is a composite monetary unit, made up of a basket of EC national currencies in varying amounts. The exact amount of each national currency that goes into the ECU basket is determined by each country's share of the total amount of EC trade and gross national product.

From 1 March 1979 until 1 September 1984, the ECU's basket contained all the EC national currencies except the Greek drachma. After 1 September 1984, the drachma was incorporated, and the amounts of the other nine were altered accordingly. Although Spain and Portugal entered the EC on 1 January 1986, it will be several years before the peseta and the escudo are incorporated into the ECU. The value of the ECU in each of the national currencies fluctuates, and the EC calculates and publishes daily its value in terms of each national currency. The ECU's value in terms of $US also fluctuates, due to the constant changes in the exchange rates between the specific national currencies against the dollar (it stood at $US 1.045 as of 1 December 1986).[20] Table 3.2 presents the composition of the ECU, both for the time prior to the incorporation of the drachma and the current basket (that does not yet include the peseta and the escudo).

The ECU is now the only unit of account employed within the Community framework. It is the unit of value in the EC's general budget; the CAP and the EAGGF are expressed in ECUs; the activities of the European Development Fund, the Regional Development Fund, and the European Investment Bank are stated in ECUs; it is the exchange medium to settle accounts between various EC institutions and national governments; the European Court of Justice levies fines in ECUs; the EC even pays some of its bills in ECUs.[21]

Community Revenues

Prior to 1 January 1975, the European Community was dependent for most of its revenues on financial "contributions" from the member-governments. But it was not a situation in which each government contributed a fixed share in advance and then the EC had to stay within the total amount. Rather, the EC would pass a budget and spend and *then* the governments would contribute their share to cover the expenditures. Such a budgetary process does not lend itself to fiscal prudence because, in theory, there was no limit to the amounts the EC could spend—the governments' "contributions" would cover the deficit.

This process was altered in stages between 1971 to 1974 and, from 1 January 1975, the Community has been dependent on its "own resources" for revenue, and its budget must reflect fiscal realities. There are obviously problems con-

Table 3.2
The European Currency Unit

Country	Unit	1 March 1979– 31 August 1984	Post 1 September 1984
Belgium	franc	3.66000	3.71000
Denmark	krone	0.21700	0.21900
France	franc	1.15000	1.31000
Greece	drachma	–	1.15000
Ireland	pound	0.00759	0.00871
Italy	lira	109.00000	140.00000
Luxembourg	franc	0.14000	0.14000
Netherlands	guilder	0.28600	0.25600
United Kingdom	pound	0.08850	0.08780
West Germany	mark	0.82800	0.71900
Total		1 ECU	1 ECU[a]

a. The value of one ECU was approximately $US 1.132 as of 17 March 1987.

nected with this process since the EC, similar to most other governmental units, usually finds that expenditures rise faster than income. But now the EC cannot rely on the national governments eating the deficit. Table 3.3 contains the revenue sources and amounts for the Community.

As the table indicates, total revenues of the EC were approximately 28.4 billion ECUs in 1985 and a projected 35 billion ECUs in 1986. Unable to levy direct taxes on the European population (except upon those who work for the Community in lieu of national income taxes—a miniscule amount), the EC receives its funds from four major but indirect sources: agricultural import levies, sugar and isoglucose levies, customs duties, and a share of the value-added-tax (VAT) receipts. The national governments administer and collect these funds, but then transfer set amounts to Brussels. For the agricultural levies (the charges placed upon imports from non-EC countries), the sugar and isoglucose levies

Table 3.3
European Community Revenue (million ECUs)

Source	1983	1984	1985	1986 (Projected)
Agricultural Levies	1,347.1	1,946.7	1,081.6	1,584.9
Sugar and Isoglucose Levies	948.0	1,003.3	1,025.0	1,113.8
Customs Duties	6,988.7	7,623.5	8,596.1	9,700.5
VAT	13,699.0	14,565.9	15,198.1	22,183.6
Financial Contributions	217.7	–	263.5	204.4
Previous Surplus	1,486.7	–	–	–
Advances	–	–	1,981.6	–
Miscellaneous	243.0	222.1	287.4	263.4
Adjustments	– 186.9	–	–	–
Total	24,743.3	25,361.5	28,433.3	35,050.6

Source: The Europa Year Book: A World Survey, Volume I, Part One, "International Organizations" (London: Europa Publications, Ltd, 1985, 1986), p. 151 and p. 153, respectively.

(charges placed upon manufacture and importation), and for the customs duties (under the common external tariff), the EC receives 90 percent of all funds collected. The national governments retain 10 percent to cover the administrative costs.

But the largest single source of revenue for the EC is its share of the value-added-tax (VAT or, after its French term, TVA). The VAT accounts for some 63 percent of the total revenue, and it is the European consumer who eventually pays the VAT. The VAT has been described in better terms elsewhere;[22] but, briefly, it is a very regressive type of sales tax. The value added at each stage of the manufacturing process is liable to the tax, and each payee simply adds it to the selling price at the next stage. The ultimate payee is the consumer, and the listed retail prices include the VAT rather than having the tax added separately to the purchase. The VAT is also levied on certain services as well (e.g., hotel rooms, rental cars). The final retail price of some products may contain as much as 35 percent VAT. Different products are taxed at different rates, but the entire system is reasonably harmonized across the entire Community.

The EC receives the revenues of a 1.5 percent rate of VAT (*not* 1.5 percent of the VAT revenue). In other words, if the final VAT rate on a product is, say, 5 percent, and the product had a value added of $20, the total VAT would be $1.00. The EC receives the rate of 1.5 percent (1.5% of $20 = 30¢), *not* 1.5 percent of the revenue (1.5% of $1.00 = 1.5¢). The national governments retain the difference. This 1.5 percent rate may not appear high but, nonetheless, it generates billions for the European Community (as well as for the national governments), payed for by the European consumer.

Community Expenditures

The EC's 1986 draft budget calls for approximately 35 billion ECUs (about $US 36.5 billion) in expenditures. Table 3.4 contains the most recent budget figures. It breaks down the expenditures into six broad categories: (1) support for agricultural markets (the EAGGF), (2) structural policies, (3) research, energy, and industry, (4) refunds and reserves, (5) development cooperation and non-member countries, and (6) staff and administrative expenses.

The largest category by far is the support for the agricultural markets under the EAGGF of the CAP. This single sector accounts for some 20.6 billion ECUs, or about 60 percent of the total budget. This is the direct, observable cost of the CAP; the almost equal but hidden indirect costs to the European consumer of the CAP are discussed in Chapter 7. In a very distant second place is the structural policies sector, with 6.5 billion ECUs (19 percent). Within this sector, the Regional Fund and the Social Fund are the largest areas. The fourth-largest sector of Community expenditures is administrative overhead (1.66 billion ECUs, or 4.7 percent). It is here that much criticism has been leveled at the EC—the EC staff is seen by many to be overstaffed, overpaid, underworked, and fiscally inefficient (e.g., the traveling road show of the European Parliament, the level

Table 3.4
Community Expenditure by Sector (million ECUs)

Sector	Appropriations for Commitments			Appropriations for Payment		
	1984	1985	1986a	1984	1985	1986a
Support for Agricultural Markets (EAGGF)	16,500.0	19,315.0	20,688.0	16,500.0	19,315.0	20,688.0
Structural Policies	5,296.4	5,870.1	7,718.2	3,705.3	4,421.9	6,571.4
EAGGF Guidance	723.5	843.3	934.0	595.6	856.8	865.0
Other Agricultural Measures	86.6	94.9	85.6	79.5	83.0	81.4
Fisheries	159.1	181.1	279.7	112.4	139.7	236.0
Regional Fund	2,140.0	2,250.0	3,433.0	1,412.5	1,642.5	2,600.0
Other Regional Measures	45.7	227.7	289.2	42.3	62.7	192.9
Transport	81.7	111.7	126.6	33.7	35.7	73.6
Social Fund	1,846.0	1,940.0	2,441.0	1,220.0	1,376.0	2,399.0
Other Social Measures	175.0	189.0	69.2	174.2	187.9	65.9
Education and Culture	18.9	20.4	34.8	18.9	20.4	34.8
Environment and Consumers	19.9	21.0	29.1	16.2	17.2	22.8
Research, Energy, and Industry	1,018.2	1,146.9	988.9	719.3	777.4	778.5
Energy	183.0	156.5	186.0	124.6	91.9	50.2
Research and Investment	743.8	914.8	704.2	509.6	614.0	637.7
Information and Innovation	27.4	23.2	23.4	23.2	15.5	21.3
Industry and Internal Market	64.0	52.4	75.3	61.9	56.0	69.3

Refunds and Reserves	2,310.5	1,079.0	3,693.3	2,310.5	1,079.0	3,693.3
Refunds to Member-States	1,057.3	1,047.1	1,239.9	1,057.3	1,047.1	1,239.9
Other Refunds	46.2	26.9	2,053.4	46.2	26.9	2,053.4
Reserves	1,207.0	5.0	400.0	1,207.0	5.0	400.0
Development Cooperation	1,022.8	1,459.0	1,602.0	897.2	1,151.7	1,651.8
Food Aid	506.1	671.9	1,007.9	505.1	492.4	954.0
Cooperation with Non-Associated Developing Countries	237.0	325.2	341.5	131.3	173.8	235.7
Specific Measures	113.2	70.0	78.3	95.2	71.0	74.8
Cooperation with Mediterranean Countries	108.0	32.66	106.7	105.1	349.2	318.7
Other Cooperation Measures	58.5	65.3	68.6	93.5	65.3	68.6
Staff and Administration	1,229.1	1,358.2	1,667.5	1,229.1	1,358.2	1,667.5
Commission	803.5	920.1	1,097.9	803.5	920.1	1,097.9
Other Insititutions	425.6	468.1	569.6	425.6	438.1	569.6
Total	27,377.0	30,228.2	36,357.9	25,301.4	28,103.2	35,050.5

a. Projected

Source: The Europa Year Book: A World Survey, Volume I, Part One, "International Organizations" (London: Europa Publications, Ltd., 1985 and 1986), p. 150 and p. 152, respectively.

of salary paid to chauffeurs, the insistence of having to translate every piece of paper—even telephone numbers!—into the nine Community languages). Development cooperation is in fifth place, with 1.65 billion ECUs. The smallest sector is research, energy, and industry, with some 778 million ECUs.

As mentioned above, these amounts are miniscule when compared to the national budgets—the United States deficit itself is more than the total EC budget—but the sums in absolute terms are not paltry. The actual direct costs associated with the EC are higher—the national governments still fund some of the expenses (the salaries of the members of the Parliament and the Council of Ministers/COREPER)—but this does not add a significant amount.

Economic and Monetary Cooperation

The *theoretical* objective of economic and monetary cooperation within the European Community is a full economic and monetary *union*—a single currency in use throughout the entire Community.[23] The intermediate step to this single currency would be fixed (nonfluctuating) rates of exchange between/among the various national currencies. With a full union, the national governments would no longer have the ability for independent action because there would exist a European-wide, single integrated economic unit with a common inflation rate (i.e., the United States). It should go without saying that the Community is still a long way away from fixed exchange rates, let alone a single currency. In fact, surveys have shown that a majority of the European population is not in favor of a single European currency in place of the national currencies.[24]

The closest the EC has moved in this direction was the establishment of the European Monetary System (EMS) in March 1979. Various countries have joined—and then left—and then rejoined the EMS at various times and, currently, eight of the 12 EC currencies are included (Spain, Portugal, Greece, and the United Kingdom are still outside the mechanism). The main component of the EMS deals with exchange rates against the $US among the national currencies. The rates are not fixed and are allowed to fluctuate, but the permissible daily rate of fluctuation is limited: + or − 2.25 percent of the central rate (+ or − 6.00 percent for Ireland and Italy). This mechanism is popularly known as the "snake in the tunnel."

The currencies can freely float within this + or − 2.25 percent area (+ or − 6.00 percent for the Irish pound and Italian lira). If any currency surpasses the margin vis-à-vis another currency, the central banks and the European Monetary Cooperation Fund (EMCF) are expected to intervene, buying or selling (depending on the direction of the float) the currency to keep it within the margin. The margins are the sides of the "tunnel"; the "snake" is the acceptable float as illustrated in Figure 3.2.

The EMS and the "snake in the tunnel" mechanism has had a mixed result. It has been able to limit the day-to-day exchange rate changes among the eight currencies, but it has not been able to lead to any convergence of inflation rates

Figure 3.2
The Snake in the Tunnel

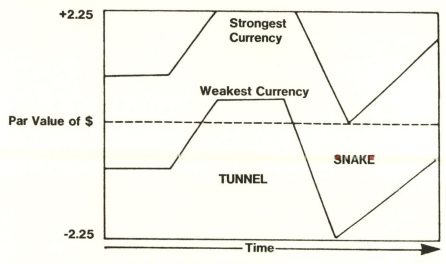

Source: Wittich and Shiratori, "The Snake in the Tunnel," 10 *Finance and Development* (June 1973), p. 12.

or prevent the devaluation of a nation's currency. And with a third of the EC members not participating (the United Kingdom being the most significant by-stander), a full monetary and economic union remains a distant goal for the European Community.

NOTES

1. See G. Edwards and Helen Wallace, *The Council of Ministers of the European Community and the President-in-Office* (London: Federal Trust, 1977); A. Morgan, *From Summit to Council: Evolution in the EEC* (London: Chatham House–PEP, 1976); and C. O'Nuallain, ed., *The Presidency of the European Council of Ministers* (Beckenham, Kent, UK: Croom Helm, 1985).

The EC Council of Ministers should not be confused with the European Council. The Council of Ministers is usually (but not always) the foreign ministers of the EC member-states; the European Council is the institutionalized meetings of the EC heads of state or government (the prime ministers, but, in France's case, the president of the Fifth Republic).

2. Stanley Henig, "The European Community's Bicephalous Authority: Council of Ministers–Commission Relations," chapter 2 (pp. 9–20) of Juliet Lodge, ed., *Institutions and Policies of the European Community* (New York: St. Martin's, 1983), p. 13.

3. Emil Noel, Secretary-General of the Commission of the European Communities, *Working Together: The Institutions of the European Community* (Brussels: Commission of the European Communities, n.d.), p. 5.

4. EEC Treaty, Article 148 (as amended).

5. See John Newhouse, *Collision in Brussels: The Common Market Crisis of 30 June 1965* (New York: W. W. Norton, 1967).

6. EC Council of Ministers, Decision of 29 January 1966, 3 *Bulletin of the EEC* (March 1966), 8–9.

7. See David Coombes, *Politics and Bureaucracy in the European Community: A Portrait of the Commission of the EEC* (London: Allen & Unwin, 1970); Stanley Henig, "The European Community's Bicephalous Authority: Council of Ministers–Commission Relations," loc. cit.; and Glenda G. Rosenthal, *The Men Behind the Decisions* (Lexington, Mass: D. C. Heath, 1975).

8. A few examples will be sufficient: Sicco Mansholt and Altiero Spinelli (Italy), Etienne Davignon (Belgium), Gaston Thorn (Luxembourg), Walter Hallstein (West Germany), Roy Jenkins (United Kingdom), and Jacques Delors, Raymond Barre, and Claude Cheysson (France).

9. There is an extensive literature on the European Community's civil service. See, for example, the following: John A. Armstrong, *The European Administrative Elite* (Princeton, N.J.: Princeton University Press, 1973); Mattei Dogan, ed., *The Mandarins of Western Europe: The Political Role of Civil Servants* (New York: Wiley, 1975); Hans J. Michelmann, *Organizational Effectiveness in a Multinational Bureaucracy* (Aldershot, Hants, UK: Saxon House, 1978); R. L. Peterson, "Personnel Decisions and the Independence of the Commission of the European Communities," 10 *Journal of Common Market Studies* (December 1971), 117–137; and Altiero Spinelli, *The Eurocrats* (Baltimore, Md.: Johns Hopkins University Press, 1966).

10. In conjunction with the 1965 Merger Treaty, a protocol ("Protocol on the Privileges and Immunities of the European Communities") was agreed to, reaffirming and enlarging the immunities of EC personnel. Although "officials and other servants" of the EC may be exempt from national income taxes, Article 13 of the Protocol specifies that they "shall be liable to a tax for the benefit of the Communities on salaries, wages and emoluments paid to them by the Communities" Sweet & Maxwell's Legal Editorial Staff, eds., *European Community Treaties* (London: Sweet & Maxwell, 1975), pp. 229–232.

11. The Joint Research Center (JRC) was established by the EURATOM Treaty, but it no longer deals solely with R & D in the nuclear field. Directed by the EC Commission with the objective of greater scientific and technological cooperation among the member-states, the JRC has four sites: Ispra (Italy), Petten (the Netherlands), Karlsruhe (West Germany), and Geel (Belgium). For a discussion of European scientific cooperation, see the following: Ronald Brickman, "National Science Policy Coordination in the European Community," 31 *International Organization* (Summer 1977), 473–496; Roy Gibson, "Aerospatial Cooperation: The European Space Agency," and John Goormaghtigh, "Scientific Cooperation: The European Science Foundation," chapters 3 and 6, respectively, of Leon Hurwitz, ed., *The Harmonization of European Public Policy* (Westport, Conn.: Greenwood Press, 1983), pp. 55–84 and 129–157, respectively; and Roger Williams, *European Technology: The Politics of Collaboration* (Beckenham, Kent, UK: Croom Helm, 1973).

12. Anthony J. C. Kerr, *The Common Market and How It Works* (Elmsford, N.Y.: Pergamon, 1983), p. 50.

13. Ibid., pp. 52–53.

14. The comments in this section are based on Werner J. Feld, "The European Community's Civil Service: Bureaucracy in Crisis," paper presented at the Annual Meeting of the Southern Political Science Association, Memphis (5–7 November 1981), 22 pp.;

and David M. Wood, "Future Technocrats? Recruits to the Higher Civil Service of the European Community," chapter 5 of Leon Hurwitz, ed., *The Harmonization of European Public Policy* (Westport, Conn.: Greenwood Press, 1983), pp. 103–127.

15. Sir Roy Denham, *London Times* (15 April 1980), 7.

16. Werner J. Feld and John K. Wildgen, *Domestic Political Realities and European Unification* (Boulder, Colo.: Westview Press, 1976), p. 126.

17. Werner J. Feld, "The European Community's Civil Service: Bureaucracy in Crisis," pp. 15–16.

18. For a detailed discussion of the financing framework, see the following: David Coombes and I. Wiebecke, *The Power of the Purse in the European Communities* (London: Chatham House–PEP, 1972); Isaac E. Druker, *Financing the European Communities* (Leyden: Sijthoff, 1975); and Helen Wallace, *Budgetary Politics: The Finances of the European Communities* (London: Allen & Unwin, 1980).

19. Only Belgium and Luxembourg have a nonfloating exchange rate between their two separate currencies: 1FB = 1FLUX.

20. Some past values of the ECU are as follows: $0.936 (18 October 1982), $0.920 (1 May 1983), $0.738 (30 September 1984), $0.784 (20 September 1985), $0.887 (31 December 1985), and $0.962 (7 March 1986). The determination of the ECU's value in $US is a simple (if tedious) calculation: each of the national currencies' amounts are translated into their dollar value and then summed. The value of the ECU in terms of any national currency is equal to the sum of the equivalents in that currency of the amounts of each of the other currencies plus the specific national currency.

21. It is not difficult to cash a check written in ECUs at a large bank in one of the EC capital cities. The value of the ECU is posted daily, and one receives its value in the local currency. It is somewhat more difficult to cash an ECU check at a local branch of a bank in the United States.

22. See K. V. Antal, "Harmonisation of Turnover Taxes in the Common Market," 1 *Common Market Law Review* (June 1963), 41–57; Donald J. Puchala, *Fiscal Harmonization in the European Communities: National Politics and International Cooperation* (London: Frances Pinter, 1984); and T. M. Rybczynski, ed., *The Value Added Tax: The U.K. Position and the European Experience* (London: Basil Blackwell, 1969).

23. See Karl Brunner and Allan Meltzer, eds., *Monetary Institutions and the Policy Process* (Amsterdam: North Holland, 1980); Peter Coffey and John R. Presley, *European Monetary Integration* (New York: St. Martin's, 1971); D. C. Kruse, *Monetary Integration in Western Europe: EMU, EMS and Beyond* (Sevenoaks, Kent, UK: Butterworth, 1980); Giovanni Magnifico, *European Monetary Unification* (New York: Wiley, 1973); Donald J. Puchala, *Fiscal Harmonization in the European Communities: National Politics and International Cooperation* (London: Frances Pinter, 1984); M. Sumner and G. Zis, eds., *European Monetary Union: Progress and Prospects* (New York: St. Martin's, 1982); and Philip H. Trezise, ed., *The European Monetary System: Promise and Prospects* (Washington, D.C.: Brookings Institution, 1979).

24. See Elisabeth Noelle-Neumann, "Phantom Europe: Thirty Years of Survey Research on German Attitudes Toward European Integration," chapter 3 (pp. 53–74) of Leon Hurwitz, ed., *Contemporary Perspectives on European Integration* (Westport, Conn.: Greenwood Press, 1980), Table 3.5, "Attitude Toward a European Currency," p. 57.

4

The European Parliament

BACKGROUND

The European Parliament (EP) began life in 1952 as the Common Assembly, established by the 1951 Treaty of Paris.[1] The original Common Assembly had 78 members, each chosen by, from, and responsible to their own respective national parliament. Compared to the Council of Europe's Consultative Assembly, which was (and still is) only a forum for symbolic debate, the ECSC's Common Assembly had real, although limited, political responsibilities and power. This power was due to its mandate of supervising the activities of the ECSC's executive—the High Authority.

The single most important power that the original Common Assembly had within the ECSC structure was the ability to force the High Authority, as a collective body, to resign (a vote or censure or nonconfidence). Even though the current Parliament likewise has the authority to force the resignation of the EC Commission, the original assembly had a relatively greater role within the ECSC framework than does the EP within the EC framework.[2] The High Authority was responsible for most of the real decision making within the ECSC and thus, by threatening a vote of collective censure, the assembly could exert some measure of political control over the High Authority and, by extension, could influence the content of ECSC policy. The current Parliament, however, has no influence over the primary decision-making unit within the European Community—it is the Council of Ministers and not the Commission who wields effective power within the EC. The Commission may still be collectively "responsible" to Parliament, but the Council of Ministers are individually responsible to the home governments. Moreover, even if Parliament were to agree on a vote of nonconfidence in the Commission, the Council of Ministers would simply appoint a new Commission on its own, without any input whatsoever from Parliament—the European Parliament does not have any "advise and consent" functions similar to the US Senate.

From the very first session in 1952 of the original Common Assembly, the members were chosen by their respective national parliaments to reflect the approximate party composition of each national parliament and the members, once in the assembly, did not opt to sit as do most other delegates-representatives to intergovernmental organizations; that is, as national delegations. Rather, the members of the assembly sat as party groups, not as country groups, and the first such transnational party groups to be organized and recognized were the Christian Democrats–Christian Socialists, the Liberals, and the Socialists. Other transnational party groups (or caucuses) have since been organized, and the current Parliament, elected in June 1984, has recognized (in addition to the three groups above) the Greens, the Communists, the Conservatives, and the Progressive Democrats.

The organizational context changed somewhat with the signing of the EEC and EURATOM Treaties in 1957. Rather than having a most illogical arrangement—separate parliamentary assemblies for each of the three Communities—it was decided that the original Common Assembly would function within all three Communities (ECSC, EEC, and EURATOM). The Common Assembly was transformed into the European Parliamentary Assembly in 1957, and its membership, still appointed by and from the six national parliaments, was enlarged to 142. This European Parliamentary Assembly was, in turn, transformed into the European Parliament in 1962, and, when the United Kingdom, Denmark, and Ireland joined the EC in January 1973, its membership increased to 198.

DIRECT ELECTIONS

As noted above, the members of the European Parliament were appointed by, from, and were responsible to their own respective national parliaments even though there had been plans from the very beginning of the ECSC to hold direct popular elections. The possibility of direct elections was provided for in the ECSC Treaty, but direct elections were made explicit in the EEC Treaty (Article 138, Paragraph 3): "The Assembly shall draw up proposals for elections by direct universal suffrage in accordance with a uniform procedure in all Member-States. The Council of Ministers shall, acting unanimously, lay down the appropriate provisions, which it shall recommend to Member-States for adoption in accordance with their respective constitutional requirements."

The Parliamentary Assembly produced a draft proposal soon thereafter, but it was never considered very seriously by the Council of Ministers (or by anyone else, for that matter). In fact, Article 138(3) was ignored by the Council and the member-governments until the end of 1974. At the Paris Summit Conference (9–10 December 1974), it was decided to institutionalize the meetings of the European heads of state and government; the result was the European Council (not to be confused with the EC Council of Ministers). At the same meeting, the decision was taken to finally pursue direct elections for the European Parliament as Article 138 envisaged. The Final Communiqué (Paragraph 12) of the 1974 Paris Summit Conference of the European Heads of State and Government (the European Council) stated:

The heads of government [European Council] note that the election of the European Assembly by universal suffrage, one of the objectives laid down in the Treaty, should be achieved as soon as possible. In this connection, they await with interest the proposals of the European Assembly, on which they wish the Council to act in 1976. On this assumption, elections by direct universal suffrage could take place at any time in or after 1978. Since the European Assembly is composed of representatives of the peoples of the states united within the Community, each people must be represented in an appropriate manner.

The Parliamentary Assembly developed a new proposal that was subjected to extensive discussions throughout 1975 and 1976 by the European Council at successive summit meetings and by the EC Council of Ministers. Agreement was finally reached, and, on 20 September 1976, the European Council issued the 1976 European Elections Act:

Article 1. The representatives in the assembly of the peoples of the states brought together in the Community shall be elected by direct universal suffrage.
Article 2. . . .
Article 3. Representatives shall be elected for a term of five years.
Article 4. Representatives shall vote on an individual and personal basis. They shall not be bound by any instructions and shall not receive a binding mandate.
Article 5. The office of representative in the Assembly shall be compatible with membership of the parliament of a member-state [dual mandate members].

An agreement could not be reached, however, on the requirement in Article 138(3) of a "uniform procedure in all Member-States" and thus each of the (then) nine European Community members established its own electoral process. The first direct elections were held in June 1979, and the elections marked a symbolic milestone in the European integrative process. Approximately 112 million voters (about 62 percent of the electorate) participated across the nine-country European Community and elected representatives to the first directly elected supranational parliament in history.[3] The membership of the Parliament was increased to 410 for the June 1979 elections. The membership was again increased by 24 in January 1981 when Greece became the tenth member of the Community.

It was widely assumed that one of the very first accomplishments of the elected Parliament would have been to adopt a "uniform procedure" in time for the second election in June 1984. This did not happen, and the 434 seats in 1984 were again contested under differing national electoral systems (most countries employed some variation of proportional representation). The third direct election is scheduled for June 1989; there is considerable doubt whether the Parliament will be able to agree on a "uniform procedure"—mandated in 1957—even by 1989.

A comparative survey of the rules governing direct elections to the European Parliament show wide variation across the member-states:

Voting Day: Denmark, Ireland, the Netherlands, and the United Kingdom vote on a Thursday; Belgium, France, Italy, Luxembourg, and West Germany vote on a Sunday. This requires that the results of Thursday's voting not be announced until Sunday's voting is completed.

Electoral System: Proportional representation is employed in all the countries except for the United Kingdom (but not in Northern Ireland, where proportional representation is also used). The majority-plurality system is used in England, Scotland, and Wales. Even though proportional representation is (almost) the Community norm, there exist sufficient significant variations among the specific types of proportional representation used.

Constituency Boundaries: The entire country serves as one large single electoral district in Denmark, France, Luxembourg, and the Netherlands. In Belgium, Ireland, Italy, and the United Kingdom, the country is divided into a number of constituencies. In West Germany, the parties may submit either tickets (lists) for small areas (the *Länder*) or a single list for the entire country.

Order of Names on Tickets/Lists: No split tickets (cross-party voting) or preferential votes are permitted in West Germany or France. However, preferential voting—changing the order of names on the list—is permitted in Belgium, Denmark, Italy, and the Netherlands. Cross-party voting is allowed in Luxembourg. Only in the Irish Republic and the United Kingdom do the electors vote for individual candidates.

Voting Age: Except for Denmark, where the age is 20, all countries have established 18 years as the requirement.

Eligibility to Run: All candidates must be a citizen of the state in which he or she runs, but the minimum age varies: 18 in West Germany; 20 in Denmark; 21 in Belgium, Ireland, Luxembourg, and the United Kingdom; 23 in France; and 25 in Italy and the Netherlands.

Nominations: Three states—Denmark, West Germany, and the Netherlands—restrict nominations to the political parties and/or political organizations. No independent or unattached candidates are permitted in these three countries.

Deposits: In France, Ireland, the Netherlands, and the United Kingdom, a candidate has to provide a deposit of varying amounts that is forfeited unless a certain percentage of the vote is received.

Seat Qualification: Three countries require a minimum percentage of the vote before a seat can be awarded: 4 percent in the Netherlands and 5 percent in France and West Germany.

It is obvious that the above differences in electoral laws and procedures are more than "minor differences" (e.g., proportional representation is seen in the United Kingdom—as it is also seen in the United States—as an alien process totally antagonistic to the traditional political culture). It is equally obvious that Article 138(3)'s insistence on a "uniform procedure in all Member-States" is more a statement of intent than an actual legal requirement. It is even more obvious that a uniform procedure will *not* be in place in time for the June 1989 direct election.

Although somewhat related to the size of the national populations, the 434 seats in the European Parliament are not allocated strictly along the lines of equal-sized constituencies. If they were—and if Luxembourg were used as the base—the Parliament would have some 5,000 members! The districts definitely do not meet the US Supreme Court's ruling of not more than + or − 1 percent deviation from the mean for congressional districts, but the malapportionment does not give rise to any real concern in the Community. The seats allocated to each country roughly approximate each country's population: France, West Germany, Italy, and the United Kingdom each are allocated 81 seats; the Netherlands 25; Belgium and Greece each at 24; Denmark at 16; Ireland at 15; and Luxembourg is allocated 6 seats. Membership increased to 518 on 1 January 1986 with the addition of 60 Spanish and 24 Portuguese MEPs.

The elections across the Community in June 1979 did not generate a very high level of interest among the European electorate (Table 4.1). Voter turnout varied widely from country to country in 1979: from a high of 88.9 percent in Luxembourg to a low of 32.3 percent in the United Kingdom. The overall 1979 turnout was approximately 62 percent—higher than American elections but lower when compared to European national elections. In fact, the turnout for the first election in 1979 in all but one country was significantly lower than that for the most recent national parliamentary election (Luxembourg was the exception, where the turnout was about the same, but this was due to the fact that the two elections were held at the same time). For example, the United Kingdom had a drop of 43.7 points when the EP election is compared to the turnout in the previous national parliamentary election; even Denmark, a consistent advocate of the Community and the European integrative process, showed a decrease of 41.1 points; West Germany's decline was 25 points.

This lack of interest or, more to the point, lack of knowledge, can be illustrated by the situation in West Germany a short time before the 1979 election. Table 4.2 shows that a full 63 percent of over 1,000 German respondents—when asked the question of whether or not a European Parliament existed—answered either "No" or "Don't Know." In addition, of those 37 percent who at least knew that the European Parliament existed, only about 16 percent were able to identify correctly the process of determining the German representatives. In other words, only about 6 percent of the more than 1,000 people questioned had precise knowledge, and 63 percent were not even aware of the existence of the European

Table 4.1
The European Elections: Distribution of Votes, June 1984 (June 1979)

	Valid Voters (Percent of Electorate)	Turnout in Most Recent National Election	Extreme Right	PD	LIB
Belgium	82.3 (80.0)	87.6 (94.6)	- (-)	- (-)	18.0 (16.3)
Denmark	52.4 (47.8)	88.4 (88.9)	- (-)	3.5 (5.7)	12.5 (14.4)
France	56.7 (60.7)	74.5 (82.8)	11.0 (-)	20.9 (15.5)	13.6 (15.7)
Greece	77.2 (78.6)	78.7 (81.3)	2.3 (-)	- (-)	- (-)
Ireland	47.6 (63.6)	73.2 (76.9)	- (-)	39.2 (34.7)	4.9 (6.7)
Italy	84.9 (83.4)	89.0 (89.9)	6.5 (5.4)	- (-)	6.1 (6.2)
Luxembourg	86.8 (88.9)	87.3 (90.1)	- (-)	- (-)	21.2 (28.1)
Netherlands	50.6 (58.1)	80.6 (87.5)	- (-)	- (-)	18.9 (16.2)
United Kingdom	32.6 (32.3)	73.0 (76.0)	- (-)	1.6 (1.8)	19.1 (12.6)
West Germany	56.8 (65.7)	89.1 (90.7)	- (-)	- (-)	4.8 (6.0)

	ED	PPE	Other	SOC	COM & Allies	Greens
Belgium	— (-)	27.4 (37.7)	14.5 (19.2)	30.4 (23.4)	1.5 (2.7)	8.2 (3.4)
Denmark	20.8 (20.1)	6.6 (6.2)	28.0 (26.8)	19.4 (22.1)	3.2 (4.7)	— (-)
France	— (-)	8.4 (10.5)	10.7 (11.4)	20.7 (22.3)	11.2 (20.5)	3.4 (-)
Greece[a]	— (-)	38.1 (31.3)	3.0 (11.4)	41.1 (40.1)	15.0 (18.1)	— (-)
Ireland	— (-)	32.2 (33.1)	14.8 (11.0)	8.4 (14.5)	— (33.1)	0.5 (-)
Italy	— (-)	33.0 (37.0)	6.4 (6.4)	14.7 (15.4)	33.3 (29.6)	— (-)
Luxembourg	— (-)	35.3 (36.1)	3.0 (9.0)	30.3 (21.7)	4.1 (5.0)	6.1 (-)
Netherlands	— (-)	30.0 (35.6)	11.8 (16.1)	33.7 (30.4)	— (1.7)	5.6 (-)
United Kingdom	39.1 (49.3)	— (-)	3.6 (3.4)	35.9 (32.7)	— (-)	0.5 (0.2)
West Germany	— (-)	46.0 (49.2)	3.7 (0.4)	37.4 (40.8)	— (0.4)	8.2 (3.2)

a. Greece did not enter the European Community until January 1981 and thus the figures in parentheses for Greece refer to the Greek election for the EP in 1981.

Source: "Forging Ahead: Thirty Years of the European Parliament" (Luxembourg: Directorate-General for Research and Documentation of the European Parliament, 1983), pp. 39-46; European Parliament, Directorate-General for Information, Elections '79: The Results (July 1979), p. 3; Le Monde, Dossiers et Documents, Les Premières Elections Européennes: Juin 1979 (Paris: 1979); and Paul Jowett, "The Second European Elections," West European Politics, 8 (January 1985), Table I, p. 111; Keesings Contemporary Archives (London: Keesing's Publications/Longman, 1982, 1983, 1984).

Table 4.2
Extent of Knowledge about the European Parliament (in percent)

Question: "Do you happen to know whether there is a European Parliament?"

	Total	Education	
		Elementary	Secondary
Yes, there is	37	32	48
No, there isn't	24	21	32
Don't know	39	47	20
Total	100	100	100

Follow-up question to persons who knew that the European Parliament exists: "And could you tell me how the representatives of the Federal Republic come to be in the European Parliament, who appoints or elects them?"

	Total	Education	
		Elementary	Secondary
The Bundestag	6	4	10
The government	5	3	6
The political parties	3	3	5
Elected by the people	2	2	3
Other reply	1	1	1
Don't know	20	19	23
Not given question	63	68	52
Total	100	100	100
Total number	1,013	695	317

Source: Elisabeth Noelle-Neumann, "Phantom Europe: Thirty Years of Survey Research on German Attitudes Toward European Integration," in Leon Hurwitz, ed., Contemporary Perspectives on European Integration (Greenwood Press, 1980), Table 3.12, p. 62.

Parliament! It is not unreasonable to assume that similar surveys would have produced similar responses in the other Community countries.

The figures for the June 1984 direct elections showed much of the same relative lack of interest. In six of the ten countries, the rate of turnout was lower in 1984 than in 1979. The Irish Republic showed the largest drop (16 points), with West Germany (-8.9) and the Netherlands (-7.5) also showing significant decreases. Only four countries showed an increase in turnout in 1984 compared to 1979—Denmark ($+4.6$), Belgium ($+2.3$), Italy ($+1.5$), and the United Kingdom ($+0.3$)—but these are not significant increases, especially when the United Kingdom's rate in 1984 was a dismal 32.6 percent. Across the EC as a whole, turnout dropped to below 60 percent.

It was obvious that even after experiencing one direct election campaign and after having the Parliament in session for a full five years, the 1984 elections came and went quietly, with very few people noticing. And, as was the case in 1979, all countries in 1984 showed a lower rate of turnout for the EP election than for the most recent national parliamentary election. This continuing large difference between the turnout in national elections and the European elections can only mean that, quite simply, the European Parliament is not yet perceived to be of much political salience or importance by the European peoples. This lack of public respect is a major obstacle to the EP's desire to achieve a greater role in the European Community decision-making process.

The distribution of seats in terms of the transnational party groupings in the Parliament fairly represented the European ideological spectrum in 1979 and did not change significantly in 1984 (Table 4.3). The center-right majority lost some strength but not overly so. There were two major winners and two major losers, however, when the 1984 seat distribution is compared to that in 1979: (1) The grouping "Extreme Right" went from five seats in 1979 to 16 in 1984. This was a direct result of the very strong showing of the extreme right in France whose representation in 1979 was zero but went to ten in 1984. (2) The "Greens"—an extremely loose coalition of environmentalists, consumer advocates, and antinuclear armaments—went from being unrepresented in the 1979–1984 Parliament to having 11 seats in the 1984–1989 session. West Germany contributed seven of the Greens, while Belgium and the Netherlands each contributed two. (3) The communist grouping lost six seats (48 to 42). The Italian Communists gained three (24 to 27), but this was more than offset by the dismal showing of the French Communists: The PCF had 19 seats in 1979 but dropped to ten in 1984; and (4) The Conservative delegation from the UK also had a dismal run in 1984—their strength went from 61 seats to 46.

Several commentators have noted that the 1984 elections to the European Parliament were concerned less with electing the members of Parliament and more with the political performance, or lack thereof, of the national governments. The 1984 elections are better interpreted as a referendum on the national governments and in those countries where the electorate was dissatisfied with the majority party or with the governing coalition, the opposition lists were able to

Table 4.3
The European Elections: Distribution of Seats, June 1984 (June 1979)

	Extreme Right	PD	LIB	ED	PPE	Others	SOC	COM & Allies	Greens	Total
Belgium	- (-)	- (-)	5 (4)	- (-)	6 (10)	2 (3)	9 (7)	- (-)	2 (-)	24
Denmark	- (-)	- (1)	2 (3)	4 (3)	1 (-)	4 (4)	4 (4)	1 (1)	- (-)	16
France	10 (-)	20 (15)	13 (17)	- (-)	8 (9)	- (-)	20 (21)	10 (19)	- (-)	81
Greece(a)	1 (1)	- (-)	- (-)	- (-)	9 (8)	- (1)	10 (10)	4 (4)	- (-)	24
Ireland	- (-)	8 (5)	1 (1)	- (-)	6 (4)	- (1)	- (4)	- (-)	- (-)	15
Italy	5 (4)	- (-)	5 (5)	- (-)	27 (30)	5 (5)	12 (13)	27 (24)	- (-)	81
Luxembourg	- (-)	- (-)	1 (2)	- (-)	3 (3)	- (-)	2 (1)	- (-)	- (-)	6
Netherlands	- (-)	- (-)	5 (4)	- (-)	8 (10)	1 (2)	9 (9)	- (-)	2 (-)	25
United Kingdom	- (-)	1 (1)	- (-)	46 (61)	- (-)	1 (1)	33 (18)	- (-)	- (-)	81
West Germany	- (-)	- (-)	- (4)	- (-)	41 (42)	- (-)	33 (35)	- (-)	7 (-)	81
Total	16 (5)	29 (22)	32 (40)	50 (64)	109 (116)	13 (17)	132 (122)	42 (48)	11 (-)	434

a. Greece did not enter the European Community until 1 January 1981 and thus the figures in parentheses for Greece refer to the Greek election for the EP in 1981.

Source: "Forging Ahead: Thirty Years of the European Parliament" (Luxembourg: Directorate-General for Research and Documentation of the European Parliament, 1983), pp. 39-46; European Parliament, Directorate-General for Information, Elections '79: The Results (July 1979), p. 3; Le Monde, Dossiers et Documents, Les Premières Elections Européennes: Juin 1979 (Paris: 1979); and Paul Jowett, "The Second European Elections," West European Politics 8 (January 1985), Table II, p. 112.

gain seats in the European Parliament. One example of this referendum nature of the 1984 European elections is given by Paul Jowett:

In West Germany, the Liberals (FDP), whose leaders had been troubled by scandals over bribes received from companies for party funds and divisions over the direction of party policy, failed to get over the five per cent electoral threshold. As a consequence, they lost all [four] of their seats in the European Parliament. The West German Greens, by contrast, achieved representation [seven seats] in Strasbourg for the first time and improved their chances of stealing the balance of power in Bonn from the Liberals.[4]

Direct elections to the European Parliament have not as yet had the desired result of making the Parliament a salient political institution within the Community's decision-making process. Some 60 percent of the European voters might have participated but, it appears, such participation was for reasons *not* linked to the process of furthering European political integration or of strengthening the European Parliament. Paul Jowett again comments:

It would be wrong to say that the European elections made a substantial impact upon the politics of the Community. Indeed, the elections represent at best ten national referendums on the popularity of the member state governments rather than a Community-wide verdict on the balance of power between the parties in the European Parliament. The drop in turnout lends further weight to the argument expressed by many both in and out of Community government that the institution of direct elections to the European Parliament may have been premature.[5]

ORGANIZATION AND POWERS

The European Parliament meets once a month in plenary session throughout the year for roughly one week at a time. Special meetings may be convened by the president of the Parliament at the request of a majority of its members or at the request of either the EC Commission or the Council of Ministers. The EP's president is elected by the entire body—Simone Veil of France was the elected Parliament's first president in 1979, and in October 1984, Pierre Pflimlin, a former French prime minister, became president—as are the 12 vice-presidents. These 13 (the president and the 12 vice-presidents) comprise the bureau, responsible for the day-to-day administrative and housekeeping functions. Although not formal members of the bureau, the chairpersons of the recognized transnational party groupings usually participate in most bureau meetings. In contrast to national parliaments, the European Parliament does not create a prime minister or the accompanying cabinet members.

The Parliament has 18 specialized standing committees, roughly approximating the main areas of Community activity as described in the treaties and the distribution of portfolios among the members of the Commission. Each member of Parliament belongs to several committees and the committees cover the following general areas:

1. Political affairs;

2. Legal affairs and citizens' rights;

3. Economic and monetary and monetary affairs and industrial policy;

4. The Community budget;

5. Social affairs and employment;

6. Agriculture, fisheries and food;

7. Regional policy and planning;

8. Transport;

9. The environment, public health, and consumer protection;

10. Energy, research, and technology;

11. External economic relations;

12. Development and cooperation;

13. Rules of procedure and petitions;

14. Budgetary control;

15. Youth, culture, education, information, and sport;

16. Verification of credentials;

17. Institutional affairs; and

18. Women's rights.

The membership demographics of each committee attempts to reflect the national and political characteristics of the Parliament as a whole.

This national origin–party affiliation distribution scheme within the major standing committees has often meant that individuals are assigned to specific committees solely on the basis of nationality and/or party grouping without taking into account the member's interest and/or expertise and/or constituency needs. This practice, very similar to a quota system, has obviously reduced the effectiveness of some committees, but most observers agree that the advantages outweigh the more publicized defects. Very few people across the Community would, for example, be content if the membership of the environmental and consumer protection committee were composed solely of the Greens. It is not a question of the Greens's approach and devotion to the protection of the environment; it is a question of balance.

The European Parliament is very similar to the US Congress in that most of Parliament's work (what there actually is) is performed by these committees. The committee reports form the parameters for the debates in the plenary sessions. The position of committee chair is a full-time position, and these people are in frequent contact with the Commission and the Council of Ministers. Since the Commission and Council of Ministers are based in Brussels, the EP committees often (and the chairs always) are also housed in Brussels. This is a major problem with the European Parliament for, as discussed below, the standing committees are based in Brussels, but the EP's plenary sessions rotate between Brussels and Strasbourg (and, until very recently, Luxembourg Ville).

The powers of the European Parliament are more symbolic than real; "potential influence" would be a more descriptive term than "political power." All too often (to the European media's delight) does Parliament expend valuable time and energy on what is purely symbolic politics—areas in which the Parliament has absolutely no mandate or competence to act. The EP has spent considerable time bemoaning the fate of the Indo-Chinese boat people—a worthy sentiment but totally beyond the political reach of Parliament. The Parliament did not want the Community members to send their athletes to the 1980 Summer Olympic Games in Moscow, but, unfortunately, the decision was not Parliament's to make; each country's independent national Olympic committee had the authority to make the decision. Also, in what was perhaps the most ridiculed parliamentary resolution, the death of several cows in France and West Germany due to severe flooding was duly noted (but with opposition—several members of Parliament did *not* agree to express sorrow over the dead cows).

Thus, even though the directly elected Parliament may possess an imputed political legitimacy that the former appointed Parliament never had (an *elected* body is usually more legitimate than an *appointed* body), this legitimacy is still in the future. And even though the European Parliament since direct elections has (unsuccessfully) attempted to move out of its traditional role as a consultative assembly and into a position of claiming the ability to participate meaningfully and as an equal partner in the European Community decision-making process, the fact remains that the EP's "power" is nonexistent, and even its influence is open to question. Symbolic politics may soothe the psyche, but it does not accomplish real-life goals.

There are some areas where the Council of Ministers must consult with the Parliament before reaching a decision. This may permit Parliament to shape the content of Community legislation before its adoption by the Council but—and this reflects actual behavior—there is absolutely no obligation or requirement that the Council accept any of the Parliament's advice. That is to say, consultation has rarely led to influence in the past. As Michael Palmer comments: "Only too often members of the European Parliament have had the impression that the Council has hardly even bothered to open the envelope and read the text of Parliament's opinion when it arrives at the Council's mail registry before announcing a decision prepared by the Permanent Representatives and the expert Committees well in advance."[6]

The Parliament has the explicit mandate to "monitor" the activities of the Commission (the Commission is "responsible" as a collective body to Parliament). Parliament can force the Commission to resign as a body through a vote of censure. This vote of censure or nonconfidence must be carried by two-thirds of the votes cast, representing a majority of the total membership. A number of such votes have been proposed over the past two decades, but none has ever taken place. In reality, however, it would make little difference in the power of the Parliament even if such votes of censure were to be passed and the Commission were forced to resign. This would no doubt paralyze for some time the decision-making process but, as mentioned above, it is the Council of Ministers and not the Commission who holds the effective power of decision making within the Community. Forcing the Commission's resignation might generate some symbolic or psychological satisfaction for Parliament, but it would bring very little, if any, real change in policy unless the Council itself decided to pursue alternative strategies. In addition, Parliament's "control" over the Commission does not extend to any role in naming or appointing a new Commission. Even if the Parliament were to censure the Commission, the national governments would simply nominate a new Commission of their own choosing and the Council of Ministers would confirm them in office. The ability to force the Commission out of office has very little practical meaning for the Parliament.

Some other "powers" of the European Parliament continue this consultative or bystander role. These powers are written in language such as "Parliament is to be kept informed" or "receive reports" or "maintain contact"—political power is not woven from such fabric. Some of the activities here include the following:

Parliament can submit written or oral questions to the Commission.

Parliament's dealings with the Commission have greatly increased since 1970 when it gained a bit larger role in the budgetary process and the President of the Commission meets regularly with Parliament to report on the budget and to answer the MEPs' questions.

Parliament is to be kept informed of the trade negotiations conducted by the Commission and can track such negotiations through the reports of its committee on external economic relations.

Parliament maintains contact with parliaments of other countries by means of exchanging visiting delegations and observers. Additional contacts are organized in the framework of the agreements signed by the Community such as the Lomé Convention. The Lomé Convention established its own Consultative Assembly, with equal representation from the European Community (the Parliament contributes some of the EC's delegation) and from the ACP (African, Caribbean and Pacific) states.

It is only with certain parts of the Community budget that Parliament's opinion is binding on the Council of Ministers—the EP has the power to reject the entire budget by a majority vote of its members. In December 1979, Parliament rejected the Community's 1980 draft budget in its first real show of strength following direct elections. The rejection was based on the refusal of the Council to accept the amendments proposed by Parliament in the Common Agricultural Policy (CAP) and the Regional Fund sectors of Community activity. The amounts of money in question were not large, and an eventual compromise was reached. But Parliament made its point: it acted with (rare) determination and was able to exert some influence over the budgetary process.

Parliament has the final say only in certain "nonobligatory" expenditures, so called because they are not mandated in the treaty. These expenditures represent approximately 17 percent of the total budget, and Parliament has the power to increase these nonobligatory expenditures by as much as 20 percent. These expenditures concern regional affairs, social questions, energy, and environmental matters. But real and effective political power does not come from the ability to vote *more* money for certain budget lines; it comes from the ability to *reduce* the available funds or to *cut off* entire programs. The European Parliament does not enjoy these last prerogatives.

Parliament's influence over the budgetary process should not be exaggerated or overestimated, whether it concerns rejecting the entire budget or tinkering with some nonobligatory expenditures. The following remarks by Lord Bruce of Donington, Parliament's rapporteur on the Community accounts, illustrate that Parliament still has a long way to go before achieving control of the Community's budget. Lord Bruce comments that after the budget procedure has been concluded,

the Commission and the Council proceed to do as they please. On the basis of spurious legal arguments and as a result of inertia, Parliament's amendments are almost systematically not implemented. Vast movements of funds within the budget knock it out of recognition as regards to budget as originally adopted. Sums are added, subtracted and transferred with the barest Parliamentary involvement and the sums concerned are far greater than the minute amounts over which Parliament went into battle during the original procedure. Parliament's amendments . . . show more clearly than anything else that Parliament is left to fight for control of the petty cash while the Commission and Council are free to determine without any democratic control the use or misuse of thousands of millions of units of account.[7]

Each member of the European Parliament receives an annual salary equal to that of a member of his or her national parliament. Dual mandate members—members of both the EP and the national parliament—receive one salary only. Only dual mandate members from Ireland receive a double salary. The national governments fund this salary rather than the EC itself. There is a wide discrepancy in the salaries paid: from a low of approximately $18,800 in Ireland (this might explain why Irish dual mandate members—13 of the 15—receive a double salary) and $21,000 in the United Kingdom to an approximate high of $43,000 (West Germany) and $48,000 (France). This state of affairs is due to the Council's inability (or refusal) to agree on a single salary level for all members. The Parliament itself has begun to work out a proposal to establish such a level—most members agree that the principle of "equal pay for equal work" should also apply to themselves— but a solution has yet to be attained. All EP members, including the 130 or so dual mandate members, receive per diem allowances (about $100), travel allowances (an average of approximately 32¢/km or about 53¢/mile), and close to $40,000 per year for research and secretarial assistance. The European Parliament funds these allowances.

One additional problem with the European Parliament concerned its seat of business. The long-standing arrangements defied the logic of efficiency, morale, and financial prudence, but they did, however, satisfy the logic of national prestige. The administrative headquarters of the Parliament was (and remains) located in Luxembourg Ville; the parliamentary committees usually meet in Brussels because the Commission and Council are (usually) in Brussels; the actual plenary sessions of Parliament rotated among Brussels, the Palais de l'Europe in Strasbourg (France), and the Centre Européen in Luxembourg Ville. In 1979, it cost the EP approximately $25 million (about 15 percent of its total budget) just to pay for the constant shuffle of staff, equipment, and documents among Brussels, Strasbourg, and Luxembourg. In 1981 this cost escalated to $40 million; the 1985 direct and indirect costs of having three homes was estimated at $65 million.

The obvious and logical conclusion is that the four main Community institutions—the Council, the Commission, the Court, and the Parliament—should be located together and share the same seat or capital. But vested national interests make it difficult to change the status quo. Belgium has a strong interest to maintain the Council and Commission, along with the 12,000 or so officials who work for the EC and contribute to the local economy, in Brussels. Brussels's Schuman Place would become quite empty if the EC moved out. Similarly, the French and Luxembourg governments also wished to maintain a Community presence in Strasbourg and Luxembourg Ville, respectively. The situation was that each city attempted to outdo the others in the availability of the amenities (accommodations, complimentary food and drink) offered to the members of the EP, and each constructed new buildings to hold the Parliament.

Luxembourg Ville's 22-story Centre Européen was completed in 1979 at a cost of some $100 million to back up its claim as the joint seat of the EP along with Strasbourg (very few plenary sessions are held in Brussels). Unfortunately, at least for Luxembourg, the Strasbourg city fathers outdid their neighbors in the lavish wooing of the MEPs, and the EP finally decided to hold all of their plenary sessions in Strasbourg's Palais de l'Europe. Luxembourg now has a new $100 million deserted building, described by an MEP (who wishes to remain anonymous) in the following terms: "An inspection of the interior of the huge chamber put up for the European Parliament is an eerie experience on most days of the year. The place is kept brightly lit and spotlessly clean, but one can walk through it for ages without seeing a single other person. It's like a spaceship that sails on indefinitely, long after the entire crew has been vaporized by aliens."[8]

The Luxembourg government is pursuing a claim in the EC's Court of Justice to force the EP to return, but very few people are optimistic; in addition, there is also the fear that Luxembourg Ville could lose to Strasbourg the EP's Secretariat as well. If this were to happen, another building would have a "For Rent" sign—the current status of the Centre Européen.

MEP CHARACTERISTICS

A recent study by Emil J. Kirchner of the first directly elected Parliament (1979–1984) presents a detailed analysis of the demographic characteristics and actual behavior within the Parliament of the individual MEPs.[9] Space does not allow for more than a brief discussion of some (sex, age, previous political experience, current political experience) characteristics, and Table 4.4 contains the relevant data. One of the more interesting findings presented by Kirchner concerns the number of women MEPs. As Table 4.4 shows, approximately 16 percent (70/434) of the EP membership were women during 1979 to 1984; this is more than double the 7.5 percent (388/5,118) found within the ten national parliaments across the European Community. This 16 percent figure is by no means high, but it does give some evidence that the parties are attempting to add more women to the electoral lists. Only one country (Ireland) has a larger percentage of women in its national parliament than in its delegation to the European Parliament (10.78 percent compared to 6.66 percent); two countries (Denmark and the Netherlands) show roughly the same amounts; the remaining seven all show a higher percentage of women MEPs than the percentage of women in the national parliaments (both houses).

The mean age of the MEP in 1979 to 1984 was approximately 51 years; this is almost identical to the mean age of MPs in the ten national parliaments across the Community. This demonstrates that the European Parliament is drawing from roughly the same age pool as the national parliaments, contradicting the perception that the EP appeals only to ready-to-retire older people and/or inexperienced younger people. Almost half (47 percent) of the MEPs had some previous political experience at the national level, either as an MP and/or experience as a government minister. This figure increases to 87 percent when regional, local, and/or party political experience is added. Only 13 percent of all EP members had no political experience at any level prior to entering the EP; these figures compare very favorably to the national parliaments within the EC. Finally, about 30 percent of the MEPs are classified by Kirchner as having ''current'' political experience in that these were dual mandate members. This dual mandate representation has increased the political acumen and abilities of the EP as a whole.

Some of the demographic characteristics (age, previous and current political experience) are emphasized because they serve to refute several often-repeated and widely believed charges against the European Parliament. These charges are related to one another and all stem from the generally accepted fact that the EP is indeed a weak parliament:

1. Because the European Parliament is considered a weak parliament, it attracts weak members in terms of previous political positions and career backgrounds.

2. There is an absence of competent politicians in the European Parliament because it is a weak parliament.

Table 4.4
MEP Characteristics

| Country | Sex | | Age | Previous Political Experience | Current Political Experience |
	Percent of Women MEPs[a]	Percent of Women MPs in National Parliaments[b]	Average Age of MEPs[c]	Percent of MEPs with National Political Experience[d]	Percent of MEPs with Dual Mandate[e]
Belgium	25.00	8.37	50y 1m	54.16	79.17
Denmark	25.00	23.46	48y 6m	50.00	37.50
France	22.22	4.64	54y 3m	48.15	27.16
Greece	8.33	3.66	56y 7m	62.50	29.16
Ireland	6.66	10.78	49y 9m	93.33	86.67
Italy	12.35	6.98	56y	60.49	30.86
Luxembourg	16.66	10.17	50y 4m	83.33	83.33
Netherlands	20.00	19.11	50y 1m	56.00	8.00
United Kingdom	13.58	5.58	46y 7m	16.04	4.94
West Germany	14.81	8.33	51y	43.21	34.00
Total	16.13 (70/434)	7.58 (388/5118)	51y 7m	47.23 (205/434)	30.24 (131/434)

a. For the period July 1982- July 1983.

b. For April 1982. Includes both houses of the national parliaments except for Denmark, Greece, and Luxembourg.

c. For the period 1979-1983.

d. For mid-1982. Previous national political experience include service in the national parliament (either house) and/or ministerial-government experience.

e. As of July 1979.

Source: Emil J. Kirchner, The European Parliament: Performance and Prospects (New York: Gower, 1984): Table 2.1, Table 2.3, Table 2.5, Table 3.1, and Table 3.3.

3. The increased recruitment of younger members in 1979 to the European Parliament can be associated with less prestige or lack of experience of the EP.[10]

The European Parliament may be a weak parliament, but the personal characteristics of the MEPs, as charged above by Dewachter and De Winter, are *not* the cause of its ineffectiveness. In fact, as Kirchner so ably demonstrates, those charges are simply not true. Approximately 50 percent of the EP's membership has previous national political experience and, when adding local, regional, and/ or party experience, this figure increases to 87 percent. Any parliament that has only 13 percent of its members without previous political experience—and with about 30 percent also members of a national parliament—cannot be characterized as "attracting weak members" or having an "absence of competent politicians." The younger mean age of the directly elected Parliament, when compared to the previously appointed European Assemblies, can work both ways: it is possible that the lack of prestige of the EP appeals to less experienced (i.e., younger) candidates, but this is balanced by the possibility of the younger members having more drive and stamina for fighting the political wars than older MEPs. Moreover, the average age of the MEPs compares favorably to that of the national parliaments. The European Parliament *is* a weak parliament, but this is due to the *institutional* framework and not to the imputed liabilities of the *individual* members.

MEP VOTING BEHAVIOR: CONFLICT-CONSENSUS, COHESION, AND PARTISAN IDEOLOGY–NATIONAL IDENTITY

The representatives to the European Parliament are from 12 separate, sovereign states—each with its own culture, national identity, and political values—and they have formed several major transnational party "groups" within the Parliament.[11] This section attempts to: (1) offer some comments on the general level of conflict-consensus in the EP as a whole; (2) note the degree of voting cohesiveness within each of the country delegations and the transnational party groups; and (3) identify the degree to which the MEPs vote along partisan ideological lines compared to national identity lines. The fact that some beginnings have been made to formulate transnational party platforms across the EC and that the groupings have been established in the Parliament lead to the hypothesis that transnational party affiliation will be a stronger explanatory variable for the observed voting differences than will national identity (e.g., a Socialist will agree more with other Socialists, regardless of country, than with fellow nationals of different parties).

The analysis will also allow some comments regarding possible future conflict-consensus within the Parliament, depending upon the scope of bloclike behavior and voting similarities. Strong transnational party groups may encourage Community interest groups to use their electoral strength to bargain for changes. A more balanced representation of interests at the European level might then be secured, for, currently, the most influential interest groups are producers and employers. Cohesive parties in Parliament—at least those on the left—may be more sympathetic to trade unions and consumer and environmental groups.

This analysis will also permit some comments on the scope of the erosion of long-held national mind-sets by Europeans and the emergence of truly trans-national attitudes. It would be significant for the future of Europe if the MEPs actually behave (vote) as *European* Socialists or Christian Democrats than as, say, Germans, Danes, or Italians. This would intimate that nationalism is breaking down, and, while not necessarily decreasing levels of conflict in the short run—ideological conflict would be substituted for nationalism—elite consensus and cooperation appear to be more readily attainable when based upon explicit and bargainable political goals than when based upon the subconsciousness of national identity.

Methodology

The accepted techniques of legislative roll-call analysis are employed to note the general level of conflict-consensus in the European Parliament as a whole and the degree to which the MEPs vote along partisan ideological or national identity lines. Three basic procedures are employed: (1) Riker's Coefficient of Significance;[12] (2) the Rice-Beyle Index of Voting Cohesion;[13] and (3) Rice's Index of Voting Likeness between Groups.[14]

Riker's Coefficient of Significance

Riker's Coefficient of Significance is used for two purposes: (1) to generate data relating to the general level of conflict-consensus in the European Parliament as a whole, and (2) as a means of selecting a sample of the roll calls for additional analysis. Riker's Coefficient of Significance is an empirical index mathematically derived from the level of participation (the number of legislators present and voting on any specific roll call) and the level of conflict (the degree to which the outcome of a specific roll call is contested).[15] The most "significant" (a value of 1.00) roll call in any voting body would be one in which every member was present and voting with the maximum possible conflict (only one vote would separate the two sides); the least "significant" (a value of 0) roll call would be one in which only a bare quorum all voted the same way. In addition to noting the degree of conflict-consensus within the EP, Riker's Coefficient is used to select a sample of EP roll calls for additional analysis. Only the more "significant" roll calls will be examined—a vote in which only a quorum all vote the same way presents very little information on the explanatory value of partisan ideology/national identity since everyone agrees with everyone else.

The Rice-Beyle Index of Voting Cohesion (IVC)

There are a number of studies in the literature dealing with the identification of voting blocs or groups and the measurement of such blocs' degree of cohesive behavior or voting agreement in legislative bodies.[16] But since this particular analysis of the EP need not identify by any methodological or empirical procedure the existence of any specific bloc or group—that the country delegations and that the major transnational party groupings in the EP each constitute (or should constitute) a group is an a priori theoretical determination—this analysis is not required to examine the voting behavior of *all* the MEP pairs (over 100,000 separate pairs or calculations for each roll call!). Rather, only the voting behavior of the MEP pairs found within each of the predetermined country groups and transnational party groups need to be examined. The Rice-Beyle Index of Voting Cohesion (IVC) produces an index of voting agreement between pairs of voters by pairing every voter within each group to every other voter in the same group on every vote.[17] The IVC values range from 0 (denoting maximum disagreement) to 100 (denoting maximum cohesion).

Rice's Index of Voting Likeness Between Groups (IVL)

Rice's Index of Voting Likeness between Groups (IVL) measures the degree of voting similarity between and among the national delegations and the major transnational party group within the European Parliament.[18] The Index is calculated by comparing the percentage of each group's members voting pro on any specific roll call, and the IVL ranges from 0 (maximum disagreement between any two groups) to 100 (maximum voting likeness/similarity between any two groups).

Data Presentation and Analysis

The temporal scope of this roll-call analysis is from July 1979 (the first session subsequent to the first direct election across the EC) to December 1980.[19] The data was generated from an examination of the European Parliament's plenary roll-call votes as reported in the *Official Journal* of the European Communities. No precise count of all the votes taken in the EP was made because many of them were by hand/voice/standing or passed "without objection." These types of votes are not amenable to the proposed methodology, and only those plenary votes that identified how each individual MEP voted could be examined—a total of 103 roll calls were so identified. Riker's Coefficient of Significance was then calculated for each of these 103. The (very arbitrary) cutoff point was set at 0.4 and above. Only 19 roll calls were at Riker's 0.4 or above, and these 19 were further examined by noting how each individual MEP (first assigned to a national delegation and then to one of the major transnational party groups) voted (pro, con, abstain, or absent).

Conflict-Consensus in the European Parliament

The application of Riker's Coefficient of Significance to the 103 roll-call votes shows that the general level of elite consensus is quite high within the European Parliament or, conversely, that there is a relatively low level of conflict. The results on the 0-to-1 scale range from a low of .06 to a high of .63, with .30 as the mean. Although no really good comparative data exist, it appears—based upon an intuitive judgment of the figures and upon an examination of the nature of the roll calls' content—that the mean of .30 is quite low. The MEPs simply do not exhibit much conflict in their aggregate voting behavior.

The reason for this level of high aggregate consensus/low conflict is reasonably obvious: the European Parliament is still not yet an "important" legislative body with real political power. The EP's "decisions" are only statements of intent or desire without any binding force in Community law, and the organization appears to function more like a social club with sporadic attendance than as a legislative body. The formal limits on its power have reduced the Parliament to passing resolutions that bemoan the fate of the Indo-Chinese boat people and express concern and sorrow over a few dead French and German cows! Again, political conflict is not woven from such fabric, and it is not surprising that people of goodwill—even from nine different countries and 55 separate national political parties—agree on such matters.

This rather low level of conflict within the EP may, however, increase dramatically over the next several years. The addition of Greece, Spain, and Portugal, along with the presence of Ireland and a growing number of Greens and extreme-right members, may militate for greater cleavages and discord along a whole series of policy variables. Greece, Spain, and Portugal will argue for not only maintaining the common agricultural policy but will, in all likelihood, attempt to increase the expenditures to aid their large agricultural populations. Ireland will join this group in issues of economic development and regional policy; one can see the beginnings of a split within the EC between "rich" and "poor." Increased representation of the Greens is likely to bring severe conflict over environmental issues and nuclear-generated energy. Splits in external relations—particularly over the EC's Mediterranean policy and its stance toward Israel and the Arab states—seems likely to increase. The greater representation of extreme-right MEPs—echoing the strident views of Jean Le Pen's National Front in France—can only lead to greater conflict and division in areas dealing with immigration, migrant workers, and citizenship requirements. This conflict has not yet surfaced within the Parliament, but the ingredients are present; the almost idyllic nature of the debates and resolutions may not continue for very long. The European Parliament has enough problems in establishing its legitimacy and influence when it is a cohesive institution; a highly fractionalized and conflictual Parliament would be totally ineffectual.

Level of Voting Cohesion (IVC)

As discussed above, only those roll calls that were at .4 or above on Riker's scale were selected for additional analysis ($n = 19$). The following discussion of the voting behavior within and among the various groups thus isolates what kind of conflict exists from what is otherwise a rather high level of consensus. Also, as noted above, the IVC, by pairing every member of a specified group

Table 4.5
Index of Voting Cohesion (IVC) by Country Delegation

Country	N	IVC
United Kingdom	81	76.45
Ireland	15	68.76
France	81	65.50
Denmark	17	64.43
Italy	81	62.48
Belgium	23	61.92
Luxembourg	6	59.99
West Germany	81	59.20
Netherlands	25	56.55

to every other member of the group on every vote, can provide data on the general level of voting cohesion/degree of "bloclike" behavior. These calculations have been performed for three different categories: (1) each of the nine national delegations, (2) each of the six major transnational party groupings, and (3) each of the 13 largest specific country-party subgroups.

Table 4.5 contains the IVCs for the nine separate country delegations which, it must be remembered, are fractionalized into the six transnational party groupings. Do the values reported in Table 4.5 evidence "cohesive" or "bloclike" groups? This is a difficult question to answer. As in the situation with Riker's Coefficient, no good comparative data exist on the use and interpretation of the IVCs, and any cutoff point established between cohesive/noncohesive would be arbitrary at best. These comments notwithstanding, however, the reported IVCs *do* appear to be low—none are at the 80+ level and this level (80+) would seem to be a reasonable cutoff point for the definition of a "bloc." Only one country delegation (the United Kingdom) is at the 70+ level; this is a direct result, as can be seen in Table 4.7 below, of the makeup of the British EP delegation. Of the 81 UK MEPs, 61 are Conservative (1979–1984), with an IVC of 85.23. The remaining eight country delegations range between 68.76 (Ireland) and 56.55 (the Netherlands). The only conclusion reached here is that the country delegations are not cohesive and do not exhibit a high degree of bloclike behavior.

Table 4.6 contains the IVCs for the six separate major transnational party groups which, it must be remembered, are fractionalized into the nine country

Table 4.6
Index of Voting Cohesion (IVC) by Transnational Party Group

Group	N	IVC
European Democrat (ED)	64	81.75
Progressive Democrat (PD)	22	78.57
European Peoples Party (EPP)	107	76.88
Communist/Allies (COM)	44	69.66
Liberal Democrat (LIB)	40	67.48
Socialist (SOC)	113	65.04

delegations. But the interpretation of these IVCs is subject to the same caveat above: no good comparative data exist and cutoff points are arbitrary. Nonetheless, the transnational party groups' IVCs are *higher* (more cohesive) than the national IVCs. They range from a high of 81.75 (ED) to a low of 65.04 (SOC). The parties may not be monolithic entities with everyone voting the identical way, but they are at least "more" cohesive than the country delegations. This lends some support to the hypothesis that transnational party affiliation is more important than national identity in explaining EP voting behavior and that we may be witnessing the beginnings of strong European transnational political parties.

Table 4.7 presents the IVCs for the 13 largest country-party subgroups in the European Parliament. Again, while it is difficult to define these subgroups as blocs, the reported IVC values are, not surprisingly, generally higher than those contained in Tables 4.5 and 4.6. The range is from 87.96 (the French Communists) to 71.18 (the French Liberal Democrats).

In looking at Tables 4.5, 4.6, and 4.7 as a whole, it can be seen, with only four exceptions, that the IVC values are highest for the specific country-party subgroups and lowest for the country delegations. The four exceptions are the French Progressive Democrats, the French Socialists, the British Socialists, and the Belgian European Peoples Party (the Christian Socialists/Christian Democrats). The identified groups in the European Parliament are relatively cohesive, with the party groupings a bit more "bloclike" than the national delegations.

Voting Likeness Between Groups: Country Comparisons

Table 4.8 contains the IVLs for each of the nine countries compared to the other eight. Table 4.8 shows that the Belgian contingent to the European Parliament has the highest mean IVL (81.39) across the remaining eight. At the

Table 4.7
Index of Voting Cohesion (IVC) by Country-Party Subgroup

Group[a]	N	IVC
French COM	19	87.96
British ED	61	85.23
West German SOC	35	81.48
West German PPE	42	78.24
Dutch PPE	10	77.95
Italian PPE	29	77.78
Italian COM	23	77.19
French PD	16	77.06
French SOC	21	74.83
British SOC	17	74.72
Belgian PPE	10	73.33
Italian SOC	13	71.51
French LIB	16	71.18

a. Only those subgroups where N ≧ 10 are included.

other extreme is the contingent from the United Kingdom, with a mean IVL of 59.09 across the remaining eight country groups. Belgium's score is not surprising to those who have studied the European integrative process over the years. The Eurobarometers have shown that Belgium—a small but prosperous and humane society—consistently has given the idea of integration and international cooperation strong support: the Belgian representatives to the European Parliament, irrespective of party, are ready to agree with their European colleagues on *most* issues. The IVL for the United Kingdom (59.09), on the other hand, is relatively low, calling into question once again the degree of British attachment to the European Community. But these comments on the United Kingdom must be qualified: approximately 61 of the 81 British MEPs (1979–1984) are Conservatives, and it is this latter group that exhibits a different aggregate voting behavior within the EP. The UK score is low because the Conservatives are different from the other transnational party groupings within the Parliament.

Table 4.8 also shows that there are some high (and low) IVL scores for specific

Table 4.8
Index of Voting Likeness (IVL)—Country Comparisons

Country	All	Belgium	West Germany	Netherlands	Italy	Luxembourg	France	Denmark	Ireland	United Kingdom
Belgium	81.39	-	87.86	86.95	89.33	82.37	84.14	79.46	81.30	59.77
West Germany	80.22		-	91.35	81.39	82.87	75.49	77.78	74.89	70.11
Netherlands	79.90			-	81.87	81.85	77.28	76.33	74.38	68.40
Italy	79.36				-	79.17	82.70	82.90	78.50	59.03
Luxembourg	77.01					-	77.68	74.76	79.33	58.08
France	76.98						-	82.25	87.53	48.79
Denmark	76.13							-	74.41	61.12
Ireland	74.76								-	47.75
United Kingdom	59.09									-

A-B country pairs. The three highest pairs are West Germany–the Netherlands (91.35), Belgium-Italy (89.33), and Belgium–West Germany (87.86). These three pairs evidence similar voting behavior in the aggregate, and these MEPs show a rather high level of intercountry group consensus. The three lowest individual *A-B* country pairs all contain, not surprisingly, the United Kingdom: Ireland-UK (47.75), France-UK (48.79) (these are what one should expect—the Irish and the French, regardless of party affiliation, simply do not agree with the British), and Luxembourg-UK (58.08). If these three latter country pairs were composed solely of national delegations, it would appear that severe conflict exists between these specific national delegations. But these country groups are composed of different parties that crosscut the countries: it is this party difference that accounts for the relatively low IVL values in Table 4.8.

Table 4.8 contains another significant pattern. The three countries who entered in 1973 (Denmark, Ireland, and the United Kingdom), as a group, have a significantly lower mean IVL toward the other EC members than the original Six (69.99 compared to 79.13). These three still appear to be "different" from the original Six although, as mentioned above, these comments only apply to national voting behavior in the aggregate. As Table 4.10 will show, specific parties within these three (the UK Socialists, for example) exhibit a higher level of voting agreement with fellow party members from different countries than those shown by the entire national group. The Danes as a *national* group may not agree very much with other *national* groups, but the specific parties within the Danish contingent to the EP do agree with the other members of the same transnational party group.

Voting Likeness Between Groups: Party Comparisons

Table 4.9 contains the IVLs for each of the six major transnational party groupings within the 1979–1984 EP. These values are lower than those for the country groups and show that the level of consensus among the party groups is less than among the aggregate country groups. The Liberals have the highest value (71.10) while the European Democrats (i.e., the British Conservatives) have the lowest at 52.40. The Liberals and the European Peoples Party (Christian Democrats) have the highest score (87.70) for individual pairs while the Progressive Democrats–European Democrats have the lowest (41.00).

The figures in Table 4.9 must be interpreted with caution, however. The IVL is really a surrogate measure for lack of internal cohesion: the higher the mean IVL score for each party, the closer that party is to a 50 percent yes vote. The Liberals, for example, are indecisive as a *group* and, therefore, their 71.10 value means they split their vote (yes-no) vis-à-vis other parties. The European Democrats, on the other hand, are much more cohesive internally and thus the lower IVL score.

Partisan Ideology or National Identity?

The previous sections attempted to give a brief overview of the aggregate levels of voting cohesiveness and voting agreement for each of the country groups

Table 4.9
Index of Voting Likeness (IVL)—Party Comparisons

	All	LIB	PPE	PD	COM	SOC	ED
Liberal (LIB)	71.10	-	87.70	84.80	70.90	62.50	49.60
European Peoples Party (PPE)	68.02		-	77.00	65.60	56.30	53.50
Progressive Democrat (PD)	67.56			-	72.80	62.20	41.00
Communist (COM)	65.02				-	67.40	48.40
Socialist (SOC)	63.58					-	69.50
European Democrat (ED)	52.40						-

and party groups considered separately. This section now combines them and tries to identify whether partisan ideology or national identity is stronger. Table 4.10 contains the data for the 12 largest specific country/party groups.

The hypothesis put forth at the beginning of this section—that partisan political ideology (defined as membership in one of the transnational party groups) will be a stronger explanatory variable for the observed voting differences than will national identity (defined as country of representation)—is seen to be "correct" in nine of the 12 specific groups analyzed. The difference in IVL values between party identification and national identification for the nine "confirmed" cases range from a high of 48.31 (the West German PPE) to a low of 2.11 (the UK Socialists). The three groups that do not agree with the hypothesis are the French Communists (−5.89), the Italian Communists (−6.75), and the French Socialists (−16.53). These three groups show a higher level of voting agreement with the rest of their country representatives than with the rest of their transnational party group in the EP.

The data in Table 4.10 could be explained at length, but this section will discuss only a few of the more meaningful results. The most striking aspect of Table 4.10 is the degree to which the West Germans (at least 77 of 81 West German MEPs) exhibit the least amount of nationalism. The 42 West German PPEs have an IVL value of 47.43 against the remaining West German MEPs— a 48.31 IVL difference when compared to their IVL against the other (non–West German) PPE MEPs; the 35 West German Socialists have an IVL value of 42.63 against the remaining West German MEPs—a 27.63 difference compared to other (non–West German) Socialist MEPs. The West Germans appear to be approaching the votes in Parliament *not* as West Germans but as members of transnational party groups—the party ideology of Christian Democracy and of Socialism has, at least for the West Germans, surpassed the national mind-set.

But as the West Germans are deemphasizing nationalism, the French and the Italians, especially the Communists and the French Socialists, appear to value national identity more than transnational party ideology. This is doubly striking since our conventional wisdom has the parties of the left as more monolithic, coherent, and internationally oriented. The French Socialists's IVL compared to the rest of the French delegation is 16.53 points higher than the rest (non-French) of the Socialist group in Parliament.

The degree to which the French and Italian Communists agree more with other French/Italian MEPs than with other Communist MEPs is also striking. The low IVLs are directly attributable to the Italy-France pair (Italy and France have 42 of the 44 Communists in the 1979–1984 EP). The French Communists show a low IVL with other Communists because they do not agree with the Italian Communists; just the obverse is true with the Italian Communists. One possible reason for this could lie in the differences in the political outlook and behavior of these two parties, both in their respective domestic environments and their international positions. The French have been much more isolated domestically and more Moscow-oriented than the Italians; the Italian Communists are more

Table 4.10
Index of Voting Likeness (IVL)—Country and Party Comparisons

Group(a)	N(b)	IVL to Rest of Party(c)	IVL to Rest of Country(d)	Difference
West German PPE	42	95.74	47.43	+48.31
West German SOC	35	70.26	42.63	+27.63
Dutch PPE	10	93.05	65.60	+27.45
Italian PPE	29	91.70	64.86	+26.84
Belgian PPE	10	91.78	71.26	+20.52
French PD	16	88.09	80.55	+7.54
French LIB	16	87.63	82.88	+4.75
Italian SOC	13	78.99	76.83	+2.16
British SOC	17	78.29	76.18	+2.11
French COM	19	63.70	69.59	−5.89
Italian COM	23	64.71	71.46	−6.75
French SOC	21	62.04	78.57	−16.53

a. The UK Conservatives are not included in this table. The UK Conservatives represent 61 of the 64 members of the European Democrat group in Parliament. The remaining 3 EDs are simply too small to compare to the 61 UK EDs.

b. Only those groups with at least 10 members are analyzed.

c. This IVL is calculated by comparing the specific group's voting to the same transnational party group less the specific group's members.

d. This IVL is calculated by comparing the specific group's voting to the same country group less the specific group's members.

integrated in Italian domestic politics and they are the leading voice for Eurocommunism.

CONCLUSIONS

The European Parliament has been described in various terms—some descriptions are not very flattering; others are a bit more positive. The problem is that both descriptions are accurate: the negative comments describe its present lack of power and its ineffectiveness; the positive comments emphasize the future and Parliament's potential to assume a greater role within the European Community framework.

The European Parliament is, unfortunately, an opera buffo with over 500 characters (the MEPs), twelve acts (the EC member-states), and seven plots (the transnational party groupings). Nine languages are spoken but none are listened to, and the EP is engaged in the symbolism of politics without its essence. Too many of the resolutions debated and passed (without a high degree of conflict) deal with areas far removed from the European Community, let alone the Parliament itself. Resolutions bemoaning the fate of the Indo-Chinese boat people or expressing sorrow over some French and German cows drowned in a flood do not political influence make. And, when the Parliament does deal with EC matters, its voice is only an opinion without any binding force in Community law. This excludes, of course, the removal of the Commission and rejection of the budget—two relatively useless ''nuclear'' weapons when the deployment of ''conventional arms'' would be better suited to establish a normal political role. This negative view of the EP has been summarized by David Curry, himself an MEP from the United Kingdom:

The European Parliament has received a bad press. It deserves quite a lot of it. Its procedures are ill-disciplined. Its ability to stick to timetable virtually non-existent. Attendance is erratic and generally poor, leading to inconsistency and frequently incoherence in its opinions. Limited in power, it tends to adopt the declamatory rather than the responsible position. Some of these faults are inevitable for a new institution. The concepts of what Parliaments are there to do, and how they relate to the executive branch, vary across Europe. The unexcitement of its debates reflect the deadening effect of translation and the fact that the essential debate is at group, not plenary level. Other faults stem from a lack of belief in their own institution by its own members—particularly the absentee members who have simply lent their names to a list to enhance its voter-appeal without the intention of playing more than a perfunctory role in the Parliament's affairs. It is notoriously difficult to identify Parliamentary power structures and influence. The most voluble are not usually the most effective; the most profligate in resolution or question-tabling may not achieve the most useful results. The committees and the plenary resemble a bazaar of shifting attendance: much of what happens does so by accident.[20]

The inability of the European Parliament to determine for itself some basic housekeeping questions—salary, elections—only underscores its real lack of power in the political decision-making process. Nonetheless, the Parliament exists, it does vote on a wide range of resolutions, its influence may increase in the future; it is an institution that may provide popular democratic control over the European Community.

The transnational political groups in the EP do attempt to work out common positions on the major policy issues, but the degree of internal cohesiveness—although higher for the political groups than for the country delegations—does not reach significant levels. It is all too obvious that the MEPs frequently vote counter to their party's majority view. The very fact of direct elections, welcomed in most quarters, may have contributed to this comparative independence of the individual EP. No longer responsible to the party hierarchy in the home parliament, the MEP has much more leeway when responsibility is now to an amorphous electorate.

But it is not realistic to expect a very high degree of cohesiveness or degree of bloclike behavior from members of a political group who have been elected, not as a member of a *European* political party, but, rather, as a member of one of some 55 separate *national* parties. The groups in the EP are only broad coalitions/alliances composed of different national parties. The transnational political groups in the European Parliament may develop into transnational parties in the future, but in order to do so they will first have to present candidates for the EP across the EC's member-states under a single label and with a single, common platform. At present, there are three parties linked at the European level—the Socialists, Liberals, and the European Peoples Party (the Christian Socialists/Christian Democrats). These loose federations attempted to coordinate the 1979 and 1984 campaigns, and they attempt to maintain links between the EP groups and the national political parties. But these federations still cannot be called transnational political parties.

The very nature of the European Parliament and factors such as its lack of any real political power, its atmosphere of a congenial club with much food and drink, its nonbinding roll calls, its emphasis upon the symbolism of politics rather than substance, all combine to detract from the significance of whatever the MEPs do or do not do in Parliament. But after these limiting conditions are accepted, the MEPs do show a remarkable degree of transnational party agreement and a deemphasis of national identity. It just may be that the traditional national mind-sets are breaking down, strengthening the integrative process. These transnational parties can serve as new political forces in Europe when and if the European Parliament enlarges its power vis-à-vis the Council of Ministers and the Commission. This power enlargement does not appear to be imminent although the groundwork has been laid. The fact is, simply, that the European Parliament's future has not yet arrived.

NOTES

1. There is now an extensive literature on the European Parliament. See, for example, J. G. Blumler, ed., *Communicating to Voters: Television in the First European Parlia-*

mentary Elections (Beverly Hills, Calif.: Sage, 1983); Sir Barnett Cocks, *The European Parliament: Structure, Procedure and Practice* (London: Her Majesty's Stationery Office, 1973); C. Cook and M. Francis, *The First European Elections* (New York: Macmillan, 1979); John Fitzmaurice, *The European Parliament* (Aldershot, Hants, UK: Saxon House, 1978); Valentine Herman and Juliet Lodge, *The European Parliament and the European Community* (New York: Macmillan, 1978); Emil J. Kirchner, *The European Parliament: Performance and Prospects* (Aldershot, Hants, UK: Gower, 1984); Michael Palmer, *The European Parliament: What It Is, What It Does, and How It Works* (Elmsford, N.Y.: Pergamon, 1981); Geoffrey Pridham and Pippa Pridham, *Transnational Party Co-operation and European Integration* (London: Allen & Unwin, 1981); and Paula Scalingi, *The European Parliament* (Westport, Conn.: Greenwood, 1980).

2. Michael Palmer, *The European Parliament*, p. 20.

3. Ronald Inglehart and Jacques-René Rabier, "Europe Elects a Parliament: Cognitive Mobilization, Political Mobilization, and Pro European Attitudes as Influences on Voter Turnout," chapter 2 (pp. 27–51) of Leon Hurwitz, ed., *Contemporary Perspectives on European Integration: Attitudes, Non-Governmental Behavior, and Collective Decision-Making* (Westport, Conn.: Greenwood Press, 1980), esp. Table 2.1, "Rates of Electoral Participation for the Election of the European Parliament and for the Most Recent National Election," p. 29.

4. Paul Jowett, "The Second European Elections: 14–17 June 1984," 8 *West European Politics* (January 1985), 109–110.

5. Ibid., p. 110.

6. Palmer, *The European Parliament*, p. 31.

7. Lord Bruce of Donington, as cited in ibid., pp. 40–41.

8. 295 *Europe* (September 1986), p. 4.

9. Emil J. Kirchner, *The European Parliament: Performance and Prospects* (Aldershot, Hants, UK: Gower, 1984).

10. W. F. J. Dewachter and L. De Winter, "Het verlies van het machtspotentieel van een swak parliament," 21 *Res Publica* (1979), 115–125; P. Lemaitre, "Un quart de siècle d'inexistence," *Le Monde* (27–28 March 1983) cited by Kirchner, *The European Parliament*, pp. 138–139.

11. This section borrows from Leon Hurwitz, "Partisan Ideology or National Interest: An Analysis of the Members of the European Parliament," chapter 9 of Leon Hurwitz, ed., *The Harmonization of European Public Policy: Regional Responses to Transnational Challenges* (Westport, Conn.: Greenwood, 1983), pp. 197–217.

12. William H. Riker, "A Method for Determining the Significance of Roll Calls in Voting Bodies," in John C. Wahlke and Heinz Eulau, eds., *Legislative Behavior: A Reader in Theory and Research* (New York: Free Press, 1959), pp. 377–384.

13. As presented and amended by Arend Lijphart, "The Analysis of Bloc Voting in the General Assembly: A Critique and a Proposal," 57 *American Political Science Review* (December 1963), 902–917.

14. Stuart A. Rice, *Quantitative Methods in Politics* (New York: Knopf, 1928), as discussed by Leroy N. Rieselbach, "Quantitative Techniques for Studying Voting Behavior in the UN General Assembly," 14 *International Organization* (Spring 1960), 291–306.

15. Riker's Coefficient of Significance is expressed as follows:

$$v(aij) = n - qij - m + 2 + \left(\frac{n - ri + 1}{n - t + 2}\right), \text{ where}$$

aij = any possible outcome,

$v(aij)$ = value of aij,
n = number of members of the legislature,
ri = number of voting on a roll call in which the outcome is aij,
qij = number on the losing side of aij,
m = minimum necessary for victory when ri participates, and
t = a quorum.

With the above expression, the higher the value of aij, the lower the significance; the lower the value of aij, the higher the significance. But these values also depend upon the size of the legislature, and different voting bodies will have different values. The least significant outcome (325) for the US House of Representatives is much different than the least significant outcome for the US Senate (77); the European Parliament's least significant outcome is 309, and its most significant outcome is 2. To remedy this situation—to make the measure comparable from one voting body to another and to make the measure have a commonsense direction (the higher the score, the more significance; the lower the score, the less significance)—Riker introduces a second step in the calculations:

$$s = -\left[\frac{V(aij) - V(all)}{V(adg) - V(all)}\right], \text{ where}$$

$V(aij)$ = the value of any specific outcome;
$V(adg)$ = the value of the least significant outcome;
$V(all)$ = the value of the most significant outcome.

S ranges from 0 (the least significant outcome) to 1 (the most significant outcome). The addition of S is much better: now a high score (1) means more significance; a low score (0) means less significance. Also, the size of the voting body no longer influences the results and the S values can be compared across different voting bodies of differing numbers of members.

16. There is an extensive literature in this area. See, for example, Lijphart, "The Analysis of Bloc Voting in the General Assembly: A Critique and a Proposal," loc. cit.; Hayward R. Alker, Jr., "Dimensions of Conflict Within the General Assembly," 58 *American Political Science Review* (September 1964), 642–647; Hayward R. Alker, Jr., and Bruce Russett, *World Politics in the General Assembly* (New Haven, Conn.: Yale University Press, 1965); Thomas Hovet, Jr., *Bloc Politics in the United Nations* (Cambridge, Mass.: Harvard University Press, 1960); Hanna Newcombe et al., "United Nations Voting Patterns," 24 *International Organization* (Winter 1970), 100–121; Rieselbach, "Quantitative Techniques for Studying Voting Behavior in the UN General Assembly," loc. cit.; Bruce Russett, "Discovering Voting Groups in the United Nations," 60 *American Political Science Review* (June 1966), 327–339; and Jack E. Vincent, "An Application of Attribute Theory to General Assembly Voting and Some Implications," 26 *International Organization* (Summer 1972), 551–582. For other roll-call analyses of the EP, see Menno Wolters, "European Interspaces: A Roll-Call Analysis of European Parliament Divisions since Direct Elections," paper presented to the ECPR Workshop on Decision-Making Processes in European Integration (Aarhus, Denmark, 1982). For an analysis of EC voting behavior within the UN, see Leon Hurwitz, "The EEC in the United Nations: The Voting Behaviour of Eight Countries, 1948–1973," 13 *Journal of Common Market Studies* (March 1975), 224–243 and Leon Hurwitz, "The EEC and

Decolonization: The Voting Behaviour of the Nine in the UN General Assembly,'' 24 *Political Studies* (December 1976), 435–447.

17. The basic Index of Voting Cohesion is the result of the following expression:

$$IVC = \left(\frac{f + .5g}{t}\right) \times 100 \text{ percent, where}$$

IVC ranges between 0 (denoting maximum
      disagreement) and 100 (denoting maximum cohesion);
f = the number of votes in which each *A-B* pair of voters votes in an identical manner
    (*A* and *B* both vote pro, con, or abstain);
g = the number of votes in which each *A-B* pair of voters display partial cohesion (*A*
    votes pro or con, *B* abstains); and
t = the total number of votes in which each *A-B* pair participates.

Aggregated *IVCs* are calculated by summing the individual *IVCs* within each group and dividing by the number of *A-B* pairs: $IVC = \Sigma IVCi/n$. For aggregated *IVCs* where the number of votes are not identical, $IVC = (IVCi \times [ti/\Sigma t])$. Absences in the EP are treated as abstentions.

18. The Index of Voting Likeness between Groups (IVL) is expressed as follows:

$IVL = 100 - |A\text{-}B|$, where
A = percentage of subgroup *A* voting pro on resolution *z*;
B = percentage of subgroup *B* voting pro on resolution *z*; and
$|A\text{-}B|$ = absolute value of *A-B*.
The *IVL* ranges between 0 (maximum disagreement) and 100 (maximum voting similarity). Aggregated *IVLs* are calculated as $IVL = \Sigma IVLiz/i$. For aggregated *IVLs* where the number of votes are not identical, $IVL = \Sigma(IVLiz) \times i/\Sigma z$.

19. The MEPs from Greece, Spain, and Portugal are not included.
20. David Curry, MEP, Foreward to Kirchner, *The European Parliament*, pp. xiii–xiv.

5
Courts, Committees, Banks, and Special Funds

This chapter deals with some of the lesser-known but important bodies within the European Community's institutional framework. Specifically, it deals with the European Court of Justice, the Court of Auditors, the Economic and Social Committee, the Consultative Committee of the ECSC, the European Investment Bank, the European Agricultural Guidance and Guarantee Fund, the European Development Fund, the European Regional Development Fund, and the European Social Fund.

COURTS

The European Court of Justice

The European Court of Justice should not be confused with either the International Court of Justice or with the European Court of Human Rights.[1] The former, also known as the World Court, is a rather ineffectual agency of the United Nations, and it sits at The Hague; the latter is the Council of Europe–created body to deal with alleged violations of the European Convention on Human Rights, and this effective and legitimate court sits at Strasbourg. The European Court of Justice (ECJ) is the European Community's judicial organ, and it sits at Luxembourg Ville.

The European Court of Justice is the only EC-wide judicial body—there are no district-level EC courts or appeals courts as there are in the US federal system. The ECJ was originally established by the ECSC Treaty and, when the EEC and EURATOM Treaties entered into force, its jurisdiction was enlarged to deal with matters falling under all three treaties.

The judges (13 in number; one from each EC member-state except the Netherlands, who currently has two in order to have an odd number) are nominated by the national governments and appointed with ''common accord'' (a unanimous vote) by the Council of Ministers for a renewable six-year term. The president of the Court is also appointed by the Council of Ministers. In addition to the judges, there are several advocates-general (analogous to the US solicitor general) who are to make submissions on cases brought before the Court. Article 167 of the EEC Treaty specifies the necessary qualifications of the judges and advocates-general: "The Judges and Advocates-General shall be chosen from persons whose independence is beyond doubt and who possess the qualifications required for appointment to the highest judicial offices in their respective countries or who are jurisconsults of recognized competence."

Although the qualifications for appointment are limited to those specified above, operating procedure and traditional practice have never seen a person from a non–EC country appointed to the Court. The treaty permits such an appointment, but it is very unlikely that such a person would be named. In addition, traditional practice also has a geographical distribution: this distribution is not mandated by the treaty (as it is with the hiring of the EC civil servants), but each country is assured at least one judge.

The Court is mandated by the treaties to represent the interests of law, justice, and equity in the interpretation and application of the three treaties, other EC texts, and Community legislation and decisions made pursuant to the treaties. Any "natural or legal person" can bring a complaint to the Court; this means that private individuals and business corporations, as well as the member-governments and the institutions of the EC (especially the Council of Ministers and the Commission), have standing before the Court.

As is true with all courts, the main task of the ECJ is to adjudicate disputes arising from the treaties' interpretation and application. If the Court finds one of the parties "guilty," however, the scope of punishment is limited. More often than not, the "sentence" will be a cease and desist order directed at the "convicted" party, without any additional sanction applied. The Court also has the ability to levy a fine as the punishment, but this type of punishment has been used very sparingly. Enforcement of the Court's decisions are governed by the rules of civil procedure in force in the specific member-state where the "guilty" party resides, and it is the national judicial structure that actually enforces the Court's rulings.

One usual type of judicial penalty however, is lacking. The ECJ *cannot* send anyone to prison. Criminal violations, and thus criminal sanctions, do not exist at the EC level, and the European Community does not have any law enforcement personnel or prisons. An activity that merits a "cease and desist" order and/or a fine at the EC level may (or may not) also entail a violation of a member-state's criminal code. If it does, it is for the national law enforcement process to prosecute; criminal prosecutions and penalties are not the tasks of the ECJ.

The Court also has the power of judicial review, analogous to the US Supreme Court's ability to declare acts of Congress and the Executive as unconstitutional. The EC does not have a "constitution" in the strictest sense of the word, but the various treaties and texts serve the same function. Article 173 of the EEC Treaty is quite explicit about this power of judicial review:

The Court of Justice shall review the legality of acts of the Council and the Commission other than recommendations or opinions. It shall for this purpose have jurisdiction in actions brought by a Member-State, the Council or the Commission on grounds of lack of competence, infringement of an essential procedural requirement, infringement of this Treaty or of any rule of law relating to its application, or misuse of powers. . . .

Any natural or legal person may, under the same conditions, institute proceedings against a decision addressed to that person or against a decision which, although in the form of a regulation addressed to another person, is of direct and individual concern to the former.

Much of the Court's work, however, does not deal with alleged violations of Community regulations or with the review of the legality of certain decisions; rather, the Court devotes a good portion of its time issuing preliminary rulings and/or advisory opinions. Whereas the US Supreme Court cannot issue such advisory opinions—it must wait until it has an actual case—the ECJ frequently is asked for such opinions. Most of these requests originate from national courts in the member-states whose presiding judge feels that the particular case under review touches upon EC matters. The ECJ does *not* decide these national disputes, but its opinion of the interpretation or application of the specific treaty article or regulation involved aids the national judge in reaching a decision.

The European Court of Justice does not enjoy a large press following or public attention and awareness in the EC. This is due to the fact that the Court deals with the administrative technicalities and definitions of the Community mechanism that, while obviously important, affects only a relatively small number of persons. The Court does not deal with cases that would immediately draw the public's attention and interest (e.g., a murder case with all the gory details or an obscenity case in which the judges had to view a film and then pronounce on its fitness for human consumption). But this low-key approach has well served the Court and the European Community—the European Court of Justice is perceived to be an effective and legitimate protector of law and justice within the limited area of the community's framework.

The Court of Auditors

The Luxembourg Ville–based Court of Auditors came into existence on 1 June 1967 with the 1965 Merger Treaty.[2] Prior to 1967, each of the three Communities had their own separate audit board responsible for examining the revenues and expenditures of the specific organization.[3] The new Court of Auditors took the place of the three separate audit boards.[4]

The 12 members of the Court of Auditors—they are really not "judges"— are appointed by the Council of Ministers by unanimous vote, after "consulting" with the European Parliament, for a six-year renewable term. The president of the court is chosen by the members themselves for a three-year term. Although not mandated by the relevant treaties, only EC nationals are appointed and the principle of geographical distribution is followed.

Each member of the Court of Auditors has the responsibility to audit specific sectors within the Community, but all decisions reached must be by a simple majority of all 12 members. Briefly stated, the court examines the books to ascertain whether all revenues have been received and that all expenditures were lawful. It can also comment on the financial management practices of the Community agencies. If the audit touches upon activities in which the national governments are involved, the audit is performed in cooperation with the national audit bodies. The Court of Auditors also has the ability to issue preliminary rulings and/or advisory opinions, if requested, on financial regulations and the internal audit procedures of the individual EC agencies.

COMMITTEES

There are some 1,500 consultative committees, specialized subcommittees, expert groups, and working parties within the EC institutional framework. This section discusses only a few of the more important of these committees not discussed elsewhere; specifically, the Economic and Social Committee, the Consultative Committee of the ECSC, and a few other committees created by treaties or Community legislation.

The Economic and Social Committee

The Economic and Social Committee (ESC) was established by both the EEC and EURATOM Treaties, each employing very similar language to describe the committee's objectives, organization, and procedure. The relevant article in the EEC Treaty, Article 193, reads: "An Economic and Social Committee is hereby established. It shall have advisory status. The Committee shall consist of representatives of the various categories of economic and social activity, in particular, representatives of producers, farmers, carriers, workers, dealers, craftsmen, professional occupations and representatives of the general public."[5]

The ESC is thus a consultative committee, composed of representatives from the organized economic and social groupings within the member-states of the Community, and it forms an integral part of the EC institutional framework and decision-making process. The ESC was established to involve, in an open and explicit fashion, the many European economic and social groups in the formulation of EC policy—an institutionalized and explicitly recognized forum for interest-group lobbying.[6] The committee also serves as a link between the organized general public and the Community's institutions.

The ESC has no power of binding decision; it can, however, influence the content of various EC-wide public policies. Under the EEC Treaty, the ESC must be "consulted" by the Commission and/or the Council of Ministers on questions relating to agriculture, freedom of movement for workers, the right of establishment and practice, transport, the harmonization-standardization of laws, social policy, vocational training, and the European Social Fund.[7]

Under the EURATOM Treaty, the committee is to be "consulted" in several specific areas within the nuclear field: research and training programs, establishment of institutes for training specialists, health and safety issues, capital investment, access to skilled jobs, and the applicability of insurance coverage against nuclear risks and hazards.[8] But, similar to all the other EC institutions, the ESC does not need to be consulted—and, in fact, is *not* consulted—on any matter that involves a member-state's (i.e., France and the United Kingdom) nuclear defense posture and behavior. The Economic and Social Committee, as well as the entire European Community process, is simply unable to advise or consult on or participate in, for example, the French nuclear-testing program in the South Pacific.

The Economic and Social Committee has the ability to produce "opinions" on its own initiative on questions that it considers relevant to the work of the Community. These "own-initiative" studies, by definition, do not require a prior request from the Commission and/or Council of Ministers. But these self-initiated advisories, as are also the requested opinions, remain advisory in nature and do not control the subsequent decision of the Council of Ministers or the Commission. The ESC produces about 120 opinions annually, the vast majority through the formal consultative process; only a few are the self-initiated variety.[9]

The committee (prior to 1 January 1986) had 156 members, distributed as follows: 24 from each of France, West Germany, Italy, and the United Kingdom; 12 from each of Belgium, Greece, and the Netherlands; nine from each of Denmark and Ireland; and six from Luxembourg. The members of the ESC are nominated by the home governments and then are appointed for a renewable four-year term.[10] The members are expected (Article 194) to serve in their personal capacity and are not to be bound by any mandate or instructions from the home governments. Also, although the members represent the various interest and functional groups, they are not supposed to be formally instructed delegates of whatever interest-professional group in which they may hold membership. For most of the ESC's members, the appointment is not on a paid, full-time basis: they live and work in the home country, but receive transportation expenses and a per diem whenever there is a meeting in Brussels.

The Economic and Social Committee is one of the few EC institutions that enjoys the luxury of a permanent and stable place of business; the committee is housed in its own building on Rue Ravenstein in Brussels and it is not required to go on the road and hold meetings in other locations. The number of days that a reasonably conscientious ESC member allocates to committee business (including travel) varies, but it averages out to approximately 70 days a year. The day-to-day organizing work is performed by some full-time personnel. There is a chairman and a bureau, both elected by and from the entire membership for a two-year term. The bureau has 24 members and is charged with organizing the committee's work. There is also the usual secretariat, a permanent full-time staff of about 500 persons providing the normal support services (clerical, translation, security, etc.).

The committee's membership is divided into three broad functional groups, and the members are seen to be representatives of the specific grouping, as follows:

I. Employers (such as UNICE—Union of Industries of the European Community);

II. Workers (such as ETUC—European Trade Union Confederation); and

III. Various Interests: agriculture (COPA—Committee of Professional Agricultural Organizations in the European Community), transport, trade, small businesses, consumers, environmentalists, and the liberal professions (SEPLIS—European Secretariat of the Liberal, Intellectual, and Social Professions).

Each of these three functional groups must have at least 30 members and, after some intentional categorizations to ensure a reasonable distribution of nationalities and functional groups, the members are then voted onto three of the nine specialized sections. These sections correspond roughly to the major fields covered by EC activity:

1. Agriculture;
2. Industry, commerce, crafts and services;
3. Economic and financial services;
4. Social questions;
5. Transport and communications;
6. External relations;
7. Energy and nuclear questions;
8. Regional development; and
9. Protection of the environment, public health and consumer affairs.

The process of rendering an opinion illustrates how European-wide and national organizations can lobby the committee as well as how the ESC, in its turn, can influence/lobby the Commission and/or the Council of Ministers. The consultative process, in four stages, is relatively straightforward and is depicted in Figure 5.1. To begin, the chairman of the ESC, after receiving the proposal from the Commission or the Council of Ministers and after then consulting with the bureau, determines which of the nine specialized sections will be responsible for producing the draft opinion.

The section to which the proposal is referred then establishes a ''study group.'' This group can range from three to a dozen or more people, evenly distributed across the ESC's functional groupings (employers, workers, and various other interests). The study group chooses its own chairman and rapporteur (the rapporteur is responsible for the actual writing of the draft opinion). It is at this point that organized interests outside the ESC have an input into the consultative process—several outside "experts" are used by the study group. The rapporteur appoints an expert; each of the three functional groups appoints an expert; any member of the study group itself can bring along an outside expert to the meetings. The Commission is also represented at the study group's meetings—it is a very interested participant in the process—and the Commission's representative frequently brings along his own outside expert. It is quite possible that a four-person study group (three ESC members and the Commission's representative) will be joined by seven outside experts. The study group usually meets three or four times, eventually approving the rapporteur's draft opinion.

This study group's draft is then referred back to the relevant specialized section to be discussed, amended, and then voted. This version is now the section's opinion which, in turn, is referred to the entire ESC at its next monthly plenary session. The draft is once again open to debate and amendment; a final version is eventually approved. This final document becomes the formal ESC opinion and is transmitted to the Commission and/or the Council of Ministers. The European Parliament also receives a copy of the final opinion or study.

The Council of Ministers and/or the Commission must wait to receive the ESC's opinion before reaching a final decision although there is no requirement to accept or follow the ESC's advice. However, these expert opinions frequently serve to shape final policy outcomes. The Economic and Social Committee has no power of binding decision in any area, but it does function as originally intended: a process by which the organized European interest groups can influence the content of Community policy.

The Consultative Committee of the ECSC

Created by Articles 7 and 18 of the ECSC Treaty, the Consultative Committee of the European Coal and Steel Community is very similar in scope and function to the Economic and Social Committee under the EEC and EURATOM Treaties. This is one of the very few areas that was not consolidated in the 1967 merger of the Community's institutions. The ESC deals with questions arising in areas covered by the EEC and EURATOM Treaties; the Consultative Committee is limited to ECSC matters.

The committee's membership is composed of three equal-sized categories: representatives from (1) the producers, (2) workers, and (3) consumers, dealers, and transporters in the coal and steel industries. Prior to 1 January 1986, the committee had 84 members, divided among the member-states in terms of each country's approximate share of the Community's coal and steel production: West Germany contributed 19 members, the United Kingdom 18, France 13, Belgium and Italy each contributed eight, the Netherlands five, Luxembourg four, and Denmark, Ireland, and Greece each contributed three members.

The members are appointed to a renewable two-year term by the Council of

Figure 5.1
The Economic and Social Committee

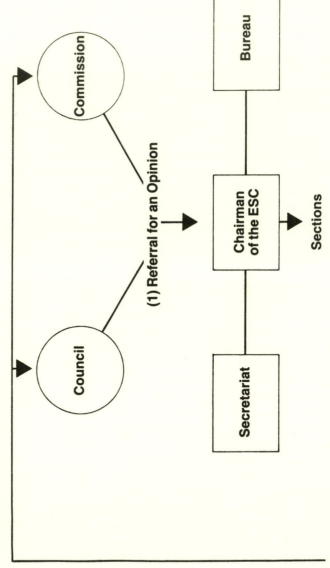

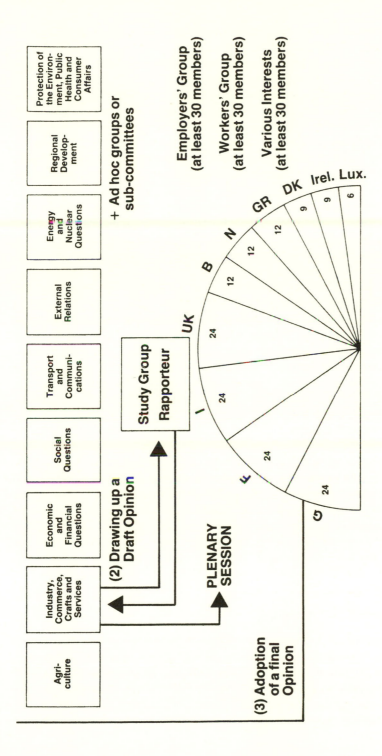

Agri-culture	Industry, Commerce, Crafts and Services	Economic and Financial Questions	Social Questions	Transport and Communi-cations	External Relations	Energy and Nuclear Questions	Regional Develop-ment	Protection of the Environ-ment, Public Health and Consumer Affairs

+ Ad hoc groups or sub-committees

Study Group
Rapporteur

(2) Drawing up a Draft Opinion

PLENARY SESSION

(3) Adoption of a final Opinion

Employers' Group
(at least 30 members)

Workers' Group
(at least 30 members)

Various Interests
(at least 30 members)

UK 24
I 24
F 24
G 24
B 12
N 12
GR 12
DK 9
Irel. 9
Lux. 6

Source: *The Economic and Social Committee* (Brussels: The Economic and Social Committee, Press - Information - Publications Division.)

Ministers—the national governments nominate the consumer/dealer/transporter representatives, but the national producer and union organizations submit a list of their nominees. Each list must contain at least twice as many nominees as there are places to be filled (Article 18 of the ECSC Treaty). The members are expected to serve in their individual capacity and, although they are representatives of the various interest groups within the coal and steel sectors of the economy, they are not to solicit or receive binding instructions from these groups or from the national governments. For most of the Consultative Committee's members, the appointment is not on a paid, full-time basis: they live and work in the home country, but receive transportation expenses and a per diem whenever there is a meeting in Brussels.

The day-to-day organizing work is performed by some full-time personnel. A president and a bureau is elected each year by the committee's entire membership. The bureau has nine members, including the president, and its members are equally distributed across the three membership categories (producers, workers, and consumers/dealers/transporters). The president is chosen from the three categories in turn, alternating between the coal and steel sectors. And, as usual, a full-time secretariat provides the support services.

The Consultative Committee usually holds about four plenary sessions a year, but special meetings have frequently been held. As with most other similar organizations, the plenary sessions are prepared in advance in the subcommittee meetings. Currently, there are four standing subcommittees: (1) general objectives, (2) markets and prices, (3) labor problems, and (4) research projects. The membership of these subcommittees reflects both the country of origin distribution of the entire committee and the maintenance of equal representation of the three functional groupings.

The Consultative Committee, similar to the Economic and Social Committee, has no power of binding decision; it can, however, influence the content of EC-wide public policies in the coal and steel sectors. The ECSC Treaty (Article 19) mandates that the Council of Ministers and/or the Commission "consult" the committee in specific areas, and the committee also has the ability to meet on its own and produce "own-initiative" opinions. But the Consultative Committee of the ECSC is exactly what its title suggests: it is an expert *advisory* committee and it does not have the power to issue any binding decision, regulation, or directive.

Other Specialized Committees

The EC institutional framework contains approximately 1,500 consultative committees, specialized subcommittees, expert groups, and working parties. Most of these provide advice and opinions to the EC Commission and/or Council of Ministers. None of these specialized committees have the power of independent and binding decision making, but much of European-wide public policy is influenced and shaped by the opinions, studies, and recommendations of these expert groups. Only a few of these committees have been created by the various treaties; most owe their existence to Community legislation. The following section presents a brief overview of just a few of these specialized committees.

Committees Established by the Treaties

A Transport Committee advises the Commission on transport problems and consists of national transport officials and experts. This committee was created by Article 83 of the EEC Treaty: "An Advisory Committee consisting of experts designated by the Governments of Member-States, shall be attached to the Commission. The Commission, whenever it considers it desirable, shall consult the Committee on transport matters without prejudice to the powers of the transport section of the Economic and Social Committee."

A Monetary Committee advises the Council of Ministers and the Commission on monetary problems. It consists of government and national central banks' officials as well as experts appointed by the Commission. The tasks of this committee are specified in Article 105 of the EEC Treaty:

In order to promote coordination of the policies of Member-States in the monetary field to the full extent needed for the functioning of the common market, a Monetary Committee with advisory status is hereby set up. It shall have the following tasks:

—to keep under review the monetary and financial situation of the Member-States and of the Community and the general payments system of the Member-States and to report regularly thereon to the Council and to the Commission;

—to deliver opinions at the request of the Council or of the Commission or on its own initiative, for submission to these institutions.

A committee referred to as Article 113 Committee (EEC Treaty) is responsible for advising the Commission regarding the latter's negotiations with third countries on trade matters. It also advises the Commission on the EC's common commercial policy, tariff rates, tariff and trade agreements, export policy, and subsidy measures. This Article 113 Committee is composed of representatives from the national governments appointed by the Council of Ministers. Finally, Article 134 of the EURATOM Treaty established the advisory Scientific and Technical Committee. Attached to the Commission, this committee is consulted on various EURATOM matters.

Committees Created by Community Legislation

Most of the committees and working groups within the EC structure have not been established by treaty; rather, their creation is based on various Community legislation and directives. The following comments briefly note some of the more important of these groups.

Standing Committee on Uranium Enrichment (COPENUR). This committee was established by the Council of Ministers in May 1973 and is composed of representatives from the Commission and representatives from European-wide public and private bodies and enterprises interested in the production and use of enriched uranium. COPENUR's tasks are as follows:

— to carry out and provide current studies of the market in enriched uranium, taking into account the production potential and the guarantees afforded by the various suppliers;

— to collect data on the fundamental technical and economic features of various technologies;

— to examine ways and means of promoting the development of the industrial capacity needed by the Community; and

— to facilitate the coordination of efforts between the interested parties.

Scientific and Technical Research Committee (CREST). This committee was set up by a January 1974 Council of Ministers' resolution, and it consists of representatives from the national governments and from the Commission. The chairman of CREST is always a Commission representative, and the committee itself is aided by experts in the scientific and technical fields. CREST's major tasks are the coordination of national policies and the definition of projects of interest to the Community. CREST maintains a close working relationship with the Strasbourg-based (but non-EC institution) European Science Foundation.

Energy Committee. Composed of representatives from the national governments and from the Commission, and assisted by outside experts, this committee was also established by a January 1974 Council of Ministers' decision. This committee assists the Commission in the preparation of energy-related proposals, particularly on the current and future energy requirements of the Community and possible energy sources.

Special Committee on Agriculture. Established in May 1960 by the Council of Ministers, this committee is composed of representatives from the member-governments. The major task of this committee is, in consultation with the Committee of Permanent Representatives, to prepare for the Council's discussions relating to the common agricultural policy.

Standing Committee on Employment. This committee is to coordinate the employment policies of the national governments, taking into account the views of the Council, the Commission, and the two sides of industry (labor and management). Composed of national experts and Commission representatives, it was established by the Council of Ministers in December 1970.

Education Committee. This committee was established by the ministers of education, sitting as the Council of Ministers, in June 1974, and was given the tasks to coordinate education measures throughout the Community and set priorities within the educational field.

Finally, four other major Community-created special committees should be mentioned:

1. The Short-Term Economic Policy Committee attempts to coordinate the day-to-day economic policies of the EC states and maintain a steady rate of economic expansion;

2. The Medium-Term Economic Policy Committee charts the probable trend of the Community's economy over a five-year period;

3. The Committee of Central Bank Governors discusses credit, money market, and foreign exchange matters; and

4. The Administrative Commission for the Social Security of Migrant Workers, which advises the Commission in areas that deal with EC citizens working in a member-country other than their own, and it consists of national officials and Commission representatives.

BANKS

The European Community does not have a central bank; there is, however, a bank within the EC institutional framework. Created by the EEC Treaty—Article 3(j)—the European Investment Bank was established to facilitate the economic expansion of the Community. The following section discusses the activities of the European Investment Bank.

The European Investment Bank

The European Investment Bank (EIB) was established by the EEC Treaty, and its powers and duties were described in precise detail in an annexed protocol.[11] Located in Luxembourg Ville, the EIB is an autonomous public institution within the European Community whose essential function is to provide, on a nonprofit basis, financing for industrial and infrastructure projects to promote a balanced and steady development within the Community.[12]

General Objectives

The EIB's principal objectives are specified in Article 130 of the EEC Treaty:

The task of the European Investment Bank shall be to contribute, by having recourse to the capital market and utilizing its own resources, to the balanced and steady development of the common market in the interest of the Community. For this purpose the Bank shall, operating on a non-profit-making basis, grant loans and give guarantees which facilitate the financing of the following projects in all sectors of the economy:

(a) projects for developing less developed regions;

(b) projects for modernizing or converting undertakings or for developing fresh activities called for by the progressive establishment of the common market, where these projects are of such a size or nature that they cannot be entirely financed by the various means available in the individual Member States; and

(c) projects of common interest to several Member States which are of such a size or nature that they cannot be entirely financed by the various means available in the individual Member States.

Management

The quoted Protocol on the Statute of the European Investment Bank (25 March 1957) defines the EIB's management structure. Obviously, the EC member-governments are members of the bank. There are three major management bodies: a board of governors, a board of directors, and a management committee.

The board of governors consists of the ministers of finance from the 12 EC member-countries. The functions of the board include the establishment of the general guidelines for the EIB's credit policies and the approval of the bank's annual report. The board of governors also appoint the EIB's board of directors and the management committee.

The board of directors is appointed by the finance ministers (board of governors) for a five-year renewable term. There are currently 22 directors and 12 alternates: France, West Germany, Italy, and the United Kingdom each nominate three directors and two alternates; Belgium, Luxembourg, and the Netherlands each nominate one director and, jointly, one alternate; Denmark, Greece, and Ireland each nominate one director and, jointly, one alternate; Spain nominates two directors and Portugal nominates one; Spain and Portugal jointly nominate one alternate; and the European Commission nominates one director and one alternate. The board of directors is charged with the following:

The Board of Directors shall have sole power to take decisions in respect of granting loans and guarantees and raising loans; it shall fix the interest rates on loans granted and the commission on guarantees; it shall see that the Bank is properly run; it shall ensure that the Bank is managed in accordance with the provisions of this Treaty and of this Statute and with the general directives laid down by the Board of Governors.[13]

The management committee is composed of the president of the EIB and four vice-presidents, each appointed for a six-year term by the board of governors on the proposal from the board of directors. The management committee is responsible for the day-to-day business of the bank and operates under the authority of the president and the supervision of the board of directors. Its major function concerns the implementation of the board of directors' decisions regarding the raising of capital and the granting of loans.

Capital Structure

The EIB's original capital funds were derived from assessments levied on the Community's member-governments. Approximately 28.8 billion ECUs were subscribed by the governments as of 1 January 1986, with about 9 percent of this amount already deposited with the bank. Table 5.1 contains the specific amounts. Not surprisingly, the four larger EC countries account for most of the subscribed capital: France, West Germany, Italy, and the United Kingdom each is at 19.1 percent.

Currently, most of the funds required by the EIB are borrowed in the capital

Table 5.1
Capital Structure of the European Investment Bank (million ECUs)

Country	Subscribed	Paid In	Percent
France	5,508.725	497.530	19.127
United Kingdom	5,508.725	497.530	19.127
West Germany	5,508.725	497.530	19.127
Italy	5,508.725	497.530	19.127
Spain	2,024.928	181.334	7.031
Belgium	1,526.980	136.742	5.302
Netherlands	1,526.980	136.742	5.302
Denmark	773.154	69.237	2.684
Greece	414.190	37.092	1.438
Portugal	266.922	23.904	0.927
Ireland	193.288	17.309	0.671
Luxembourg	38.658	3.462	0.134
Total	28,800.00	2,595.942	100

Source: The Europa Year Book: A World Survey, Volume I, Part One, "International Organizations" (London: Europa Publications, Ltd., 1986), p. 145.

markets, both within the Community and on international markets. In many cases the bank is able to raise funds at lower interest rates than apply to private industrial concerns and even some other public authorities. This interest rate advantage is the result of its high credit rating in the international markets: its reserves are high and the "shareholders" or the "guarantors" of the borrowings are the member-states of the EC itself (the national governments may be running deficits, but it is highly unlikely that the countries will fall into bankruptcy). Since the bank is to operate on a nonprofit basis (operating costs must be met and the capital reserves must be maintained, however), combined with lower borrowing costs, it can often pass on the lower interest rates to its own borrowers.

In October 1978 a borrowing and lending mechanism—the New Community Instrument for Borrowing and Lending (NCI)—was created by the EC. The objective of the NCI is to raise additional funds for the financing of structural investment projects, particularly in energy, industrial conversion, and infrastructure. NCI-generated funds are deposited with the EIB which, in turn, makes loans on behalf of the Community. Total loans granted since 1979 with NCI funds is approximately 3.922 billion ECUs, with Italy the largest recipient of NCI-generated funds (about 56 percent).

Financing Provided (Amounts)

In its early years of operation, most of the EIB's lending activities were limited to projects within the Community itself. Close to 90 percent of the total lending operations were within the EC or for projects in neighboring non-EC countries that had a direct benefit for the Community. The EIB, however, has slowly increased the amounts loaned to other countries, particularly those that have signed cooperation agreements with the EC. Countries in the Mediterranean region have received such loans for various projects: Greece, Spain, and Portugal before entering the EC; Turkey, Malta, and Yugoslavia; the Maghreb countries (Algeria, Morocco, and Tunisia); the Mashrek countries (Egypt, Jordan, Syria, and Lebanon); and Cyprus and Israel. In addition, investment projects have been funded in some of the 56 ACP (African, Caribbean, and Pacific) countries that belong to the EC-ACP Lomé Convention. Loans granted for projects in non-EC countries that are not linked to the Community by any development finance agreement or cooperation/association agreement are usually restricted to projects that provide direct benefits to the Community.[14]

The EIB is not limited by Article 130 or the protocol to make loans only to private enterprises; in fact, a high proportion of its loans are to public authorities. There has yet to be any charge that the bank's lending decisions are based on any "political" considerations; a rather frequent occurrence with international lending agencies.[15] The protocol specifies that the granting of finance is *not* dependent on the nationality of the borrower. The loans granted by the EIB are usually intended to cover only a part of the project's cost—ordinarily about 50 percent—and the difference is to be provided by the borrower's own funds and/or credits from other sources. Although the protocol does not specify any minimum amount, the EIB has been very hesitant to make any loan for less than ECU one million.

To help small- and medium-sized projects, the EIB has evolved a system called *global loans*: funds are provided to regional or national (or, sometimes, to international) financial institutions. These institutions then select projects from their own clients (in agreement with the EIB) and parcel out the funds accordingly. This is a very flexible system—a combination of the rather large financial resources of the EIB linked to local knowledge and expertise. The normal duration of an EIB loan is from seven to 12 years, but can be as long as 20 years for certain large-scale infrastructure projects.

One of the primary and most important objectives of the European Investment Bank is to foster regional development within the Community and, as Table 5.2 indicates, it should not be surprising that Italy has been the greatest beneficiary by far of EIB financing, mostly for projects in the Mezzogiorno. Italy has received

Table 5.2
Financing Provided by the EIB—by Amount (million ECUs)

Recipient	1985		1958–1984	
	Amount	Percent	Amount	Percent
Within the EC	6,524.4	90.8	33,728.6	87.70
Belgium	77.8	1.08	661.2	1.70
Denmark	332.5	4.63	1,430.9	3.70
France	1,247.4	17.36	5,121.1	13.29
Greecea	423.7	5.90	1,396.6	3.61
Ireland	174.5	2.43	2,301.4	5.95
Italy	2,978.0	41.45	15,523.6	40.33
Luxembourg	-	-	25.4	0.04
Netherlands	69.1	0.96	105.2	0.25
United Kingdom	1,130.1	15.73	5,778.0	14.99
West Germany	91.4	1.27	1,490.4	3.84
Outside the Community	660.2	9.20	4,730.8	12.30
(Direct Benefit Loans)b	(-)	(-)	(223.5)	(0.58)
(Others)c	(660.2)	(9.20)	(4,507.3)	(11.72)
Total	7,184.6	100	38,459.4	100

a. Loans provided in Greece between 1964 and 1980, before Greece entered the EC (351.4 million ECUs), are included in the figures for financing Outside the Community (Others).

b. Loans granted for energy projects in Austria, Norway, and Tunisia.

c. Includes 220 million ECUs for Spain and Portugal in 1984 and 260 million ECUs in 1985.

Source: The Europa Year Book: A World Survey, Volume I, Part One, "International Organizations" (London: Europa Publications, Ltd., 1985), p. 144; European Investment Bank, "EIB-Information" (February 1986), pp. 2, 4.

Table 5.3
Financing Provided by the EIB—by Sector (1958–1978)

Sector	Loans	Percent of Loans	Percent of Amounts Loaned
Energy	152	9.7	30.6
(Production)	(110)	(7.0)	(22.5)
(Transmission)	(42)	(2.7)	(8.1)
Transport	84	5.3	15.1
Telecommunications	51	3.2	14.6
Water Projects	60	3.8	10.5
Public Buildings	2	0.1	0.2
Industrial Projects	1,182	74.8	28.6
Agricultural	37	2.3	0.2
Tourism	6	0.3	0.1
Other	8	0.5	0.1
Total	1,582	100	100

Source: Annuaire des Communautés Européennes (Editions Delta, 1979), pp. 342–343.

approximately 40 percent of all EIB financing within the European Community. The United Kingdom is the second-largest recipient, with about 15 percent; closely followed by France, with 13 percent. No other country reaches the 10 percent level. These vast differences in funding levels have yet to give rise to claims of unequal costs/benefits (a complaint that is constantly voiced regarding the common agricultural policy) and the EIB has been (relatively) free of politics. It is accepted across the EC that, for example, southern Italy and Sicily have greater justification to claim EIB funds than, say, the Netherlands or Denmark.

Financing Provided (Sectors)

The largest part of the finance provided by the EIB within the Community has been for projects in the less developed regions and for industrial infrastructure and modernization. In recent years, projects that benefit a number of member-states have been receiving priority, particularly those involving the production of energy (nuclear and hydroelectric plants). Table 5.3 presents the sectoral breakdown of the financing provided.

As this table indicates, industrial projects (infrastructure, modernization, conversion) is the largest sector in terms of number of loans (74.8 percent of the total), but not in terms of amounts loaned (28.6 percent). The energy sector, with only 9.7 percent of all loans, receives approximately 30.6 percent of the EIB funds. This emphasis on energy production stems from the EC's desire to decrease the Community's dependence on foreign energy sources. Transport projects are next (15.1 percent), followed by telecommunications (14.6 percent) and water projects (10.5 percent). Agricultural projects received only 2.3 percent of the loans and 0.2 percent of the funding, but these low levels are readily explained. The very low amount of EIB financing for agricultural infrastructure projects is due to the operation of the European Agricultural Guidance and Guarantee Fund (EAGGF) within the EC's common agricultural policy. It is the EAGGF that expends vast sums of these projects rather than the European Investment Bank.

SPECIAL FUNDS

The European Community has established several funds with specialized objectives. This section discusses four of the more important of these special funds: (1) the European Agricultural Guidance and Guarantee Fund; (2) the European Development Fund; (3) the European Regional Development Fund; and (4) the European Social Fund.

The European Agricultural Guidance and Guarantee Fund

The European Agricultural Guidance and Guarantee Fund (EAGGF or, following the frequently used French abbreviation, FEOGA) is discussed in greater detail in Chapter 7, and comments here are only a brief overview. The common agricultural policy (CAP), through the EAGGF, finances EC activity within the agricultural sector and is administered by DG VI within the Commission. The EAGGF expenditures account for an extraordinarily large percentage of the total EC budget—some 72 percent in 1985 (20.1 billion ECUs) and a projected 60 percent in 1986 (19.3 billion ECUs). The EAGGF is directed at four related processes: (1) domestic production, (2) inter-EC trade, (3) exports, and (4) structural improvements.

In the area of domestic production of agricultural commodities, the EAGGF mechanism will intervene if open-market prices fall to or below EC-established support prices for various commodities. The intervention process is as follows:

1. The EAGGF will finance the purchase of the surplus commodities that could not be sold at (at least) the support price; and/or

2. The EAGGF will finance the costs of storage/stockpiling the commodity until a later date when, presumably, market conditions will be stronger; and/or

3. The EAGGF will finance the difference between the actual open-market realized price and the support price.

In the area of trade of agricultural commodities among the EC countries, the EAGGF, in order to maintain "harmonized" prices, will intervene with border levies, either positive or negative, that are formally termed "Monetary Compensation Amounts" (MCAs) on such trade. Agricultural commodities from a low-cost country to a high-cost country will pay a levy at the border to bring its price up to that of the importing country's level; conversely, commodities from a high-cost country will receive a subsidy at the border to allow the selling price to be lowered and thus able to compete with the lower prices in the importing low-cost EC country.

The EAGGF also finances the export subsidies on agricultural exports to non-EC countries. Since the CAP has led to artificially high prices, the world market price for many commodities is several times lower than the EC price. To compete in the world markets, the EAGGF finances the difference between the EC internal price and the lower-realized world market price. Finally, the structural improvement sector of the EAGGF, which deals with the agricultural sector's infrastructure, has the objective to make farming across the EC more efficient.

The European Development Fund

Administered by the Commission, assisted by the European Development Fund Committee, the European Development Fund (EDF) was established in 1958 in the context of the Lomé Convention and later expanded within the context of the Arusha and Yaoundé Conventions.[16] These conventions are economic trade, development, and cooperation agreements between the EC and various Third World countries.

The funds within the EDF are used not only to provide basic infrastructure projects (roads, water supplies, harbors) and social needs (schools, hospitals, medical services), but also to promote industrial growth in the countries, particularly in agricultural efficiency in order to increase their competition in the world markets.

Community aid through the EDF has emphasized the following areas:

1. Investments to increase production and modernize the economic and social infrastructure;
2. General technical cooperation measures; and
3. Measures to encourage the marketing and sales promotion of products (primarily commodities) exported by the associated countries.

There are six basic types of EDF activity: grants, special loans, risk-capital formation, a scheme to guarantee minimum export earnings (STABEX), a scheme to protect mineral producers (SYSMIN), and an extensive food aid program. It is difficult to break down the amounts allocated for these programs, but the 1986 EC draft budget lists some 1.65 billion ECUs for development cooperation. And food aid—at 954 million ECUs—is the largest category.

The European Regional Development Fund

One of the main objectives laid down in the EEC Treaty was to narrow the gap between the underdeveloped regions and the richer areas in the Community.[17] These underdeveloped or depressed areas were primarily agricultural regions or regions dependent on declining industries. Although every member of the European Community has some areas classified as "underdeveloped," the main regions are southern Italy and Sicily, the western and southwestern areas of France, northern Netherlands, parts of West Germany along the border with the German Democratic Republic, sections of the United Kingdom, Ulster, and parts of Ireland.

In October 1969, the Commission issued a major position paper that urged greater coordination and cooperation among the countries' regional policies. The major points of this 1969 memorandum were as follows:

— An annual review of the situation in regions "for which the establishment, extension or execution of development plans is particularly urgent";

— The setting up of a permanent committee on regional development to be composed of representatives from the member-states under the direction of the Commission;

— The establishment of a fund for regional development, financed by the Community's budget and administered by the Commission; and

— The provision of better information to the public and private investors.

The European Regional Development Fund (ERDF) was eventually established and began funding projects in 1975. The ERDF is administered by the Commission, assisted by the European Regional Development Fund Committee. The fund's major objective is to compensate for the unequal rate of development in the Community by encouraging investment and improving the infrastructure in the regions that needed aid. From 1975 until 1979, all funds expended by the ERDF were allocated according to national quotas, but in 1979, a nonquota section was added. This nonquota section is now approximately 15 percent of the total funds, and projects here can be initiated by the Commission. Also in 1984, the national quota amounts were made a bit more flexible (with lower and upper limits): Italy has the highest quota (31.94–42.59 percent), followed by the United Kingdom (21.42–28.56 percent), Greece (12.35–15.74 percent), and France (11.05–14.74 percent).[18] The 1986 draft EC budget has committed some 3.43 billion ECUs to the European Regional Development Fund.

The European Social Fund

The European Social Fund (ESF) was authorized by the EEC Treaty but was not established until 1960.[19] The ESF is administered by the Commission, assisted by the European Social Fund Committee (composed of representatives of the member-governments, trade unions, and employers' organizations). The fund's major objectives are to improve employment opportunities for workers and increase workers' geographical and occupational mobility within the Community.

Article 125 of the EEC Treaty specifies the ESF's activities:

On application by a Member-State the Fund shall . . . meet 50 percent of the expenditure incurred . . . by that State or by a body governed by public law for the purposes of:
   (a) ensuring productive-re-employment of workers by means of vocational retraining and resettlement allowances; and
   (b) granting aid for the benefit of workers whose employment is reduced or temporarily suspended, in whole or in part, as a result of the conversion of an undertaking to other production, in order that they may retain the same wage level pending their full re-employment.

In 1986, total EC commitments under the Social Fund amounted to some 2.44 billion ECUs. Approximately 80 percent of the expenditures were for projects in the United Kingdom, Italy, France, and Ireland, with the emphasis placed upon employment opportunities for young people. Currently, applications for ESF contributions run about 40 percent more than the available resources.

NOTES

1. See Gerhard Bebr, *Judicial Control of the European Communities* (New York: Praeger, 1962); L. J. Brinkhorst and H. G. Schermers, *Judicial Remedies in the European Communities* (London: Stevens, 1969); L. N. Brown and F. G. Jacobs, *The Court of Justice of the European Communities* (London: Sweet & Maxwell, 1977); Werner J. Feld, *The Court of the European Communities* (Amsterdam: Martinus Nijhoff, 1964); K. Lipstein, *The Law of the European Economic Community* (Sevenoaks, Kent, UK: Butterworth, 1974); and H. G. Schermers, *Judicial Protection in the European Communities* (Dordrecht: Kluwer, 1979).

2. See Isaac E. Druker, *Financing the European Communities* (Leyden: Sijthoff, 1975), esp. chapter 23, "External Audit and Discharge," pp. 335–341.

3. Article 180, EURATOM Treaty; Article 78(d), ECSC Treaty; Article 206, EEC Treaty.

4. Article 22, Merger Treaty.

5. Article 165 of the EURATOM Treaty reads: "The Committee shall consist of representatives of the various categories of economic and social activity." Other than this, there is very little difference in how the EEC and EURATOM Treaties describe the Economic and Social Committee.

6. For the linkages between the ESC and the interest groups, see Economic and Social

Committee of the European Community, General Secretariat, *European Interest Groups and Their Relationship to the Economic and Social Committee* (Aldershot, Hants, UK: Gower, 1980). See also Emil J. Kirchner, *Trade Unions as a Pressure Group in the European Community* (Aldershot, Hants, UK: Saxon House, 1977).

7. Article 198 of the EEC Treaty reads: "The Committee must be consulted by the Council or by the Commission where this Treaty so provides. The Committee may be consulted by these institutions in all cases in which they consider it appropriate."

8. Article 170 of the EURATOM Treaty is identical to Article 198 of the EEC Treaty (cited above).

9. These opinions and studies range in length—some have been only ten pages while others have approached 200 pages—and cover the full range of Community activity. Some representative titles are: "Systems of Education and Vocational Training," "Progress Report on the Common Agricultural Policy," "The Situation of Small and Medium-Sized Undertakings in the European Community," "The EEC's Transport Problems with East European Countries," "Monetary Disorder," and "Regional Policy."

10. Both Article 195 of the EEC Treaty and Article 176 of the EURATOM Treaty read: "For the appointment of the members of the Committee, each Member-State shall provide the Council with a list containing twice as many candidates as there are seats allotted to its nationals. The composition of the Committee shall take account of the need to ensure adequate representation of the various categories of economic and social activity. The Council shall consult the Commission. It may obtain the opinion of European bodies which are representative of the various economic and social sectors to which the activities of the Community are of concern."

11. Protocol on the Statute of the European Investment Bank (25 March 1957). Sweet & Maxwell's Legal Editorial Staff, eds., *European Community Treaties* (London: Sweet & Maxwell, 1975), pp. 126–134.

12. For a detailed discussion of the European Investment Bank, see Sheila Lewenhak, *The Role of the European Investment Bank* (Beckenham, Kent, UK: Croom Helm, 1982).

13. Article 11, paragraph 1, of the Protocol on the Statute of the European Investment Bank.

14. Examples of such loans include the development of Norwegian oil and gas resources and the construction of a gas pipeline across Austria.

15. An example of employing "political" considerations in the practices of international lending agencies in the United States is the Harkin Amendment to the 1976 Foreign Assistance Act. The amendment requires the US representatives on multinational economic development funds and banks to oppose any loan to countries that "engage in a consistent pattern of gross violations of internationally recognized human rights." See Leon Hurwitz, *The State as Defendant* (Westport, Conn.: Greenwood Press, 1981), esp. chapter 5, "Parliamentary Political Activity," pp. 107–134.

16. See Thomas Balogh, "Africa and the Common Market," 1 *Journal of Common Market Studies* (September 1962), 79–112; W. G. Barnes, *Europe and the Developing World* (London: Chatham House, 1967); R. Cohen, *Europe and the Developing Countries* (Rotterdam: Rotterdam University Press, 1972); Ingrid D. di Delupis, *The East African Community and the Common Market* (New York: Longman, 1970); Frank Long, *The Political Economy of EEC Relations with African, Caribbean and Pacific States* (Elmsford, N.Y.: Pergamon, 1980); Harry Stordel, *The Lomé Convention and a New International Economic Order* (Leyden: Sijthoff, 1977); Carol C. Twitchett, *A Framework for Development: The EEC and the ACP* (London: Allen & Unwin, 1981); and William

I. Zartman, *The Politics of Trade Negotiations Between Africa and the European Economic Community* (Princeton, N.J.: Princeton University Press, 1971).

17. See Sergio Barzanti, *Underdeveloped Areas within the Common Market* (Princeton, N.J.: Princeton University Press, 1968); Dudley Seers et al., *Underdeveloped Europe: Studies in Core-Periphery Relationships* (Atlantic Highlands, N.J.: Humanities Press, 1979); R. F. Talbot, *The European Community's Regional Fund* (Elmsford, N.Y.: Pergamon, 1977); and Douglas Yuill, ed., *Regional Development Agencies in Europe* (Aldershot, Hants, UK: Gower, 1982).

18. *The Europa Yearbook: A World Survey*, Volume I, Part One, "International Organizations" (London: Europa Publications, 1985), p. 145.

19. See W. R. Bohning, *The Migration of Workers in the United Kingdom and the European Community* (New York: Oxford University Press, 1972); Doreen Collins, *The Operation of the European Social Fund* (Beckenham, Kent, UK: Croom Helm, 1983); L. H. Klaassen and Willem Molle, *Industrial Mobility and Migration in the European Community* (Aldershot, Hants, UK: Gower, 1983); Michael Shanks, *European Social Policy* (Elmsford, N.Y.: Pergamon, 1977); and Jacques Vandamme, ed., *New Dimensions in European Social Policy* (Beckenham, Kent, UK: Croom Helm, 1985).

PART III

Goals and Objectives

The EEC Treaty identified several goals and objectives: some of these objectives were quite explicit, with accompanying timetables and deadlines for their attainment; others were more vague, hopes and desires without any real definition or deadlines. Article 3 of the Treaty lists the explicit goals:

(a) The elimination, as between Member-States, of customs duties and of quantitative restrictions in regard to the importation and exportation of goods, as well as of all other measures with equivalent effect;

(b) The establishment of a common customs tariff and a common commercial policy toward third countries;

(c) The abolition, as between Member-States, of the obstacles to the free movement of persons, services and capital;

(d) The inauguration of a common agricultural policy;

(e) The inauguration of a common transport policy;

(f) The establishment of a system ensuring that competition shall not be distorted in the common market;

(g) The application of procedures which shall make it possible to co-ordinate the economic policies of Member-States and to remedy disequilibria in their balances of payments;

(h) The approximation of their respective municipal law to the extent necessary for the functioning of the common market;

(i) The creation of a European Social Fund in order to improve the possibilities of employment for workers and to contribute to the raising of their standard of living;

(j) The establishment of a European Investment Bank intended to facilitate the economic expansion of the Community through the creation of new resources; and

(k) The association of overseas countries and territories with the Community with a view to increasing trade and to pursuing jointly their effort towards economic and social development.

These eleven goals and objectives were (are) the explicit ones; some, especially the creation of a customs union by eliminating artificial barriers to trade (tariffs, duties, quotas), had stages of attainment with timetables and deadlines included in the body of the treaty. Most of the listed goals and objectives, however, were economic and commercial in nature. Very little can be found in the body of the treaty itself about political integration or political unification—an entirely different matter than, say, agreeing on the tariff levels to be imposed on Israeli citrus products during the winter months. It was generally recognized, though (implicitly, if not explicitly), that the idea of political integration and future political unification under some form of a European federal system underlay the entire process. This unstated goal was hinted at in the treaty's preamble: "DETERMINED to establish the foundations of an ever closer union among the European peoples, and DECIDED to insure the . . . progress of their countries by common action in eliminating the barriers which divide Europe."

This hoped-for future "ever closer union" and "common action in eliminating the barriers which divide Europe" are the vehicles through which *political* (rather than economic) harmonization and coordination attempts have taken place within the EC and among its member-states. That a full political union or European political federation (a "United States of Europe," perhaps) is still far off is not disputed; also not disputed is the fact that the EC and its member-states have made some efforts, with varying levels of success, to achieve some political cooperation, common positions on political issues, and (in some limited areas) achieved a common foreign policy. There *is* some evidence that national attachments and identities are breaking down, leading to a "European" mind-set that seeks "European" solutions to transnational challenges.

Space does not allow for a detailed discussion of all the goals and objectives identified above. Rather, Part III presents three illustrative cases: (1) the free movement of persons within the European Community (Chapter 6); (2) the inauguration and operation of the common agricultural policy (Chapter 7); and (3) European political cooperation and the hoped-for "ever closer union among the European peoples" (Chapter 8).

6

The Free Movement of Persons

Article 3(c) of the EEC Treaty established the general objective: "The abolition, as between Member-States, of the obstacles to the free movement of persons, services, and capital." This general objective was made a bit more specific in Title III of the treaty, particularly by Articles 48, 52, 57, 59, and 60. These articles deal with movement, establishment, mutual recognition of qualifications, and the right of actual practice.

Article 48 specifies this right of movement within the Community:

1. Freedom of movement for workers shall be secured within the Community by the end of the transitional period at the latest.
2. Such freedom of movement shall entail the abolition of any discrimination based on nationality between workers of the Member States as regards employment, remuneration and other conditions of work and employment.
3. It shall entail the right, subject to limitations justified on grounds of public policy, public security or public health;
   (a) to accept offers of employment actually made;
   (b) to move freely within the territory of Member States for this purpose;
   (c) to stay in a Member State for the purpose of employment in accordance with the provisions governing the employment of nationals of that State laid down by law, regulation or administrative action;
   (d) to remain in the territory of a Member State after having been employed in that State, subject to conditions which shall be embodied in implementing regulations to be drawn up by the Commission.
4. The provisions of this Article shall not apply to employment in the public service.

Article 52 guarantees the right of establishment:

restrictions on the freedom of establishment of nationals of a Member State in the territory of another Member State shall be abolished by progressive stages in the course of the transitional period. Such progressive abolition shall also apply to restrictions on the setting up of agencies, branches or subsidiaries by nationals of any Member State established in the territory of any Member State. Freedom of establishment shall include the right to take up and pursue activities as self-employed persons and to set up and manage undertakings, in particular companies or firms . . . under the conditions laid down for its own nationals by the law of the country where such establishment is effected.

Article 57 provides for the mutual recognition of the qualifications of self-employed persons (the liberal professions):

In order to make it easier for persons to take up and pursue activities as self-employed persons, the Council shall, on a proposal from the Commission and after consulting the Assembly, acting unanimously during the first stage and by a qualified majority thereafter, issue directives for the mutual recognition of diplomas, certificates and other evidence of formal qualifications. . . .

In the case of the medical and allied, and pharmaceutical professions, the progressive abolition of restrictions shall be dependent upon coordination of the conditions for their exercise in the various Member States.

Finally, Articles 59 and 60 guarantee the right of actual practice (freedom to provide services for remuneration):

Within the framework of the provisions set out below, restrictions on freedom to provide services within the Community shall be progressively abolished during the transitional period in respect of nationals of Member States who are established in a State of the Community other than that of the person for whom the services are intended. . . .

Services shall be considered "services" within the meaning of this Treaty where they are normally provided for remuneration, in so far as they are not governed by the provisions relating to freedom of movement for goods, capital and persons.

The transitional period referred to above was a 12-year period, divided into three 4-year stages (Article 8), set to expire on 1 January 1970. The Council of Ministers had the authority to extend the length of a particular stage, but this could be done only by a unanimous vote and only after the proposal was made by the Commission; in any case, the transitional period could not extend for more than 15 years (1 January 1973). The Council did not extend any stage, and the transitional period did, in fact, expire on 1 January 1970.

The major regulations on the free movement of persons within the Community became effective on 4 May 1964, with the following principal provisions:

(a) Equal right of access to employment was provided throughout the Community for all wage earners, especially for seasonal and frontier workers.

(b) A Member-State could, in certain circumstances, impose temporary restrictions on the ability of non-nationals to compete with nationals in the labor market.

(c) The period of assimilation of foreign workers in the country of employment was reduced from four to two years.

(d) Foreign workers had the right to vote in, and stand for election to, representative bodies in the firm in which they were working.

(e) The worker had the right to be accompanied by all dependent relatives and any other relative living in the worker's home.[1]

Some additional provisions were implemented from 1968 to 1970: the abolition of work permits, the circulation of job openings across the Community, and the right of the worker and the worker's family to remain in the host country after employment ceased.[2] The free movement of persons within the Community was thus achieved by the end of the transitional period, but the regulations applied only to wage earners (mostly manual laborers/unskilled workers).[3] Free movement might have been possible but, except for seasonal workers and frontier crossers, very few individuals took advantage of the opportunity: a factory worker in, say, Bordeaux, was (and still is) not likely to move the entire family in search of work in, say, Copenhagen (a city with a different life-style, language, and culture).

The free movement of persons only applied to wage earners—the regulations cited above did *not* apply to the liberal professions and/or those for whom licensing requirements existed. European status might have been available for the assembly-line worker, but such status was not available for physicians, dentists, attorneys, architects, pharmacists, veterinarians, investment brokers, and all the other liberal, social, and intellectual professions. It was only within the past decade—almost 20 years after the Rome Treaty—that one of the liberal professions received European status/free movement: physicians. The illustrative case presented below traces the development of the decision to grant physicians free movement, establishment, and practice across the European Community; the illustrative case also presents some empirical results of such movement.

THE FREE CIRCULATION OF PHYSICIANS WITHIN THE EUROPEAN COMMUNITY

The Development of a European Health Community

The idea, if not the reality, of a European health community far predates the Rome Treaty and the establishment of the European Community.[4] The original health community may not have been grounded in legal and institutionalized bureaucratic directives, but it existed nonetheless. The free circulation of tradesmen, artisans, and professionals was commonplace during the Middle Ages— the stonecutters for the great cathedrals and court musicians are but two examples—and there were no passport controls, border restrictions, residence requirements, or relicensing exams. Physicians, too, enjoyed free circulation, and one such physician, Paracelsus, was renowned throughout Europe for his art and science.

In France, for example, the ideals of the Revolution recognized explicitly the free circulation of individuals and goods. Article 2 of the Law of March 2 and 17, 1791, stated that "every person is free to engage in trade or practice any profession or art he chooses." These Revolutionary principles were later whittled away by more restrictive measures arising from nationalism but, a "community of ideas" still existed. Throughout the 1800s and 1900s "there were no restrictive measures preventing physicians from one country to travel and exchange opinions with their colleagues in neighboring countries, and it was a common and well-accepted practice—even as it was at the time of Paracelse [Paracelsus]—to observe some medical team and then return home with the knowledge gained."[5]

The formal status of physicians who happened to be in another country on a temporary basis (vacation, research, additional training or education) also pre-dates the European Community. A physician in such a situation who provided medical care during the temporary stay usually received special permission from the host country to do so, and, if the medical aid were rendered in an emergency situation, the special permission could be granted retroactively. Physicians in another country on a temporary basis usually enjoy most of the rights that a "legally" established physician has. In France, for example, such a physician has access to the health insurance system and can treat insured persons without any preliminary formalities: the health insurance system will view the visiting physician's fees and prescriptions in the same manner accorded to an established physician, and the normal reimbursement rates and policies would apply.

The Brussels Convention of 1910 is another example of the free circulation of physicians predating the Rome Treaty and the EC. Signed by Belgium and France, the 1910 Convention is an agreement that allows a physician in border areas to cross the frontier and treat patients on the other side if there is no host-country physician in the designated area. Each country, on an annual basis, establishes a list of frontier localities qualifying for these border crossings, and the Brussels Convention appears to have worked well for 77 years.

The idea of a European health community—at least a "community of ideas"—thus existed prior to the Rome Treaty. But the establishment of the European Community and the stated goal of the abolition of obstacles to the free movement of persons marked an important turning point: European physicians could now consider very seriously the possibility of true free circulation and establishing a practice in another EC country. Article 3(c) of the treaty promised to change the conditions that physicians had to satisfy before receiving authorization to practice as an "established" physician in any specific country; these conditions being (1) that one had to be a national of the country of practice, and (2) that the medical degree had to be earned in the country of practice.

Instruments of Community Action

Although Article 145 of the Rome Treaty gives to the Council of Ministers the essential decision-making authority within the EC structure and Article 155 gives to the Commission the authority to enforce Council decisions (it was the

Council that passed the 1975 Directives on free circulation), much of the real work in European health care policies, including the free-circulation decision, is performed by three advisory bodies: the Permanent Committee of Physicians of the EC, the Consultative Committee for Medical Education, and the Committee of Public Health Officials.

The Permanent Committee of Physicians of the EC was established in Amsterdam on 23–24 October 1959. It is a European-wide group composed of representatives from the recognized national medical associations in each EC country.[6] Some members of the Permanent Committee serve as the group's representatives to the European Secretariat of the Liberal, Intellectual, and Social Professions (SEPLIS) and participate in the activities of this group. SEPLIS, in its turn, contributes several of its members to the EC's Economic and Social Committee. The Permanent Committee is organized into several subcommittees and has dealt with a variety of issues that eventually played a role in the decision that gave free circulation/European status to physicians.

One such relevant document generated by the Permanent Committee was the Charter of Hospital Physicians, unanimously adopted at its 21–22 April 1967 meeting in Berlin. This charter identified certain guarantees that hospital physicians (hospital physicians, distinguished from those in private practice with hospital affiliations, constitute a large percentage of the physicians in several EC countries) had the right to expect from their status: guarantees on professional, economic, political, and social independence. This charter also defined the terms by which the various service heads were to be chosen, and it insisted that hospital physicians should have an effective role in the management and decision-making process within the hospital (one physician/one vote).

A second well-known document from the Permanent Committee is the Nuremberg Charter, unanimously adopted at its 24–25 November 1967 meeting in Nuremberg. Cognizant of immediate past history—the Nazis chose Nuremberg to promulgate their infamous Race Laws—the Permanent Committee also chose Nuremberg to reaffirm the basic principles of European medical ethics: freedom of the patient to choose an individual physician, respect for human life and the individual personality, and medical care that is provided in accordance with acceptable procedures. The Nuremberg Charter, moreover, included some economic and social considerations in the medical ethics statement: "economic expansion finds its major human justification in the improvement of the resources allocated to health care" and that the medical profession "should do its best to improve medicine's human and social effectiveness."

Other areas of concern of the Permanent Committee have included continuing medical education in the EC; the various social security systems, particularly the health insurance systems; industrial medicine; and, in cooperation with the European Union of General Practitioners (UEMO), specific educational requirements for a European GP. The Permanent Committee, through SEPLIS and the EC's Economic and Social Committee, is also involved in the constant process of representing the interests of the medical profession within the EC.

The Consultative Committee for Medical Education was created in 1975 by a Council of Ministers' decision.[7] The Consultative Committee is expected to identify and maintain the standards for all physicians (GPs and specialists) within the EC. This Committee forwards its opinions, recommendations, and suggestions concerning proposed amendments on medical education requirements to the EC Commission and to the government of each EC member. The Consultative Committee is composed in equal strength of representatives from the medical profession, the universities, and the national administrations.

The Committee of Public Health Officials was also established by the 1975 Council of Ministers' decision.[8] This committee has a threefold function:

1. To anticipate and analyze the possible difficulties that the implementation of directives in the health care area may face;
2. To gather and disseminate information on how general and specialized health care is delivered under different situations within the EC; and
3. To formulate proposals for submission to the Commission for the latter's use in the implementation and/or the amending of the health care directives.

This committee is composed of high-level administrative officials who have direct responsibilities in the area of public health within each of the EC countries.

The Free-Circulation Decision

The 1975 Council of Ministers Directives that established free circulation or "European" status for EC physicians derived from three articles of the EC Treaty cited above:

1. The right of free movement (Article 48);
2. The right of establishment, whereby the migrant can establish himself in the host country under the same conditions that apply to the host-country's nationals (Article 52); and
3. The right of actual practice, whereby the migrant is entitled to practice his profession under the same conditions that apply to the host-country's nationals (Article 59).

The two separate but related directives dealt with (1) the mutual recognition of diplomas, degrees, certificates, and other medical titles and contained measures aimed at facilitating the right to establish a practice; and (2) the regulatory and administrative oversight of the physician's activities.[9] In reference to the mutual recognition of diplomas, the directive states that "each Member-State recognizes diplomas, certificates, and other titles issued by, and held by citizens of, Member-States." The recognized equivalents are specified in the directive for both the GP level and for the specialist.[10]

These directives were the result of failure to achieve harmonization across the

Community about the content of medical education. Attempts were made to harmonize the medical school curriculum (subjects, hours, clinical experience, etc.), but one common standard could not be attained. Thus the EC opted for full faith and credit—the standards of each EC country would be recognized in the others, allowing for the free-circulation decision.

One of the first barriers that comes to mind when dealing with the free circulation of physicians—as opposed to stonecutters or musicians or soccer players—is language. Except for Ireland and the United Kingdom, France, and parts of Belgium and Luxembourg, none of the 12 EC countries have a language in common. In addition, except for English, French, and German, and, to a much lesser extent, Italian, the other EC languages do not appear to be very popular with non-nationals. But the 1975 Directive states that "the Member-States will see that the beneficiaries [of the free-circulation decision] acquire, in their own interest and in the interest of their patients, sufficient language ability that may be necessary to practice in the receiving country."[11] The text of the directive is vague, however, and the words "sufficient language ability that may be necessary to practice" are not seen as a formal legal obligation of a migrant physician. In fact, it is not even accepted that a migrant physician could be refused entry, and thus the right to practice, into another EC country solely on the grounds of not having "sufficient" language ability.

Such a denial could be considered as an illegal restriction on the rights of establishment and practice (guaranteed by Articles 52 and 60 of the Rome Treaty) or, perhaps, discrimination based on citizenship (prohibited by Article 20). As a last resort, the denial of entry on linguistic grounds could perhaps be seen as a violation under the European Convention of Human Rights (Article 14 of the ECHR prohibits discrimination based upon various grounds, including language and national origin). The assumed language barrier is not a legal barrier, but it may nonetheless restrict the migratory flow. As Rolf Wägenbaur comments, it is simply inconceivable that a physician—whose civil and criminal liabilities are tremendous—would treat patients without being able to understand their complaints and thus risk malpractice suits.[12]

Thus, prior to December 20, 1976 (the date when the free-circulation directives became operational), physicians within the EC had to satisfy two conditions before receiving authorization to practice in a specific country: (1) the physician had to be a national of the country of practice, and (2) the medical degree had to be earned in the country of practice. This situation was changed drastically by the granting of European status. Briefly stated, the directives gave the right of movement, establishment, and practice to physicians in any EC member-state, regardless of nationality and/or country of training. The migrant physician must of course register with the appropriate host-country licensing authorities before being able to practice, but this right of establishment does not require any additional licensing examinations, medical training, or language proficiency examinations.

Method of Analysis

The standard techniques of transaction flow analysis are employed to examine the characteristics of the migrant physician phenomenon within the EC. Transaction flow analysis is a descriptive process applied to observable and quantifiable exchanges or flows between/among various actors or units within a defined system (e.g., tourists, mail, labor, capital, trade, etc.). In this case study, the sending/receiving units are the individual EC countries and the exchanges/flows/transactions are the migrant physicians. Four separate but related processes are employed: (1) absolute raw transaction volumes;[13] (2) percentage and proportion transformations;[14] (3) relative acceptance–relative intensity measures;[15] and (4) a geographical concentration–fractionalization index.[16] These measures, applied to the approximately 10,250 physicians who have taken advantage of the free-circulation decision since 20 December 1976, are supplemented by the results of a limited number of personal interviews in Belgium and France with such migrant physicians.[17]

The Migratory Flow

Absolute Transaction Volumes

Table 6.1 presents the raw aggregate figures across the EC as a whole. These figures most likely do not reflect the current status of the migratory presence since (1) additional physicians have migrated since 1984, and (2) many of these physicians have probably returned to their country of origin. Several observations follow from Table 6.1.

The three least developed EC countries—Ireland, Greece, and Italy—show the largest absolute number of physicians leaving (2,067, 1,582, and 1,376, respectively; these account for 49.1 percent of the total flow of 10,250). It would appear at first glance that physicians also may not be immune from economic considerations, and such migration may be related to economic variables. The figure for Greece (1,582) is most significant for, compared to the other nine countries where the data span eight years, the time span for Greece is only four years. If this trend continues, Greece will, in a few short years, be the largest exporter of physicians in the European Community. Large exports of olive oil and fish undoubtedly aid the Greek economy; there is some question as to the benefits of exporting physicians. The three countries with the smallest outflow in absolute terms are Denmark (269), Luxembourg (287), and the Federal Republic of Germany (778).

The three countries that exhibit the largest inflow are the United Kingdom (4,254), West Germany (3,997), and—a distant third—France (608). The United Kingdom and West Germany alone import 80.5 percent of all the migrant physicians within the EC; with France, the percentage increases to 86.4. The three countries with the smallest absolute number of arrivals are Greece (34), Denmark

(67), and Luxembourg (80). As discussed above, language ability may not be a formal legal requirement for the migrant physician, but it is obvious from Table 6.1 that language does indeed play an important role in the migratory process. The three largest importers (countries of attraction) of migrant physicians are those whose language (English, German, French) is relatively widespread beyond national borders. Conversely, the two smallest importers have a language that is (figuratively) confined within the national frontier (Greek and Danish). Economic considerations may be important, but it seems equally obvious that few EC physicians migrate to Greece (in spite of the rather attractive climate of the Greek islands compared, say, to Hamburg or Manchester) or Denmark because few people outside these two countries speak Greek or Danish. Language ability may not be the controlling variable, but its importance cannot be overlooked.

On a more specific level of analysis, Table 6.1 shows that there are several relatively large unilateral directional flows. The five largest one-way flows are: Ireland → UK (2,015); Greece → West Germany (1,054); Netherlands → West Germany (671); Italy → UK (591), and Italy → West Germany (587). These five one-way flows, out of a total of 90 possible directions, account for 48 percent of the total EC flow. Conversely, there are several nonexistent one-way directional flows. For the entire time span of this study, 13 one-way directional flows show 0: Denmark → Greece, Luxembourg, Netherlands; France → Ireland; Greece → Netherlands; Ireland → Luxembourg, Greece; Luxembourg → Denmark, Ireland, Greece, Italy; Netherlands → Greece; and UK → Greece.

The last observation to be made from Table 6.1 is that there are many bilateral transactions that are extremely low or even nonexistent. The following figures represent the two-way flow between specific pairs of countries (those physicians from A entering B and those from B entering A): Denmark ↔ France (4 ↔ 5); Ireland ↔ Italy (2 ↔ 7); Greece ↔ Ireland (7 ↔ 0); Belgium ↔ Denmark (4↔ 2); Italy ↔ Luxembourg (6 ↔ 0); Luxembourg ↔ Netherlands (4 ↔ 2); France ↔ Ireland (0 ↔ 5); Ireland ↔ Belgium (2 ↔ 2); Ireland ↔ Denmark (2 ↔ 2); Denmark ↔ Netherlands (0 ↔ 4); Greece ↔ Denmark (2 ↔ 0); Greece ↔ Luxembourg (1 ↔ 0); and the three bilateral flows that show 0: Denmark ↔ Luxembourg; Greece ↔ Netherlands; and Ireland ↔ Luxembourg (all 0 ↔ 0).

Percentage Transformations

Table 6.2 presents the migratory flow standardized along certain variables. This transformed data permit cross-national comparisons of the transactions while controlling for the "size" of the actors within the EC system. Several observations follow from Table 6.2.

As mentioned above in relation to Table 6.1, the three least developed countries within the EC—Ireland, Greece, and Italy—contribute a combined total of 49.1 percent of the total 10,250 migrant physicians (20.3 percent, 15.4 percent, and 13.4 percent, respectively [Column B]). Thus a full one-half of all migrant physicians originate in just three countries. Also, again as mentioned above,

Table 6.1
Physician Migration in the EC: Absolute Volumes, 1976–1984[a]

To (country of arrival)

		From (country of origin)									
Country	Total Arrivals	Belgium	Denmark	France	Greece[b]	Ireland	Italy[c]	Luxembourg[d]	Netherlands	United Kingdom	West Germany
Belgium	241	–	2	70	9	2	31	4	72	17	34
Denmark	67	4	–	5	2	2	9	0	4	20	21
France	608	233	4	–	60	5	106	25	23	42	110
Greece[b]	34	3	0	4	–	0	23	0	0	0	4
Ireland	325	2	2	0	7	–	7	0	12	256e	39
Italy[c]	120	8	5	27	4	2	–	0	6	12	56
Luxembourg[d]	80	18	0	39	1	0	6	–	2	2	12
Netherlands	524	277	0	11	0	11	16	4	–	150	55
United Kingdom	4,254	207	86	170	445	2,015f	591	8	285	–	447
West Germany	3,997	389	170	524	1,054	30	587	246	671	326	–
Totals	10,250	1,141	269	850	1,582	2,067	1,376	287	1,075	825	778

a. The raw data on the number/nationality of the migrant physicians reflect the number of each country's nationals who migrated under the two 1975 Directives of the EC Council of Ministers (75-362 and 75-363 of 16 June 1975, effective 20 December 1976) and who received authorization to practice in the listed host country. There is a possibility of some double counting—the data reflects the total of actual moves and does not track specific individuals—but it is assumed that the number of such double moves is relatively small. Also, the reported numbers reflect those physicians who received authorization to practice in the host country—the figures do not represent the actual number of physicians still in the host country, for many of the migrants (could) have returned to the country of origin after a temporary stay. Such moves are not included in the migrant data. Except for Greece and Italy (noted below), the time span is from 20 December 1976 to 30 September 1984. Except for Luxembourg (noted below), the data does not include nationals of one country who qualified in another but then returned to practice in the home country—these are seen to be migrant students rather than migrant physicians. Likewise, the data does not include nationals of one country who qualified in another and remained to practice in the qualifying country—these too are seen as migrant students. The data in Table 6.1 include only those physicians who qualified in the country of nationality and then migrated to another country and those who qualified in a country other than the one of nationality but then migrated to a third country.

b. The reported figures for Greece—both the number of Greek physicians migrating out (1582) and the number of non-Greek physicians migrating in (34)—are for the time span 1 January 1981 to 30 September 1984.

c. The law transposing the free circulation Directives into Italian national legislation was not adopted until 22 May 1978. Thus the reported figure of non-Italian physicians entering Italy (120) covers the time span 22 May 1978 to 30 September 1984. The number of Italian physicians leaving Italy (1376) is for the entire time span.

d. Luxembourg is the exception to the note above concerning migrant students. All prospective Luxembourg physicians have to obtain their medical training outside Luxembourg and thus, in a sense, they are all migrant students. For our purposes, nationals of Luxembourg who remain to practice in the qualifying country or receive authorization to practice in a third country are not seen as migrant students but as migrant physicians; as such, these are reported in Table 6.1. Luxembourg nationals who return to Luxembourg are not included.

e. The reported number of British physicians migrating to Ireland (256) may include some physicians who are not of British nationality. Entry to Ireland from the UK is based upon being registered in the UK and no account is taken of nationality.

f. The reported number of Irish physicians migrating to the UK (2015) may include some physicians who are not of Irish nationality. Entry to the UK from Ireland is based upon being registered in Ireland and no account is taken of nationality.

Source: Document Nos. III/D/17/78, III/D/22/3/79, III/D/65/3/80, III/D/155/3/81, III/D/286/4/82, and unnumbered: "Migrant Physicians," EC Commission, Direction du Droit et d'Etablissement (Brussels: March 15, 1984), 6 pp., mimeo; personal correspondence from A. Tellier, Directeur Administratif, Fédération Belge des Chambres Syndicales de Médecins (Braine-L'Alleud), 22 January 1985; personal correspondence from Dr. J. Autin, Secretary-General, Ordre National des Médecins (Paris), 26 August 1985; and personal correspondence from Dr. J. Farber, Conseil National de l'Ordre des Médecins (Brussels), 17 July 1985.

Table 6.2
Physician Migration in the EC: Percentage Transformations

	Departing Physicians				Entering Physicians		
	A	B	C	D	E	F	G
	N	Percent of total	Departing MDs as Percent of all Country MDsa (Yearly Mean)	Country Share of all EC MDsa (Yearly Mean)	N	Percent of Total	Difference
Belgium	1141	11.1	0.64	3.7	241	2.4	-900
Denmark	269	2.6	0.30	1.9	67	0.6	-202
France	850	8.3	0.10	17.7	608	5.9	-242
Greece	1582	15.4	1.56	4.2	34	0.3	-1548
Ireland	2067	20.2	5.97	0.7	325	3.2	-1742
Italy	1376	13.4	0.10	28.8	120	1.2	-1256
Luxembourg	287	2.8	6.83	0.1	80	0.8	-207
Netherlands	1075	10.5	0.51	4.4	524	5.1	-551
United Kingdom	825	8.0	0.11	15.6	4254	41.5	+3429
West Germany	778	7.6	0.07	22.9	3997	39.0	+3219
Total	10250	100	0.21	100	10250	100	

a. The statistics reported are not homogeneous. For several reasons, the figures contained in Column C (Departing MDs as percent of all Country MDs [Yearly Mean]) and Column D (Country Share all EC MDs [Yearly Mean]) are only approximate and should be used only to indicate general characteristics. In most cases, the number of physicians reported represents the number actually practicing. For Italy, the Netherlands, and Luxembourg, however, the number relates to all persons entitled to practice; whether these are all in fact practicing is not known. The number of physicians reported includes all hospital physicians except for Ireland (hospital physicians are not included) and perhaps for the Netherlands (the Dutch figures do not specify whether hospital physicians are included or excluded). The number of physicians reported includes all physicians in industry, research, and administration except for Belgium and Ireland (such physicians are excluded). Military physicians are included in the Netherlands; they are excluded in the United Kingdom; the other eight countries' figures do not specify whether military physicians are included or excluded. Other medical professions are not included for any country except Italy where dentists are included. Italy does not recognize an independent dental profession. Dentistry is practiced by physicians, all of whom are registered in the Italian Medical Register, but who may or may not have followed a specialist course in dental surgery. General practitioners may also practice dentistry in Italy since it is regarded as a branch of medicine and consequently falls within the competence of a physician.

Source: Calculated from figures contained in Table 6.1, "Physician Migration in the EC: Absolute Volumes, 1976-1984"; and Number of Physicians in the Member-States of the Community, Statistical Office of the European Communities; Directorate: Demographic and Social Statistics--Agricultural Statistics; Division E-1: Employment and Labour Force Surveys; Eurostat/E1/104/84/EN/FINAL (Brussels: July, 1984), 40 pp., mimeo.

there are some obvious target countries or "importers" of this particular commodity: 86.4 percent of all migrants enter either the United Kingdom (41.5 percent), Germany (39.0 percent), or France (5.9 percent [Column F]). Deleting France, one sees that the UK and West Germany import 80.5 percent of all migrants.

Column G of Table 6.2 shows the net difference ($+/-$) of this migratory flow over the entire time span since the directives became operational in December 1976. This net flow (or balance of trade) is not approached here in terms of international trade in the sense that a favorable balance is seen as an advantage; rather, it is approached in terms that say a net outflow (exports exceed imports) represents a "loss" for the exporting country. This perception is due to the nature of the particular commodity being traded: members of a highly educated group of people who provide both necessary and highly desirable services to society (physicians *are* different than soccer players or rock musicians). This perception of the migratory flow is similar to the "brain drain" from the Third World to the developed countries. The "brain drain" scenario has not yet arrived, however, within the EC although the underlying concept is analogous. Although some of the net outflow figures appear large, it is premature to write that the migratory flow represents a danger to the continued availability of professional health care in any of the EC countries. None of the EC countries are in danger of being denuded of physicians. In fact, even those countries who show a large net outflow (e.g., Italy) have a surplus of physicians. Also, as discussed below, the actual number of migrants represents a very small percentage of national physicians, and many of these migrants probably return home after a temporary stay in the host country.

Notwithstanding the comments above, eight of the ten reviewed EC countries show a negative net flow. Again, the three least developed countries exhibit the largest trade imbalance: Ireland ($-1,742$), Greece ($-1,548$), and Italy ($-1,256$). Here are 4,546 physicians who, after receiving training in their country of origin (costs), left and provided service (benefits) in another country. Conversely, the United Kingdom and West Germany are receiving the benefits. These two are the major importers ($+3,429$ and $+3,219$, respectively), and, after having the taxpayers of other EC countries produce the commodity, the United Kingdom and Germany are receiving the immediate cost-free services. If these trends accelerate over the coming years, the United Kingdom and West Germany may wish to reassess the amount of internal financial support accorded medical education: it is far cheaper to let the other EC countries pay for the training of physicians who will practice in the United Kingdom and Germany.

Continuing with Table 6.2, Column C presents each country's departing physicians as a percentage of all national physicians (on an annual basis). The EC mean is 0.21 percent—even though over 10,000 individual physicians may have taken advantage of the free-circulation decision since December 1976, these 10,250 represent only 0.21 percent (annualized) of all EC physicians. After eight years, this figure should put to rest the fears (particularly of the French) of a *marée blanche* of physicians inundating certain countries.[18] Although there has yet to be any *marée blanche*, six countries of the EC (Belgium, Denmark, Greece, Ireland, Luxembourg, the Netherlands) show an annual mean rate of outflow that exceeds the EC norm. The three highest are Luxembourg (6.83 percent), Ireland (5.97 percent), and Greece (1.56 percent). These figures must, however, be qualified by two observations: (1) many of these migrants are only temporary and eventually return to their country of origin; and (2) this rate of "loss" is decreased by the inflow of non-national physicians. Column C also shows that four countries (West Germany, France, Italy, the United Kingdom) have an outflow rate lower than the EC mean of 0.21 percent (0.07, 0.10, 0.10, and 0.11 percent, respectively). Italy may have a large number of physicians leaving, and thus contributes a large percentage to the total EC migrant pool, but Italian physicians are less likely to migrate than any other national grouping except for West German and French physicians.

Column D of Table 6.2 presents each country's share of all EC physicians, and this column should be compared to Column B—each country's share of all the migrants. The indifference model says that each country would contribute a share of the total EC flow equal to its share of all the EC physicians; this is obviously not the case. Comparing Columns B and D, Table 6.2 shows that physicians in six countries (Belgium, Denmark, Greece, Ireland, Luxembourg, the Netherlands) have a greater tendency to migrate than those physicians in France, West Germany, Italy, and the United Kingdom (these last four show a less than expected rate than the indifference model would suggest). As above, Italy may show a high level of departing physicians and be a net exporter, but this is due to the large absolute number of Italian physicians: only a West German physician is less likely to move than an Italian physician.

Tables 6.3 and 6.4 present the breakdown (in percentages) of the specific destinations of each country's departing physicians (Table 6.3) and the specific country of origin of each country's arriving migrant physicians (Table 6.4). Several observations follow from these tables.

Table 6.3 shows that the departing physicians from all ten EC countries have a definite target/preference country or, conversely, there exists a country of attraction for specific national groupings of physicians. Some are much higher than others, of course, but even the lowest is much higher than the null or indifference model would suggest. There must be some underlying factors that explain the choice of countries for these migrants (economic conditions and language ability have been mentioned above) because the departing physicians simply do not disperse themselves across the Community according to the indifference model. Seven of the ten EC countries show a majority of departing physicians being attracted to one specific country, and the remaining three show a high plurality: 34.2 percent of all Belgian migrant physicians went to West Germany; 63.3 percent of Danes → West Germany; 57.5 percent of West Germans → UK; 61.6 percent of French → West Germany; 66.7 percent of Greeks → West Germany; 97.6 percent of Irish → UK; 42.9 percent of Italians → UK

Table 6.3
Distribution of Departing Physicians (in percentages)

Country of Arrival	Country of Origin									
	Belgium	Denmark	France	Greece	Ireland	Italy	Luxembourg	Netherlands	United Kingdom	West Germany
Belgium	-	0.7	8.2	0.6	0.1	2.2	1.4	6.7	2.1	4.4
Denmark	0.3	-	0.6	0.1	0.1	0.7	0	0.3	2.4	2.7
France	20.4	1.5	-	3.8	0.2	7.7	8.7	2.1	5.1	14.1
Greece	0.2	0	0.5	-	0	1.7	0	0	0	0.5
Ireland	0.1	0.7	0	0.4	-	0.5	0	1.1	31.0	5.0
Italy	0.7	1.8	3.2	0.2	0.1	-	0	0.5	1.4	7.2
Luxembourg	1.6	0	4.6	0.1	0	0.4	-	0.2	0.2	1.5
Netherlands	24.4	0	1.3	0	0.5	1.2	1.4	-	18.2	7.1
United Kingdom	18.1	32.0	20.0	28.1	97.6	42.9	2.8	26.6	-	57.5
West Germany	34.2	63.3	61.6	66.7	1.4	42.7	85.7	62.5	39.6	-
Total	100	100	100	100	100	100	100	100	100	100
N	(1141)	(269)	(850)	(1582)	(2067)	(1376)	(287)	(1075)	(825)	(778)

Table 6.4
Distribution of Arriving Physicians (in percentages)

Country of Origin	Country of Arrival									
	Belgium	Denmark	France	Greece	Ireland	Italy	Luxembourg	Netherlands	United Kingdom	West Germany
Belgium	-	6.0	38.4	8.8	0.6	6.7	22.5	52.8	4.9	9.7
Denmark	0.8	-	0.6	0	0.6	4.2	0	0	2.0	4.3
France	29.1	7.5	-	11.8	0	22.5	48.8	2.1	4.0	13.1
Greece	3.7	3.0	9.9	-	2.1	3.3	1.2	0	10.5	26.4
Ireland	0.8	3.0	0.8	0	-	1.7	0	2.1	47.3	0.7
Italy	12.9	13.3	17.4	67.6	2.1	-	7.5	3.1	13.9	14.7
Luxembourg	1.6	0	4.1	0	0	0	-	0.8	0.2	6.1
Netherlands	29.9	6.0	3.8	0	3.7	5.0	2.5	-	6.7	16.8
United Kingdom	7.1	30.0	6.9	0	78.9	10.0	2.5	28.6	-	8.2
West Germany	14.1	31.2	18.1	11.8	12.0	46.6	15.0	10.5	10.5	-
Total	100	100	100	100	100	100	100	100	100	100
N	(241)	(67)	(608)	(34)	(325)	(120)	(80)	(524)	(4254)	(3997)

and 42.7 percent → West Germany; 85.7 percent of Luxembourgers → West Germany; 62.5 percent of Dutch → West Germany; and 39.6 percent of the British migrants went to West Germany. The Federal Republic of Germany is the obvious country of preference, and this would seem to suggest that economic variables are more important than language ability (the economic attraction of West Germany may be constant for the other EC countries, but one cannot assume that the German language is randomly distributed throughout the EC).

Table 6.4 presents the breakdown (in percentages) of the countries of origin of each other country's arriving migrant physicians. As above, a very high percentage of each EC country's arrivals come from one other specific country. Approached from the viewpoint of the receiving/host country, the new arrivals do not represent a random distribution of other EC nationalities: an Irish patient, if seeing a non-Irish physician, has a 78.9 percent probability of being treated by a British physician and a probability of 0 of being treated by a French or Luxembourger physician; or a Greek patient, if seeing a non-Greek physician, has a 67.6 percent probability of being treated by an Italian physician and a probability of 0 of being treated by a Danish, Irish, Luxembourger, Dutch, or British physician. The specific breakdowns are as follows: 29.9 percent of the migrants entering Belgium came from the Netherlands; 31.2 percent into Denmark ← West Germany; 26.4 percent into West Germany ← Greece; 38.4 percent into France ← Belgium; 67.6 percent into Greece ← Italy; 78.9 percent into Ireland ← UK; 46.6 percent into Italy ← West Germany; 48.8 percent into Luxembourg ← France; 52.8 percent into the Netherlands ← Belgium; and 47.3 percent of the migrant physicians entering the United Kingdom came from Ireland.

Relative Intensities

Table 6.5 uses the Relative Intensity (RI) values to note the nature of each bilateral relationship. As discussed above, the RI is based on the null or indifference model, and its value ranges from −1.00 (no transactions) through 0 (actual amount equals expected amount) to infinity (actual amounts are far larger than what would be expected from the indifference model). Table 6.5 presents these RIs in terms of "Partnership," "Dependence," and "Isolation."

"Partnership" is assumed when each directional flow in a bilateral relationship ($A \rightarrow B$ and $B \rightarrow A$) has a positive RI value—each of the two transaction flows are larger than would be expected. The reported RI values represent the mean RI for the two-way flow. There are 13 two-way flows that are characterized as "Partnership"—several are quite intense (Ireland ↔ UK at a mean RI of +5.10, Belgium ↔ Netherlands at +2.81, France ↔ Luxembourg at +2.67, West Germany ↔ Italy at +2.62, and Belgium ↔ France at +2.49). Other relations, although still at the (+) level, are much less intense and are much closer to 0 (the flows are just about what would be expected from the indifference model): West Germany ↔ UK at +0.20 and UK ↔ Italy at +0.15.

"Dependence" is assumed when one directional flow ($A \rightarrow B$) in a bilateral

Table 6.5
Partnership–Dependence–Isolation

Partnership (+ ↔ +)		
Ireland	United Kingdom	+5.10
Belgium	Netherlands	+2.81
France	Luxembourg	+2.67
Germany	Italy	+2.62
Belgium	France	+2.49
Germany	Denmark	+1.88
France	Italy	+1.51
Luxembourg	Germany	+1.08
Greece	France	+0.98
Germany	Greece	+0.63
Germany	Netherlands	+0.49
Germany	United Kingdom	+0.20
United Kingdom	Italy	+0.15

Less than Expected (- ↔ -)		
Belgium	Italy	-0.22
France	United Kingdom	-0.33
Belgium	United Kingdom	-0.34
Greece	Belgium	-0.49
Belgium	Denmark	-0.58
Italy	Netherlands	-0.65
United Kingdom	Greece	-0.66
France	Netherlands	-0.70
Luxembourg	Italy	-0.72
Denmark	Netherlands	-0.72
Netherlands	Luxembourg	-0.74
Ireland	Netherlands	-0.78
Luxembourg	United Kingdom	-0.81
Ireland	Denmark	-0.81
France	Denmark	-0.87
Ireland	Italy	-0.88
Greece	Denmark	-0.90
Greece	Ireland	-0.93
Ireland	Belgium	-0.96
Greece	Luxembourg	-0.96
Ireland	France	-0.98

Dependence (+ ↔ -)		
Italy	Greece	4.85
United Kingdom	Denmark	2.98
United Kingdom	Netherlands	2.93
Germany	Ireland	1.54
Belgium	Luxembourg	1.46
Germany	Belgium	0.98
France	Greece	0.78
Denmark	Italy	0.62

Isolation (-1.00 ↔ -1.00)		
Denmark	Luxembourg	-1.00
Ireland	Luxembourg	-1.00
Netherlands	Greece	-1.00

relationship has a positive (+) RI value and the second flow ($B \rightarrow A$) has a negative (−) value. "Dependence" here relates to country B of each specific pair. The reported values in Table 6.5 for "Dependence" represent the absolute distance between the positive ($A \rightarrow B$) and negative ($B \rightarrow A$) RI values. There are eight such relationships; three of them with rather high scores, denoting a higher level of dependence: Italy ↔ Greece at 4.85, UK ↔ Denmark at 2.98, and UK ↔ Netherlands at 2.93.

"Isolation" is assumed when each directional flow, $A \rightarrow B$ and $B \rightarrow A$, shows an RI value of −1.00. Here there are no transactions at all between the pairs, and the absence of preference in each for the other is obvious. There are only three relationships seen as "isolated": Netherlands ↔ Greece, Ireland ↔ Luxembourg, and Denmark ↔ Luxembourg.

The last quadrant of Table 6.5 contains 21 bilateral relationships, where each of the flows, $A \rightarrow B$ and $B \rightarrow A$, show negative (−) RI values or less than expected amounts. At one extreme the mean RIs are closer to 0, suggesting that these country pairs approach what the indifference model would predict: Greece ↔ Belgium at −0.49, Belgium ↔ UK at −0.34, France ↔ UK at −0.33, and Belgium ↔ Italy at −0.22. At the other extreme, there are five pairs that approach −1.00. These are not totally isolated in the sense that there aren't any transactions, but the amount/intensity of the observed flows is so low that they could justifiably be characterized as isolated pairs: Greece ↔ Denmark at −0.90, Greece ↔ Ireland at −0.93, Ireland ↔ Belgium at −0.96, Greece ↔ Luxembourg at −0.96, and Ireland ↔ France at −0.98.

Concentration-Fractionalization

Table 6.6 notes the degree to which (1) each country's departing physicians concentrate themselves in one or two countries or, conversely, the extent to which they are dispersed (fractionalized) throughout the EC; and (2) the degree to which the physicians entering each specific country originate from only one or two others (concentration) or, conversely, the extent to which entering physicians originate from several countries (fractionalization). The index for this particular study ranges from +1.00 (complete concentration) to +0.11 (complete fractionalization/dispersal).

From the discussions of Tables 6.1 through 6.5, it should not be surprising that Ireland is very close to complete concentration relating to the choice of host country for departing Irish physicians (its value on the index is +.976). The overwhelming choice for Irish physicians is the United Kingdom (language is most definitely a relevant variable here), and, conversely, Irish physicians are not dispersed throughout the EC system. The most fractionalized for departing physicians is Belgium although its score (+.501) still places it on the side of concentration on the concentration-fractionalization continuum. The EC mean is at +.686, suggesting that the choice of departing physicians is not made at random, but there are certain reasons why each national group shows such a high preference for one or two destinations.

Table 6.6
Geographical Concentration–Fractionalization

Sending			Receiving	
Country	Score		Country	Score
Ireland	.976		Ireland	.799
Luxembourg	.862		Greece	.701
Greece	.724		Netherlands	.611
Denmark	.709		Luxembourg	.564
Netherlands	.683		Italy	.536
France	.655		United Kingdom	.523
Italy	.611		France	.477
West Germany	.605		Denmark	.468
United Kingdom	.538		Belgium	.466
Belgium	.501		West Germany	.398
EC	.686		EC	.554

The degree of concentration is a bit less in relationship to the country of origin of each country's entering physicians although it cannot be characterized as a fractionalized system. Ireland again shows the highest level of concentration (at +.799) because most of its entering migrant physicians turn up in one country (the UK). West Germany is the most fractionalized at +.398, adding support to the view that West Germany is by far the country of preference within the EC system.

Interview Data

The aggregate data presented above were supplemented by a very limited number of personal interviews with migrant physicians who were, or who had very recently been, in France. The few physicians involved cannot be regarded as a representative sample of any targeted population, and the following remarks relate only to these few physicians.

A composite picture of this migrant physician shows the following characteristics:

1. Relatively young (31–34), just at the beginning of his/her professional career;
2. Relatively low paid compared to the mean income of established French physicians;
3. Migrant status is only temporary—there exists the intention (but not necessarily the desire) to return to the home country;
4. Equally likely to be male or female, a GP or specialist, and in private practice or on a hospital staff;
5. Excellent language ability—fluent in at least two languages and a good working knowledge of at least a third;
6. Supports the idea of "Europe" as an admirable goal, especially to counter the perceived political dominance of the US and the USSR and the economic dominance of Japan and the US;
7. Believes that Europe's cultural heterogeneity and diversity (its "regionalism") is simply too great to superimpose a veneer of "oneness" over the area—a loose federal system that would increase political and economic cooperation, but leave cultural patterns untouched is the only viable option; and
8. The status of migrant physician is not the result of a "European" mind-set or the result of a conscious decision, as a member of a socioeconomic elite group, to build European cooperation and integration through medicine. Rather, the decision to (temporarily) be in France is based on personal and/or professional grounds—reasons that are not linked to the European idea. The free-circulation decision is interpreted solely in personal terms and not in reference to international community building.

It may be instructive at this point to present specific comments by some of these migrant physicians. These comments must not be employed to make any generalizations but, simply, to look behind the inanimate aggregate data for some individual perceptions.

A 31-year-old male Italian pediatric heart surgeon on the staff of a French hospital well known for its leadership in pediatric cardiac care and surgery:

I came to France six months ago for professional reasons and to further my surgical techniques. The department head here is well known and respected across Europe and I wanted to learn from him. I plan to return to Italy in 18 months but I'm really not that happy with the prospect. There are simply too many MDs in Italy and, assuming one can find a suitable position, the number of MDs in a hospital department is so large that each individual surgeon has a limited number of turns in the operating room. I am not overworked here but at least the rotation is satisfactory. I am not earning very much ($600–$800/month) but it is more than I would be getting in Italy ($500–$600/month). My career prospects are much better in France than in Italy but I will probably return— I see myself as a stranger here. But I would take out French citizenship and remain if I were to meet a nice French girl. But that is a different question.[19]

A 32-year-old male West German GP in private practice:

I don't have enough money to open my own private practice. I earn my keep by replacing established French MDs at night, weekends, and when they go on vacation. I am not in France for the income nor for professional reasons. Economic conditions for MDs are far better in Germany than in France. But, you see, I have this relationship with a French woman. She has a good job here, she doesn't speak German, and she doesn't want to move to Germany. I would like to return but there are various complications.[20]

A 34-year-old female West German GP authorized to practice in France, but at the time not practicing:

It is a misrepresentation of reality for anyone to say that we Germans come to France for professional opportunities or for a better standard of living. The culture is fine but the money is a joke. Germany is much better . . . but my husband is currently working for a French-based German industrial concern and thus I came to France with him. We will eventually return to Germany.[21]

A 33-year-old male Belgian, OB-GYN:

I did some post-graduate training in France. I thought the techniques in France were better than those taught in Belgium. The head of the department asked me to stay on and so I did—two years in the hospital with a small private practice on the side. The two years were sufficient [this conversation took place three days after he left France] and now [the following day] I'm leaving for Chad under a contract with WHO.[22]

Summary of the Migratory Flow

As mentioned previously, the methodology of transaction flow analysis is a useful tool for certain low-level descriptive studies—it can perhaps identify the level or nature of integration along a single dimension, but it cannot contribute to an explanatory or predictive analysis. Other methodologies and approaches are required for these objectives. Working within this general limitation, a summary of the data show the following findings:

1. The three least developed EC countries—Ireland, Greece, and Italy—show the largest absolute number of physician outflow (5,025 or 49.1 percent of the total 10,250). The three countries with the smallest absolute outflow are Denmark, Luxembourg, and West Germany.

2. The United Kingdom and West Germany receive the most migrants, with France a distant third; these three receive a total of 86.4 percent of all migrant physicians. The fewest number of migrants go to Greece, Denmark, and Luxembourg.

3. There are several relatively large one-way flows (Ireland → UK is the largest, with 2,015) as well as 13 nonexistent one-way flows). Three pairs of countries (Denmark ↔ Luxembourg, Netherlands ↔ Greece, and Ireland ↔ Luxembourg) show absolutely no transactions in either direction for the entire time span reviewed.

4. All EC countries except the United Kingdom and West Germany show a net loss of physicians; the United Kingdom gained 3,429 and West Germany gained 3,219.

5. Although increasing in absolute terms each year, the number of migrating physicians is still relatively small as a percentage of all physicians: only a annual mean of 0.21 percent physicians decide to migrate within the EC as a whole. Six countries are above this mean, with Luxembourg (6.83 percent) and Ireland (5.97 percent) the highest; West Germany, France, Italy, and the United Kingdom are below the EC mean.

6. Departing physicians do not disperse themselves across the EC—certain countries appear to attract certain national groups. Arriving physicians in most EC countries do not represent a cross section of other national groups—the entants are likely to be from a limited number of countries. West Germany's arrival group is fractionalized: West Germany attracts physicians from all nine other EC countries.

7. The 45 separate bilateral relationships can be characterized as "Partnership" (higher than expected flows in each direction) or as "Dependence" (higher than expected flows in one direction and less than expected in the other) or as "Isolation" (no flows in either direction).

8. The status of migrant physician appears not to be the result of a "European" mind-set or the result of a conscious decision, as a member of an elite group, to build European cooperation and integration through medicine. Rather, the decision to migrate is based on personal and/or professional and/or economic grounds—reasons that are not linked to the European idea. The free-circulation decision is interpreted solely in personal terms and not in reference to international community building.

THE LIBERAL PROFESSIONS AND EUROPEAN INTEGRATION

The study of migrant physicians may eventually be only a small segment in an overall examination of the liberal professions in Europe for it is likely that the EC will grant free-circulation/European status to most other liberal professions. As of now, other than physicians, nurses responsible for general care and dental practitioners also enjoy free circulation. But in December 1984 a meeting was held in Brussels, organized by the European Secretariat of the Liberal, Intellectual, and Social Professions (SEPLIS), to discuss a report from OECD dealing with the liberal professions and competition policy.[23] Although not directly concerned with the granting of free circulation—the report concerned competitive practices within the liberal professions—it was this author's perception that the eventual granting of free circulation to most liberal professions provided the underlying basis of both the report and discussions during the meeting. Such decisions may not be imminent, but the free circulation of the European liberal professions, and their resultant European status, will strengthen the "community of ideas" that existed since the Middle Ages.

NOTES

1. Keesing's Research Report, *The European Communities: Establishment and Growth* (New York: Scribner's, 1975), pp. 55–56.

2. Ibid., p. 56.

3. For a discussion of the free movement of workers within the European Community, see: W. R. Bohning, *The Migration of Workers in the United Kingdom and the European Community* (New York: Oxford University Press, 1972); and L. H. Klaassen and Willem Molle, *Industrial Mobility and Migration in the European Community* (Aldershot, Hants, UK: Gower, 1983).

4. This section is based on Roger Vaissière and Jean-Marc Mascaro, "Health Policies in the European Community: Attempts at Harmonization," chapter 8 of Leon Hurwitz, ed., *Contemporary Perspectives on European Integration* (Westport, Conn.: Greenwood Press, 1980), pp. 171–188.

5. Ibid., p. 171.

6. The recognized national groups/associations are as follows: West Germany—Bundesärztekammer; Belgium—at first the Fédération Médicale Belge and then the Fédération Belge des Chambres Syndicales des Médecins; France—Confederation des Syndicats Médicaux Français until 1961 and, since that date, joined by the Ordre National des Médecins; Italy—Federazione Nazionale degli Ordini dei Medici d'Italia; Luxembourg—first by the Syndicat des Médecins du Grand Duché de Luxembourg and then by the Association des Médecins et des Médecins-Dentistes du Grand Duché de Luxembourg; Netherlands—Koninklijke Nederlandsche Maatschappij tot Bevordering der Geneeskunst; Denmark—Den Almindelige Danske Laegeforening; Ireland—Irish Medical Association; United Kingdom—British Medical Association.

7. EC Directive 167 of 16 June 1975. *Official Journal of the European Communities* (30 June 1975), p. 17.

8. Ibid., p. 19.

9. EC Directives 75–362 and 75–363 (16 June 1975). Ibid.

10. The recognized equivalents are as follows: Belgium—the M.D. degree (in medicine, surgery, and obstetrics); Denmark—the M.D. as well as the certificate of the training stage obtained from the Health Service; France—the M.D. from a medical school or from schools combining medicine and pharmacy; West Germany—the state certificate of M.D. (signaling the end of the preparatory period); Ireland and the United Kingdom—a certificate sanctioning the individual's knowledge and clinical experience (awarded upon passing a series of exams); Italy—the M.D. issued following the state examination by the Education Ministry and a certificate issued by the Health Ministry; the Netherlands—a university M.D. The equivalents for specialists are also listed, and they all entail, in one form or another, a certificate issued by the relevant national authorities, attesting to the individual's knowledge and experience in the specific field.

11. Article 20, Paragraph 3, Directive 75–362 (16 June 1975).

12. Cited by Vaissière and Mascaro, p. 180.

13. Absolute transaction volumes present the raw, unconverted quantities—the absolute size of the observed transactions among/between the units without any standardization or any control for size. In our example, the absolute volumes report the total number of migrating physicians, the country of origin, and the destination/arrival country. Data presented in this manner give a reasonable overview of the totality of the transactions but, since the figures are not standardized and since the units (the EC countries) within the system are of different size, these absolute volumes have a limited utility. The absolute amounts do, however, provide the necessary input in the calculation of the remaining measures.

14. Percentage/proportion measures standardize for the "size" of the transacting units

and thus allow for more meaningful comparisons. Size does not necessarily mean the total population of the units; size can refer to the number of physicians within each country—those theoretically available for migration—and/or to the total number of migrant physicians across the EC as a whole. For example, for the time span of this illustrative case, France contributed some 850 migrant physicians to the total flow and Italy contributed 1,376. But when standardized against the number of physicians in each country, both France and Italy show an identical annual 0.10 percent outflow rate. The absolute volumes might be different, but, in certain circumstances, percentage transformations may be more significant.

15. The Relative Acceptance (RA) or Relative Intensity (RI) measure is based on a comparison of the observed actual transactions with the predicted or expected transactions in a random (or undifferentiated or null) model system. It is a concise measure of the intensity of the observed flows standardized for the relative "size" of the units. These RI figures show the extent to which each country's transactions deviate (positive or negative) from the expected. The RI is based on the null (or indifference) model and assumes that each country's flow (in/out) will reflect that country's share of all the transactions across the system. In other words, if Belgium contributes 11.1 percent of all the migrant physicians (which it does), we would then expect that 11.1 percent of every other country's entering physicians would be from Belgium (obviously not the case). This assumption of indifference says, in effect, that the nationality of a migrant physician has no effect on his or her choice of a new host country and, conversely, a migrant physician's arrival in a specific country is not related to the physician's country of origin. The RIs are calculated by the following expression:

$$RI_{ij} = \frac{A_{ij} - E_{ij}}{E_{ij}}, \text{ where}$$

A_{ij} = actual share of physicians from i to j, and
E_{ij} = expected share of physicians from i to j.

The values of RI range from -1.00 (no transactions at all) through 0 (actual amount equals expected amount) to infinity (actual amount is far larger than what would be expected by the indifference or null model). The RIs can form a basis for discussion of bilateral relationships such as preference, partnership, dependence, interdependence, and/ or isolation. For a full discussion of this measure, see I. R. Savage and Karl W. Deutsch, "A Statistical Model of the Gross Analysis of Transaction Flows," 28 *Econometrica* (July 1960), 551–572. For an application of the measure to tourism within the European Community, see Arend Lijphart, "Tourist Traffic and Integration Potential," 2 *Journal of Common Market Studies* (March 1964), 251–262.

16. A Concentration-Fractionalization index can note the intensity of various geographical distributions for both departing and entering physicians. This index notes specifically the degree to which: (1) each country's departing physicians concentrate themselves in one or two selected countries or, conversely, the extent to which they are dispersed (fractionalized) across the EC; and (2) each country's arriving physicians are concentrated from one or two other countries or, conversely, the extent to which the arrivals represent fractionalization (dispersal). This degree of geographical concentration–fractionalization is measured by Douglas Rae's Vote Fractionalization Index. Rae's original measure dealt with party strengths within individual political systems, but it is readily

adapatable to physician departures/arrivals. The index is calculated by summing the squared proportions of each country's transactions with all the other countries:

$$C = \sum_{I=1}^{N} T_i^2,$$

where T_i equals any country's decimal share of migrating (in/out) physicians. This index ranges from +1.00 (complete concentration—100 percent of country A's physicians who migrate go only to one other country or 100 percent of A's entering physicians originate from only one country) down to complete fractionalization/dispersal (the value approaches 0). Our example, however, has a built-in limit: since the migrant physicians can originate from/enter into only nine other units (Spain and Portugal are not included in this illustrative case study since they have been in the EC only from 1 January 1986), the maximum fractionalization score (minimum value) is 0.11. Thus the index ranges from +1.00 to 0.11. See Douglas Rae, *The Political Consequences of Electoral Laws* (New Haven, Conn.: Yale University Press, 1967), esp. pp. 53–57.

17. A limited number of physicians were interviewed in Brussels, Grenoble, and Bordeaux during December 1984. They cannot be regarded as a representative sample of any targeted population, and the interview data simply look behind the inanimate aggregate data for some individual perceptions.

18. This *marée blanche* is a direct analogy to a *marée noire* (a "black tide" literally but meaning an "oil spill"). The *marée noire* that inundated Brittany on 16 March 1978 from the Amoco Cadiz's 68 million gallons of crude oil gave visions of a "white tide" (*marée blanche*) of physicians inundating France. Vaissière and Mascaro, p. 187.

19. Personal interview, Bordeaux-Mérignac, France (22 December 1984).

20. Personal interview, Grenoble, France (17 December 1984).

21. Personal interview, Voiron-Coublevie, France (18 December 1984).

22. Personal interview, Brussels, Belgium (12 December 1984).

23. Organized by SEPLIS, the seminar was titled "The Liberal Professions and the Policy of Competition." It was held at the EC's Economic and Social Committee (Brussels: 14 December 1984). Ms. Jacqueline Rousseaux, president of SEPLIS, served as chair, and J. A. Thys served as rapporteur. OECD, Committee of Experts on Restrictive Business Practices, "Report on Competition Policy and the Professions." RPB (84) 8 (2nd Revision), W.1575F/D.0005F (Paris: October 1984), 84 pp., mimeo.

7

The Common Agricultural Policy

The European Community's Common Agricultural Policy (CAP) was perceived originally to be one of the major cornerstones or building blocks for EC economic (and possible political) integration. The CAP has, however, presented a double-sided result: on the one hand, the CAP has contributed to creating and maintaining a more than sufficient quantity and quality of foodstuffs and commodities in Europe, but, on the other hand, the CAP has also brought high economic and political costs. The EC consumers are forced to pay artificially high prices (much higher than the world market price for several commodities); the CAP usually consumes between 60 to 70 percent of the EC's annual budget; vast surpluses ("butter mountains" and "wine lakes" and "sugar lumps") have accumulated; financial fraud and chicanery have been well documented; and intense political friction has developed over the CAP's operation. The CAP has been described in greater detail elsewhere,[1] and this chapter presents only the general outlines—its basic objectives, functioning, and economic-political consequences.

THE EVOLUTION OF THE CAP

Article 3(d) of the Rome Treaty states that one of the explicit goals of the European Community is "the inauguration of a common agricultural policy." This basic objective was fleshed out somewhat in Articles 38 to 47, especially Articles 39 and 40. Article 39 states:

1. The Common Agricultural Policy shall have as its objectives:
    (a) to increase agricultural productivity by developing technical progress and by ensuring the rational development of agricultural production and the optimum utilization of the factors of production, particularly labor;
    (b) to ensure thereby a fair standing of living for the agricultural population, particularly by the increasing of the individual earnings of persons engaged in agriculture;

(c) to stabilize markets;
(d) to guarantee regular supplies; and
(e) to ensure the reasonable prices in supplies to consumers.

Article 40 states:

1. . . .
2. . . . a common organization of agricultural markets shall be effected. This organization shall take one of the following forms according to the products concerned:
   (a) common rules concerning competition;
   (b) compulsory coordination of the various national market organizations; or
   (c) a European market organization.
3. The common organization in one of the forms mentioned in paragraph 2 may comprise all measures necessary to achieve the objective set out in Article 39, in particular, price controls, subsidies as to the production and marketing of various products, arrangements for stock-piling and carry-forward, and common machinery for stabilizing importation or exportation. . . . A common price policy, if any, shall be based on common criteria and on uniform methods of calculation.
4. In order to enable the common organization referred to in paragraph 2 to achieve its objectives, one or more agricultural orientation and guarantee funds may be established.

The basic objectives, then, as contained in Articles 39 and 40, are to ensure adequate supplies at ''reasonable'' prices to consumers, but, also, to ensure rising incomes for farmers at the same time. Agricultural productivity and efficiency are also to be enhanced through various structural improvements. Most of these basic objectives have been met—there is a more than adequate supply of foodstuffs and, except for a few isolated regional pockets, the backwardness of a ''peasant'' society has disappeared from the Community. But there is serious doubt whether ''reasonable'' prices for consumers exist.

The Treaty of Rome says very little about agriculture beyond the basic objectives listed above in Articles 39 and 40. The essential nature of the CAP, the implementation of Articles 39 and 40, was left to the directives of the Council of Ministers in subsequent years and the implementing regulations by the Commission. The CAP is *not* found in one single coherent document—it evolved over the years—and the CAP is, to say the least, extremely complex.

THE IMPORTANCE OF AGRICULTURE

The agricultural sector was one of only a few limited areas singled out in the Treaty of Rome as requiring a European-wide harmonized or coordinated approach, but even within these few areas, agriculture is treated differently. Most other areas of economic activity (goods and services and capital) within the Community may be subject to some degree of EC regulatory processes or standards, but the free-market economic structure prevails: there is free trade without border restrictions; competition is encouraged in the marketplace through the

EC's competition and antitrust regulations; prices are based upon supply and demand; incomes to producers-suppliers vary with economic conditions.

But the agricultural sector in the Community is highly regulated: price controls; subsidies for production and marketing; stockpiling; common prices; and, not least, the objective of maintaining a fair standard of living for those people in the agricultural sector by increasing farm incomes throughout the Community. The European Community does not, for example, establish common prices for automobiles within the EC, nor does it guarantee by treaty to maintain and increase the earnings of automobile assembly-line workers or to guarantee sufficient automobiles at reasonable prices to consumers—why is the agricultural sector treated differently?

There are three related reasons why agriculture within the EC was not left to the open-market economy but, instead, was subject to intensive intervention, regulation, and price controls. Any one (or, perhaps, any two) of these reasons may also be applicable to other functional sectors of the economy and social framework, but it is only with agriculture that all three apply: (1) the production of food is an absolute necessity for the survival of any society; (2) a large percentage of the European population was classified as agricultural workers at the time the EEC Treaty was negotiated and signed; and (3) the politicians who devised and implemented the CAP fully realized that farmers vote and that the farm vote could swing close elections. These three factors intersected with agriculture and thus the CAP resulted.

The explicit goal to guarantee regular agricultural supplies (Article 39, paragraph 1-d) underscores the EC's commitment to surplus production. The European Community has made the conscious decision that the region would become totally self-sufficient in the basic foodstuffs and thus not be dependent upon the vagaries of imports from external sources. Such imports could be shut off for political reasons and/or prices could be increased suddenly. This was the situation with oil imports in the aftermath of the 1973 Yom Kippur War: the Organization of Arab Petroleum Exporting Countries (OAPEC, a subgroup within the larger OPEC cartel) first reduced the availability of oil to the Community (the crisis of supply) and then increased prices dramatically (the crisis of price). The CAP is intended to prevent a similar situation with agricultural commodities.

Also contributing to the different treatment of agriculture within the EC was, simply, that a very large number of people were classified as being within the agricultural sector of the economy. Any program in agriculture thus concerned millions of people and not just a handful employed in some esoteric activity. Table 7.1 contains some approximate figures since 1950 on the percentage of the EC's working population engaged in agriculture (including forestry and fishing). At the time that the CAP was established and during its early development, the agricultural sector was by far the largest sector in all the EC countries (except the United Kingdom). These percentages have decreased vastly since the 1950s and 1960s, however. The EC has experienced what the United States has experienced: fewer farmers are producing more food. This rural depopulation

Table 7.1
Percentage of Working Population in Agriculture (including forestry and fishing)

Country	1950	1955	1970	1975	1983
Belgium	12.0	9.3	4.1	3.4	3.0
Denmark	23.0	25.4	9.0	9.3	8.5
France	33.0	25.9	12.7	10.9	8.6
Greece	-	-	-	-	30.3
Ireland	42.0	38.8	25.7	23.8	19.2
Italy	41.0	39.5	13.1	15.5	13.3
Luxembourg	12.0	11.7	11.0	6.1	5.6
Netherlands	14.0	13.7	5.8	6.5	5.0
Portugal	-	-	-	-	26.7
Spain	-	-	-	-	18.9
United Kingdom	6.0	4.8	2.7	2.7	2.8
West Germany	22.0	18.9	5.6	7.1	5.9
Total	28.0 EC-6	21.0 EC-6 (1960)	14.0 EC-6 (1968)		8.1 EC-10

Source: A.M. El-Agraa, "The Common Agricultural Policy," in A.M. El-Agraa, ed., The
Economics of the European Community (New York: St. Martin's, 1980), Table
7.1, p. 136; Anthony J.C. Kerr, The Common Market and How It Works (Elmsford,
N.Y.: Pergamon, 1983), Figure 3, pp. 71, 237.

has brought with it other problems. The infrastructure of social life and the environment in many agricultural areas across the EC have been affected by this decline, and part of the CAP is targeted at these problems. But in the 1980s, only about 8 percent of the EC's working population (excluding Spain and Portugal) are classified within the agricultural sector, and the CAP is now seen by many as a vast entitlement program for a small number of people.

The third reason that explains why agriculture is treated differently than most other sectors of the economy in the EC concerns national (domestic) politics. Farmers vote and, in certain situations, can provide the margin of electoral victory for the majority party or the governing coalition. The national politicians—even in situations in which economic logic would dictate resistance to higher farm prices—have in many instances succumbed to the political logic of supporting increases in farm prices. This third reason may be more important than the effects of the first two combined. Werner J. Feld presents a most illustrative example of the relationship between West German domestic politics and West German support of the CAP during the 1970s:

An interesting example of how domestic political conditions have combined to make a minister of agriculture a most powerful champion of farm interests with respect to his ministerial colleagues is the story of Joseph Ertl . . . whose political strength stem[med] from the fact that the farm vote can swing elections. Although Ertl, a member of the Free Democrats (FDP) [did] not control more than 7 per cent of the farm vote, under the combined single-member district/proportional representation list system of the Federal Republic of Germany, the Free Democrats . . . received many of the list votes from Christian Social Union (CSU) and Christian Democratic Union (CDU) farmers, enough to account for . . . 10 percent of the total 39 FDP seats. As a consequence, Mr. Ertl, one of four FDP ministers in Chancellor Helmut Schmidt's cabinet, [had] been able to secure continually rising farm prices despite the strong opposition of the German finance, economics, and foreign ministers and even Chancellor Schmidt. . . . But for industrialized Germany, often complaining of being the "paymaster" of the Community, resistance to any farm price rise would seem to be the rational policy stand.[2]

THE OPERATION OF THE CAP

The common agricultural policy, through its European Agricultural Guidance and Guarantee Fund (EAGGF), finances EC activity within the agricultural sector. The EAGGF itself is funded by import levies on agricultural commodities, proceeds from the value-added-tax (VAT), and assessments levied on the national governments. But, as with any other public policy expenditure, it is the European consumer and taxpayer who pays for the CAP. The CAP accounts for an extraordinary large percentage of the total EC budget—some 72 percent in 1985, decreasing to a projected 62 percent in 1986. The CAP through the EAGGF is a coherent whole directed at five related processes: (1) domestic production; (2) inter-EC trade; (3) imports; (4) exports; and (5) structural improvements. The first four deal with production and marketing; the fifth deals with the agricultural sector's infrastructure.

Domestic Production

Through a long and complex process characterized by national political antagonisms and effective lobbying by European-farm interest groups, the EC establishes annually a specific "target" price for many commodities (e.g., cereals, sugar, milk, beef, butter, olive oil, wine). This "target" price establishes the rest of the process, and it is in the economic and political interest of many groups to have the "target" price set as high as possible. It is also in the economic and political interest of many groups and countries (especially the United Kingdom) to have the lowest possible "target" price. For any specific commodity under the CAP, a "support" or "intervention" price usually is 90 to 95 percent of the "target" price.

The CAP/EAGGF does not become operational if the commodity can command in the open free market a price above the support-intervention level. But due to the vagaries of supply and demand, quite often the open-market realized price falls to or below the support-intervention price. The CAP then becomes a factor in this situation. When the realized price is below the support-intervention level, the CAP mechanism will intervene (the national authorities actually intervene and provide the funding, to be later reimbursed by the EAGGF) in one (or in a combination) of three ways:

1. The EAGGF will finance the purchase of the surplus commodities that could not be sold at (at least) the support-intervention level; and/or
2. The EAGGF will finance the costs of storage/stockpiling the commodity until a later date when, presumably, market conditions will be stronger; and/or
3. The EAGGF will finance the difference between the actual realized price received in the open market and the support-intervention price.

The European Community is not *legally* bound to guarantee unlimited financing, but there has yet to be a situation in which the EAGGF has not intervened. This process gives an explicit financial incentive to the farmer to produce as much as possible—he is "guaranteed" at least the support price for his product and, if the producer believes supply will decrease the following year and/or the target price will be raised (thus increasing in turn the support price), the commodity can be stored at the CAP's expense. The CAP is quite different from the American farm program: there are very few limits set on the amount of acreage that can be farmed; there are no "payments-in-kind" to reduce surpluses; there is no program to subsidize farmers *not* to produce. Rather, as mentioned above, maximum agricultural production is encouraged economically, and this has led to vast surpluses (discussed below) of many commodities. The EC is simply producing far more than its people can possibly consume.

Inter-EC Trade in Agricultural Commodities

One of the original objectives of the CAP was to have "common" prices for foodstuffs throughout the European Community. A common price can never be achieved until a common currency is in place—a very doubtful proposition even for the long-term future—and the prices consumers pay for various products and the income levels or purchasing power of farmers vary widely across the EC. These variations are due to the different exchange rates and values of the EC currencies and the different cost factors involved in producing the commodity (e.g., labor, energy, fertilizer, machinery). A wheat producer in West Germany may in theory receive the same "support" price for his wheat as, say, a French producer, but then the West German farmer could purchase a tractor at 80 percent of the price his French colleague may have to pay. Farm incomes across the EC may be increasing, but they are not "common."

But the EC-CAP insists upon maintaining the fiction of "common" prices, and this has led to a very complex system of border controls over trade in agricultural commodities between/among EC members. It has also led (discussed below) to fraud and chicanery. The target and support prices established by the EC process is relevant here, but it is far less complex to discuss inter-EC trade without reference to these price levels. It is a question of protecting "high-cost" countries from cheaper commodities produced in "low-cost" countries and, conversely, to allow "high-cost" countries to compete effectively in the home market of "low-cost" countries. This is the lip service that the CAP pays to Article 3(a) of the EEC Treaty that mandates free trade although there is really no free market competition within the agricultural sector.

A very complex agrimonetary system ("green" rates of exchange) has been established for trade within the EC for agricultural commodities. A fictitious but illustrative example follows:

Frozen chickens from Italy are exported to West Germany. But due to the lower production costs in Italy (energy, feed, labor), a frozen Italian chicken can be delivered, even including transportation charges, and sold in Munich at a lower unit cost than West German-produced frozen chickens. The West German producers can't compete, and thus the Italians monopolize the West German market. Conversely, due to higher production costs, a West German chicken costs more in Rome than the Italian chicken. This effectively shuts out West German chickens in the Italian market, ensuring also an Italian monopoly in the domestic market.

If the product sold were under the ECSC regulations, as coal and steel are, the logical result would be the economic demise of the West German chicken producer. This obviously would benefit the Italian producer, but it would also benefit both the Italian and West German consumers by having available less expensive (Italian) chickens on the supermarket shelves. But, since this is agriculture, a different set of ground rules are in force. These rules will enable the West German producer to compete on equal terms with his Italian counterpart, both in Munich and in Rome; will take away the economic advantage enjoyed by the Italian producer; and will ensure that the Munich consumer (and, indirectly, even the Italian consumer) will pay an artificially high price for chickens. This is accomplished by border levies, either positive or negative, that are formally termed "Monetary Compensation Amounts" (MCAs) on the export-import of frozen chickens between Italy and the Federal Republic of Germany.

The low-cost Italian chicken will have to *pay a levy* at the border. The levy is set at such a level to increase its price up to that of a West German chicken.

Thus the Munich consumer—stripped of his ability to choose between a high-priced West German chicken or a low-priced Italian chicken—will have a choice only between a high-priced Italian chicken or a high-priced West German chicken. The West German consumer does *not* receive the benefit of lower prices from "free" trade and the Italian producer cannot monopolize the West German market. Conversely, the high-priced West German chicken will *receive a subsidy* for traveling to Rome. This subsidy will enable the West German producer to lower his price in order to compete with the Italian chickens. The Roman consumer may believe he is getting a good buy—less expensive chickens even if they are German—but this is not the case. It is the Italian chicken consumer who is financing the EAGGF through the VAT, import levies, and other taxes, and if these indirect costs are added to the price of the chicken, the bargain is no longer a bargain. In a real sense, the Italian consumer is paying for the subsidy that the West German exporter receives at the border.

These border levies/subsidies (MCAs) are totally counter to the nature of the EC's goal of free trade, and the MCA system presents severe disadvantages to a country with a weak currency that is also a net food exporter. But due to the importance of the agricultural sector, the mechanism continues. Although the MCAs operate for the benefit of an exporter in a strong-currency country (the West German producer, in our example), they do not provide any real economic benefits for the consumer: the West Germans are not paying any less for chickens even with the CAP/EAGGF and the Italians are (indirectly) paying more than they would in the absence of the CAP. In addition, and this is discussed below, the border levies-subsidies (MCAs) have led to fraud and chicanery, increasing even more the net price to consumers. Finally, the entire situation operates when there is a vast surplus of chickens across the EC, which, given a normal economic policy, should lead to lower prices.

Imports of Agricultural Commodities into the European Community

Many agricultural commodities are imported by the EC with no or very little import levies/restrictions applied. This category of commodities does not compete with domestic production and thus has relatively easy access to the European markets. Some noncompeting commodities do, however, face quotas: the EC has imposed national quotas under the Lomé Convention with the ACP states on the export of bananas to the EC—there were simply too many bananas chasing too few Europeans. But for products that do compete with EC-produced commodities—grains, milk products, sugar, beef, butter, wine, olive oil, for example—the amount and price of the imports are strictly regulated.

Variable import levies are imposed on the imports such that, when added to the cost, freight, and insurance of the product, the final price is no lower (and usually higher) than the CAP-established "target" price. This protectionism, for example, prevents less expensive American wheat from displacing more expensive French and West German wheat. American wheat would, in economic and political reality, be purchased only if extreme shortages of EC wheat pushed up the domestic price. Another consequence of these import levies is that the European consumer does not have the benefit of less expensive commodities. The consumer has a choice between French wheat at artificially inflated prices or American wheat (if available) at even a higher price. The import price of competitive commodities will always be more expensive than the domestic target price level.[3]

Exports of Agricultural Commodities to Non-EC Members

The financial and marketing sectors of the CAP-EAGGF, while providing for an increasing standard of living for farmers and while ensuring the security of supplies, have also led to vast surpluses of several commodities. There are "wine lakes" and "butter mountains" and "olive oil reservoirs" and "sugar lumps" across the EC, increasing in size and storage costs each year. These surpluses are due to a combination of (1) the financial incentive to produce as much as possible, and (2) the changing eating habits in Europe (more people are, for example, substituting no-fat margarine for cholesterol-laden salted butter). As Table 7.2 shows, the EC as a whole produces approximately 10 percent more of the six basic products that most Community citizens consume in one form or another nearly every day (wheat, potatoes, vegetables, sugar, butter, and meat) than its needs require. These surpluses are available for export and provide welcome foreign exchange earnings within the balance of payments equation.

But due to the artificially high prices within the EC, many of these surplus agricultural commodities cannot compete in the world market. The CAP's financial mechanisms have priced these products out of the world market: EC skim milk powder and sugar are approximately 500 percent higher than the world market price; butter, about 400 percent higher; wheat and beef, approximately 200 percent higher. To enable EC commodities to be competitive outside the EC, the CAP-EAGGF also provides "refunds" (export subsidies) to encourage exports. These subsidies make EC agricultural products a good buy just about anywhere *except* within the Community itself. The export subsidies reflect the difference between the EC price and the realized world market price. Strictly speaking, this practice is not considered to be "dumping." Dumping occurs when the product is exported and sold to a third country at a price level *below* the prevailing price in the importing country. The export subsidies enable EC commodities to be sold at prices far below EC prices, but the realized price is close to the world market price. The export refunds, as with all the other financial-marketing provisions of the CAP, are administered by the national authorities, who eventually are reimbursed by the EAGGF. The export of surplus EC agricultural commodities has become a very volatile political issue within the Community. This issue is discussed in greater detail below with reference to EC butter sales to the Soviet Union.

Table 7.2
Degree of Agricultural Self-Sufficiency

Country	Degree of Self-Sufficiency (base = 100)[a]
Denmark	168
Ireland	154
Luxembourg	140
France	137
Belgium	135
Netherlands	124
Portugal	120
Greece	101
Spain	100
West Germany	95
Italy	90
United Kingdom	60
EC-12	109

a. Weighted average of six basic products: wheat, potatoes, vegetables, sugar, butter, and meat.

Source: Anthony J.C. Kerr, The Common Market and How It Works (Elmsford, N.Y.: Pergamon, 1983), p. 237.

Structural Improvements

The structural improvement section of the CAP-EAGGF accounts for only about 4.2 percent of the CAP's total expenditure, but this represents an important activity. The main objective of the structural improvement section is to make the agricultural sector more efficient, and it includes projects such as land real-location and reclamation, hydraulic and irrigation projects, reforestation and afforestation, rural electrification, and food-processing centers and plants. Similar to the financial-marketing schemes, the national governments administer these programs and share part of the costs with the EAGGF.

The basic framework for the structural sector of agriculture was presented by the EC Commission to the Council of Ministers on 10 December 1968. The report was a ten-year plan of agricultural reform titled "Agriculture 1980" but more popularly known as the Mansholt Plan, named after the former EC commissioner for agriculture, Dr. Sicco Mansholt. The Mansholt Plan proposed a restructuring of the agricultural sector in order to increase the living standards of agricultural workers, and reduce the ever-increasing costs of the CAP. The plan aimed at the following:

1. Placing less emphasis on guaranteed markets and prices;
2. Reducing the acreage of farmland in the Community;
3. Increasing the average size of landholdings; and
4. Encouraging the movement of farmers off the land.

In April 1970, the commission submitted to the Council of Ministers six specific proposals aimed at implementing the Mansholt Plan:

1. Annual pensions of up to $600 for farmers between the ages of 55 and 65 who give up farming, providing they make their land available for extending other farms or for uses such as afforestation or national parks;
2. Interest rebates on loans to enable farmers who stay on the land to modernize their holdings;
3. Retraining facilities and social and economic advice for farmers in difficult regions;
4. Financial help to producer groups in order to improve marketing;
5. A special income subsidy of $600 a year for farmers between the ages of 45 and 55 who have small farms but no alternative to farming; and
6. A grant of $1,500 for every new job created for those leaving the land in difficult areas.[4]

After more than two years of debate, the Council of Ministers on 24 March 1972 accepted the major principles of the Mansholt Plan and issued several implementing directives for the first three of the above-cited commission proposals. The directives concerned farm-modernization projects, retirement pensions, and worker-retraining schemes. For example, aid would be given to assist consolidation of land where inheritance laws had led to fragmented farms; retirement benefits would be made available to farmers to encourage them to leave farming; and funds would be available to retrain agricultural workers for other types of employment.[5]

The Mansholt Plan was very ambitious and far reaching, but the national governments have since come to recognize that there are problems involved in reducing the number of farmers. Anthony J. C. Kerr summarizes some of these problems: "by phasing out small farmers, one alters the balance of population between the countryside, small towns, and cities. This may lead to a waste of the existing infrastructure of roads, houses, schools, and medical services, to deterioration of the land, and in times of high unemployment, to heavier burdens on the welfare state [and therefore higher taxation]."[6]

Although accepted in principle by the Council of Ministers, those with the responsibility of implementing the Mansholt Plan—the national governments and regional public authorities—have been less than enthusiastic in accelerating the elimination of small farmers. Dr. Mansholt eventually resigned from the commission (he was its president for a short time) over what he (correctly) perceived to be nonsupport for his grand proposals.

THE CONSEQUENCES OF THE CAP

The operation of the CAP-EAGGF has brought in its wake some unintended consequences. This section briefly describes some of these consequences: (1) the extraordinary high cost of the CAP; (2) activities that can best be described as outright fraud; (3) people taking daylong boat rides on the North Sea to do their weekly grocery shopping; (4) strained relations with the United States; and (5) the sale of surplus commodities to non-EC members ("buttering up" the Russians).

The Cost of the CAP

The costs of the CAP-EAGGF are enormous. In 1984, EAGGF expenditures totaled some 17.096 billion ECUs, accounting for 67.4 percent of the *entire* European Community budget. Costs in 1985 escalated to 20.172 billion ECUs, for 71.8 percent of the total budget. The 1986 preliminary budget projects a cost of some 21.6 billion ECUs, representing about 62 percent of the total budget. As Table 7.3 indicates, this 61.7 percent is much lower than earlier years when the EAGGF consumed over 90 percent of the EC budget, but the absolute costs are increasing each year. As with any other public-policy entitlement program, it is the European taxpayer who subsidizes the EAGGF.

In addition to the high absolute direct costs, the European consumers also pay artificially high prices for food purchased in the supermarket. To protect the standard of living for agricultural workers, many commodities are sold in the EC at prices that range from 200 to 500 percent higher than the world market price. The Monetary Compensation Amounts (MCAs) effectively prevent the consumers from receiving the benefits of low-cost imports from other EC countries, and the import levies prevent low-cost imports from third countries.

The export subsidies also contribute to the high costs. For example, the EC support-intervention price for sugar is about 20¢ per pound—approximately five times the current world market price. Not surprisingly, the EC's annual sugar production jumped from about 10 million tons in 1977 to 13.5 million tons in

Table 7.3
EAGGF Expenditures (million ECUs)

Year	Guarantee (Market Support)	Guidance (Structural Policies)	Total	Percent of Total EC Budget
1967	1,313	285	1,598	93.2
1970	3,149	244	3,393	92.9
1972	2,732	202	2,934	82.8
1973	4,166	229	4,395	80.3
1978	8,673	324	8,997	74.1
1981	11,571	731	12,302	67.0
1984	16,500	596	17,096	67.4
1985	19,315	857	20,172	71.8
1986a	20,688	946	21,634	61.7

a. Preliminary draft budget.

Source: For 1967-1981, John S. Marsh and Pamela J. Swanney, "The Common Agricultural Policy," in Juliet Lodge, ed., Institutions and Policies of The European Community (New York: St. Martins, 1983), Table 9, p. 70; for 1984 and 1985, The Europa Year Book: A World Survey, Volume I, Part One, "International Organizations" (London: Europa Publications, Ltd., 1985), p. 150; for 1986, The Europa Year Book: A World Survey, Volume I, Part One, "International Organizations" (London: Europa Publications, Ltd., 1986), p. 152.

1984 and a vast "sugar lump" was created. The EC began to export this surplus sugar and, since 1977, has been able to sell about 38 million tons. But the difference between the 20¢ paid and the 4¢ received comes out to about $US 320/ton "loss" on each ton exported. The European taxpayers had to pay approximately $US 2 billion in 1984 for these sugar subsidies, in addition to having to pay 20¢ for a 4¢ product.

One last example of these export subsidies—subsidies that are eventually billed to the European taxpayer—concerns a recent sale of French wheat to the Soviet Union. Due to the increased use of modern technology and cultivation procedures, many countries that were formerly grain importers have now reached internal self-sufficiency. The size of the world market is, in turn, decreasing, but the developed nations (the EC, US, Canada, Australia) are very hesitant to cut back on their own grain production. The combination of increased supply and reduced demand has obviously led to lower prices, and the developed countries are quite ready to subsidize farmers and shippers in order to sell the grain at almost any price.

On 1 August 1986, President Reagan offered 3.85 million metric tons of wheat to the Soviet Union at a price of $93/ton. The Soviet Union did not respond to the American offer because grain prices were lower from other suppliers. On 27 September 1986, the Soviet Union announced that a contract was signed to purchase 1.1 million metric tons of French wheat at $80/ton—a full $13/ton lower than the American offer, with a savings of $14.3 million. The French were able to underbid the Americans because of the CAP's export subsidies. For every metric ton of wheat sold to the Soviet Union at $80, French farmers and shippers received a subsidy of $123—a total subsidy of $135 million.[7] The Soviet Union was able to purchase inexpensive wheat; the American farmers lost the sale because President Reagan declined to match the French offer; the European taxpayer was sent a bill for $135 million.

Certain countries are hard hit by the operation of the CAP-EAGGF. As Table 7.4 indicates, the Federal Republic of Germany and the United Kingdom are by far the countries that show a negative balance. The West German and British taxpayers and consumers are subsidizing the other countries and although the West Germans have not been as vocal as their British colleagues, the situation does not make for harmonious relations. The costs—political and economic— of the Common Agricultural Policy are enormous, and they are not equally shared.

Fraud and Chicanery

Over the past several years, the EC Commission has instituted legal proceedings to recover approximately 5 to 6 million ECUs each year for sums seen to be obtained by fraudulent practices under the CAP-EAGGF. The Commission hasn't been very successful in this area—recovering only about 1 million ECUs annually—and many observers are convinced that the actual amount of fraud is several times greater than what is uncovered. Most of the fraud concerns the export of commodities from a high-valued currency/high-cost EC state to a low-valued currency/low-cost EC state. To enable the high-cost producer to compete with the lower-cost commodity in the low-cost market, the Monetary Compensation Amounts (MCAs—border subsidies) will be paid to the exporter.

The fraud occurs when the exporter, after having received the export subsidy, does not dispose of the product in the low-cost country. Rather, the product is surreptitiously brought back into the high-cost country. A new set of documentation is prepared and the export—with the resulting subsidies—"travels" again. One such example concerned a herd of Irish cows that were legally exported to Northern Ireland (high cost to low cost) and the exporter duly received the subsidy. The cows didn't linger very long in Northern Ireland, however. They were brought back to Ireland under the cover of darkness, and the next day, with false documentation attesting to the fact that these were different cows,

Table 7.4
CAP's Net Budgetary Effects (million ECUs/estimated)

Country	1980	1981
Belgium	255	388
Denmark	331	302
France	423	624
Greece	-	123
Ireland	644	591
Italy	735	619
Luxembourg	232	282
Netherlands	441	223
United Kingdom	−1,521	−1,505
West Germany	−1,540	−1,647

Source: John S. Marsh and Pamela J. Swanney, "The Common Agricultural Policy," in Juliet Lodge, ed., _Institutions and Policies of the European Community_ (New York: St. Martin's, 1983), Table 10, p. 71.

were again exported to Northern Ireland and the subsidy was paid. And the next day . . .[8]

A variation of this scam has low-cost products smuggled into high-cost countries and, after "documenting" that the commodity was actually produced in the high-cost country, then legally exported back into the low-cost country (and receiving the subsidy). One of the more embarrassing cases occurred several years ago: the _same_ truckload of butter made the rounds of the Community. The truck would surreptitiously enter high-cost countries, but then proudly produce the required documentation each time it entered a low-cost country from a high-cost state. This particular butter truck netted over $US 1 million before its luck ran out.

The opportunities for such fraudulent activities are limited only by the imagination of those who engage in it. False documentation is not very difficult to manufacture, and it is quite a simple matter to cross EC frontiers without being subject to border controls. The EC has an antifraud unit in operation, but the sums recovered represent only a small fraction of the actual amounts improperly paid out.

Grocery Shopping on the High Seas

Due to the high domestic prices for agricultural products within the EC and due to the export subsidies available, the situation has resulted that EC foodstuffs are a good bargain just about anywhere except within the Community itself. But because traveling to Moscow to purchase some butter is inconvenient and expensive, a phenomenon known as "butter boats" has arisen.[9] The boats leave a Dutch port, briefly stop at Borkum (West German territory), and then sail the North Sea for a few hours. After Borkum, the boats are technically in international waters and thus whatever they sell on board is considered exports.

These boats are mobile supermarkets, catering to some 10 million passengers a year who do their grocery shopping on the high seas. The process has been described in the following terms:

Beyond the lee at Borkum, the wind picks up, the sea swells, and the ship begins to roll. It's time to go shopping. Below decks, customs seals on the supermarket doors are broken and the doors thrown open. Passengers leave their seats and make their way, holding on to tables and pillars, to the end of a long line. The ship heaves and the line staggers. . . . Jostling for position while struggling to keep standing, the shoppers inch along a passageway and down into the supermarket, which might better be described as a cattle chute with shelves. Everyone takes a basket and sets to heaping it, not just with liquor and cigarets but also with olives and canned tomatoes and coffee creamer and tuna fish and butter. . . . Sniffing at the salamis and testing the cheeses with their thumbs, the passengers are herded toward the checkout counter.[10]

A strange sight indeed, but at least one can combine grocery shopping with a very inexpensive boat ride (the ship makes its profit on the goods sold, not on the cost of the tickets). This is not fraud—it is very similar to airport duty-free stores—but its very existence points out the illogic of the CAP.

Strained Relations with the United States

The combination of the CAP's export subsidies (undercutting the American price in world markets), the variable import levies placed on agricultural products (preventing less expensive American commodities from competing in the EC domestic market), and the expansion of the EC to 12 countries have contributed to increased tension within the Atlantic Alliance over agricultural trade. Space does not permit a discussion of all the various so-called trade wars between the US and the EC (e.g., the "chicken war," the "lemon war," the "pasta war"). Rather, this section concentrates on the implications of Spain's and Portugal's entry to the EC on future US agricultural exports to the EC.

Spain and Portugal entered the EC on 1 January 1986—an event long favored by the United States on political grounds. Accession to the EC, and the subsequent (spring 1986) Spanish referendum to continue in NATO, ended decades of isolation of the Iberian peninsula. Spain and Portugal finally put to rest the authoritarianism of the Franco and Salazar regimes and turned toward full participation in the European democratic integration process. The *political* ramifications of this are clearly positive for the United States; the *economic* implications are far less favorable and may even be quite negative.

Spain and Portugal were relatively good customers for US agricultural products, especially corn to Spain and wheat and corn to Portugal. In 1985, Spain purchased approximately $2.6 billion of American exports and Portugal approximately $1 billion. But due to the common external tariff and the variable import levies, EC grain in all likelihood will be substituted for the American grain. In addition, in 1985, the United States sold approximately $500 million of nuts, fruits, and horticultural products to the EC of the Ten—a market that is bound to shift to Spain and Portugal for supplies. The United States thus faced a potential loss of some $4.1 billion in exports as of 1 March 1986, the effective date of the EC-imposed restrictions. The situation after Greece's entry to the EC strengthened US fears—Greece increased substantially its imports from other EC countries while imports from the United States declined.

The simmering quarrel became public in spring 1986. The United States announced that unless the EC rescinded the quotas on grain shipments to Spain and Portugal, and unless compensation was provided for the increased tariffs, the United States would retaliate by placing quotas and raising tariffs on a wide range of EC products entering the United States. The announced retaliatory measures, to be effective 1 May 1986, dealt with some $1 billion of food-and-drink products (wine, beer, cheese, meat, fruit, cookies, canned ham, and whiskey) from the EC.[11] Not unexpectedly, the EC judged these threats as unjustified, and the Commission then prepared a list of US agricultural products (soybean cake and meal, corn gluten feed, dried fruit, corn, and sorghum) that would be subject to counter-retaliatory moves if the United States did, in fact, implement its threats. The Commission's list was submitted to, and approved by, the Council of Ministers on 21 April 1986. At the time, Willy De Clercq, the EC commissioner responsible for external relations, was quoted as saying: "If the United States does take the steps it has spoken of, it must be clear that the EC will firmly defend its lawful interests. As judged by the Commission, what counts most is that the list be symmetrical, that is to say, constitute a tit-for-tat reply to whatever the U.S. ultimately decides."[12]

But cooler heads prevailed, and on 2 July 1986, the United States and the EC reached a temporary agreement that averted the imposition of the retaliatory and counter-retaliatory measures. The United States agreed to suspend its plans to increase tariffs on the listed EC food-and-drink products and the EC agreed to drop its threatened countermeasures. In addition, the Community agreed to guarantee at least 234,000 metric tons a month of US exports to Spain of corn, sorghum, corn gluten feed, and brewing residues (the average monthly level during 1985). If the US exports fell below this level, the EC agreed to reduce the variable import levies to enable the shortfall to be sold in other EC countries.[13]

This agreement, however, was only temporary, with a 31 December 1986 expiration date. Negotiators on both sides hoped that this six-month grace period would allow an equitable and permanent solution. But any successful resolution—successful from the American viewpoint—would necessarily call into question the provisions of the enlargement treaty and the basic principles of the CAP. The EC does not appear ready to repudiate either, and the trade war seems likely to continue.

"Buttering Up" the Russians

The sale of surplus Community agricultural commodities, especially butter, to the Soviet Union, deserves some mention. It now appears that the same type of price advantages the Soviet Union was able to obtain with its vast wheat purchases from the United States in the early 1970s were also present for some time with their purchases of surplus butter from the European Community.

As discussed above, the CAP has contributed to vast (!) surpluses of many agricultural commodities within the EC, especially butter. The CAP has set prices so high that dairy concerns are financially encouraged to produce as much as possible—an amount far beyond what the Europeans currently consume— and combined with the contemporary understanding that low-fat/low-cholesterol margarine is preferable to artery-clogging butter comes the realization that there is simply *too much butter in Europe*. There is a "butter mountain" of approximately 400,000 metric tons (almost a billion pounds), and the increasing refrigeration costs has raised the price of storing the butter (and other surplus milk products) to approximately $US 3.5 billion a year.

As part of a rational process of trying to reduce the surplus (but not attempting to reduce production), the butter is exported at a cut-rate bargain price—a price well below the market price within the European Community. The difference between the realized-export sale price and the EC-fixed price is made up by an export subsidy from the EAGGF (i.e., the European taxpayers). Concerned over the ever-increasing surpluses and the ever-increasing storage costs, it is seen by many within the EC as good economic policy to sell whatever can be sold at whatever price realized.

The Soviet Union, recognizing the obvious, moved in, and in 1979, for example, purchased approximately 135,000 metric tons of EC butter at an average price of around 65¢/pound compared to the average EC price of about $US 2/ pound. One might reasonably argue that such a policy makes little sense even in the best of times—production should be decreased to reduce the surplus and/ or the artificially high EC political support price should be lowered to encourage higher domestic consumption. But due to domestic political factors (lower support prices translate into less income for voters in the agricultural sector) and other factors (more and more Europeans simply will not eat butter even if it were given away free), the surplus exists, and the Soviet Union is buying cheap butter subsidized by the European taxpayer. But in the aftermath of the Soviet invasion of Afghanistan in December 1979 and the resultant (but later rescinded) US embargo on grain sales to the USSR, the European Community had to take a long and hard look at its policy of "buttering up" the Russians.

This reevaluation, however, illustrated the extent to which the EC was divided on what to do. Of the 12 EC member-states, only the United Kingdom has demanded that all butter export–sales to the Soviet Union be stopped. The British position stems from two separate but related facts: (1) the United Kingdom has been much more militant than the other Community countries in its commercial approach to the Soviet Union and has generally supported American initiatives to punish the USSR for "bad behavior"; and (2) the United Kingdom sees itself as having nothing to gain from the butter exports (distinguished from its support of the pipeline deal, where the UK did have quite a large economic interest). Partly as a reaction to the Soviet stance in international affairs, but mostly because the British (correctly) perceive that much of the real economic costs of selling cheap butter to the Soviet Union is paid by the British taxpayers via the CAP, the United Kingdom has argued strongly against the sales.

The producing (and selling) countries—especially France and Denmark (who account for approximately 50 percent of all EC butter exports) and Ireland—are located at the opposite end of the argument. These countries have butter to sell and they have insisted that "traditional" trade flows be maintained, if not increased. They argue strongly against any reduction in surplus butter sales to the USSR and totally oppose a complete stoppage.

These antagonistic views are mirrored in Community policy (or lack thereof). The Council of Ministers, reflecting the views of the producing and exporting countries, agreed to the principle of maintaining the traditional trade flows and thus refuses to halt the butter sales. The European Parliament, on the other hand, passed yet another symbolic resolution on 15 February 1980 that called for an immediate and total halt of sales of *all* (not just butter) surplus EC agricultural commodities to the Soviet Union. The divergent views of the Council and the Parliament have placed the Commission in a difficult and tenuous position.

In March 1980, the EC Commission attempted to carve out the middle ground and, by so doing, displeased practically everyone. The Commission rebuffed the European Parliament and the British by not calling for a halt to the sales; it also rebuffed the producing-exporting countries by declaring that the EC would not fill the gap created by the American-sponsored trade embargo imposed after the Soviet invasion of Afghanistan. Sales of surplus EC agricultural commodities to the Soviet Union would continue, but the amount of permitted butter exports was set at a much lower level than the 140,000 metric tons sold in 1979. The level established in 1980—approximately 80,000 metric tons—was roughly the average of butter exports in the 1970s (but excluding 1979). The Commission also suspended the guaranteed subsidies on the butter exports.

These two 1980 Commission decisions—limiting the amount of butter that could be sold to the Soviet Union to about 80,000 metric tons annually and the suspension of the butter export subsidies (banning, in effect, sales at a price below the EC level)—brought still another actor into the fray: Jean-Baptiste Doumeng. A long-standing member and financial backer of the French Communist Party and known in France as the "Red Millionaire," Doumeng controls Interagra, the EC's largest agribusiness concern. In 1983, Interagra made about $US 5 million profit on approximately $US 2.2 billion of sales, one-third of its revenues coming from trade with the Eastern bloc, but especially with the Soviet Union.

Originally specializing in importing Eastern bloc agricultural equipment and food products, Interagra then began selling agricultural products to Eastern Europe. This shift was the result of growing Soviet demand just at the time the protectionist CAP was creating the vast surpluses. It appears that Interagra has a monopoly on such sales (to the envy of competing EC firms) because of Doumeng's affiliation with the PCF. In 1973, for example, Interagra sold some 200,000 metric tons of surplus butter to the Soviet Union at a price 80 percent below the Community price; 150,000 metric tons of beef were sold in 1974; another 50,000 metric tons of butter in 1975. In 1979, the year of the Soviet invasion of Afghanistan, Doumeng sold the Soviets 130,000 metric tons of butter at prices well below the EC level.

The March 1980 decisions by the Commission obviously did not meet with Doumeng's approval. Doumeng was reported to have decided to fight the Commission decisions by all possible means, and he had the alleged support of French agricultural organizations and the French government itself.[14] Doumeng was quoted as saying:

The Commission has exceeded its powers. It has taken decisions on meat and milk which are purely Malthusian, and a disgrace when half the world is under-nourished. Europe should not align itself with the American embargo. To resort to the food weapon is a disgrace for our civilization. It is a policy based on an appreciation of Soviet policy in Afghanistan or elsewhere which is quite unjustified.[15]

The entire issue of surplus Community agricultural commodities was simply dismissed by Doumeng as a false problem. No doubt convinced that Interagra would continue to profit from the sale of such surpluses, Doumeng said that the real "problem" was that there were not enough surpluses available for export: "Take milk surpluses. They only account for 6 per cent of total Community production. I would like them to rise to 20 per cent. I wish Europe had more surpluses so that it could have a dynamic food export policy."[16]

Doumeng was not able to get the Commission to rescind the 1980 decisions, and butter exports to Eastern Europe are limited to 80,000 metric tons/year without the export subsidies. Doumeng, however, has been accused several times, mainly by the British, of violating these restrictions (a relatively easy matter), but no overt violations have yet been proven.[17] Interagra continues to dominate the export of surplus EC agricultural products to Eastern Europe. In July 1984, the Soviet Union bought some 1,800 metric tons of inexpensive table wine from Interagra. This particular deal was warmly welcomed by both the French government and the French wine industry as a step—however small—to drain the ''wine lakes'' in France and reduce the record and ever-increasing wine glut. Also in 1984, Interagra sold the Soviet Union 1.5 million metric tons of French wheat, 120,000 metric tons of French flour, and 50,000 metric tons of French meat—approximately $US 280 million worth of surplus French agricultural commodities.[18] These exports do not fall under the 1980 restrictions and thus the export subsidies are available: the Soviet Union pays less than the EC price and the difference is subsidized by the CAP-EAGGF.

The French government supports Doumeng's aggressive export policy, but across the Channel, the British government is extremely dissatisfied. The United Kingdom perceives the entire situation as one in which the British taxpayers are subsidizing two totally unacceptable groups: (1) the French farmers, and (2) the Soviet armament industry (by paying less for food, the Soviet Union has more funds available for its missile program). Even the institutions within the European Community are at odds, with the European Parliament and the Council of Ministers at opposite ends and with the Commission attempting to hold the middle ground. The sale of surplus EC agricultural commodities, especially butter, to the Soviet Union has only a marginal impact on the reduction of these surpluses, but it is having a much more than marginal impact on the political relationships among certain Community members.

PERFORMANCE AND PROSPECTS OF THE CAP

The Common Agricultural Policy has had mixed results: agricultural production is guaranteed but this had led to vast surpluses; the remaining farmers have seen income levels and standard of living steadily increasing, but at a cost to the European consumer having to pay artificially high prices; a strong food export policy is in operation but with severe political antagonisms. Moreover, the CAP-EAGGF accounts for approximately 60 to 70 percent of the Community's total budget.

The inner logic of the CAP has resulted in staggering agricultural overproduction, even with only about 8 percent of the EC's population now engaged in agriculture, compared to some 25 percent at the time of the CAP's formation. This overproduction can be evidenced by the following figures:[19]

1. At the start of the 1970s, the EC was a net importer of over 20 million metric tons of grain annually. But by 1985, EC net exports of grains and feed reached 18.3 million metric tons—a shift of some 38 million metric tons.

2. EC wheat and wheat flour exports increased some 500 percent since 1970, reaching 17 million metric tons in 1985.

3. The EC's share of world wheat and wheat flour trade increased from 6 percent in 1970 to about 16 percent in 1985.

4. The EC has gone from a net importer of white sugar in 1977 to the world's largest exporter in 1985, with some 5.4 million metric tons.

5. Prior to 1974, the EC was a net importer of beef and veal. The EC is now the largest exporter of beef and veal products.

6. In the mid–1960s, the EC was the world's largest importer of poultry meat; the EC is now the largest exporter, accounting for approximately 36 percent of the world poultry trade.

7. Prior to the inception of the CAP for eggs in 1967, the EC was the world's largest importer, taking in some 1.5 billion eggs annually. The EC is now the world's largest egg exporter, shipping some 2.7 billion eggs annually.

8. The EC is the world's largest dairy exporter, accounting for about 60 percent of world trade.

9. The long-term trend has been for EC production to increase by 1.5 to 2.0 percent annually; consumption has increased by only 0.5 percent. The agricultural surpluses are not going to disappear.

The accession of Greece in January 1981 to the EC and the accession of Spain and Portugal in January 1986 only exacerbate the existing problems. Greece, Spain, and Portugal all have a much higher percentage of farm workers than the other EC countries, and many of the farms are inefficient and in need of modernization. The financial demands on the structural-improvement sector of the EAGGF are rapidly increasing, and the United Kingdom, after complaining for years that it was subsidizing the French farmer, will now have to subsidize the Spanish and Portuguese farmers as well. In addition, the agricultural sector of Greece, Spain, and Portugal only adds to the already vast surpluses of certain commodities (wine and olive oil, in particular).

The CAP will most likely survive although in a modified form. Its real costs—political as well as economic costs—are such that national governments more and more are ready to consider proposals for reform.

NOTES

1. See, for example, William F. Averyt, *Agropolitics in the European Community* (New York: Praeger, 1977); Ian R. Bowler, *Agriculture Under the Common Agricultural Policy* (Manchester, UK: Manchester University Press, 1985); Allan Buckwell et al., *The Costs of the Common Agricultural Policy* (Beckenham, Kent, UK: Croom Helm, 1982); Gordon R. Foxall, *Agricultural Marketing in European Agriculture* (Aldershot, Hants, UK: Gower, 1982); and Brian E. Hill, *The Common Agricultural Policy: Past, Present and Future* (New York: Methuen, 1984).

2. Werner J. Feld, "Two-Tier Policy Making in the EC: The Common Agricultural Policy," chapter 6 (pp. 123–149) of Leon Hurwitz, ed., *Contemporary Perspectives on European Integration* (Westport, Conn.: Greenwood Press, 1980), p. 137.

3. For an extended analysis of this process, see R. F. Talbot, *The Chicken War: An*

International Trade Conflict between the United States and the EEC (Ames, Iowa: Iowa State University Press, 1978).

4. Keesing's Research Report, *The European Communities: Establishment and Growth* (New York: Scribner's, 1975), pp. 82–84.

5. Ibid.

6. Anthony J. C. Kerr, *The Common Market and How It Works* (Elmsford, N.Y.: Pergamon, 1983), pp. 70, 72.

7. As reported by Keith Schneider, "A Grain Glut Has Growers Skirmishing for Markets," *The New York Times* (5 October 1986), Section IV, p. 5.

8. Kerr, p. 218.

9. Barry Newman, "West Germans Take Voyage to Nowhere to Save on Butter," *The Wall Street Journal* (4 September 1981), pp. 1, 10.

10. Ibid., p. 10.

11. H. Peter Dreyer, "U.S., E.C. Exchange Threats on Trade," 256 *Europe* (May 1986), p. 13.

12. Willy De Clercq, cited in ibid.

13. "U.S.–E.C. Farm Trade Accord," 259 *Europe* (September 1986), p. 41.

14. As reported in the *London Times* (8 April 1980), p. 5.

15. Ibid.

16. Ibid.

17. As reported by Paul Lewis, *New York Times* (19 August 1984), pp. F6-F7.

18. Ibid.

19. Doug Bereuter, "Farm Trade: A U.S. Viewpoint," 255 *Europe* (April 1986), p. 14.

8

European Political Cooperation
and a Closer Political Union

The Treaty of Rome is quite explicit about the competence of the European Community as a separate legal entity—an internationally recognized intergovernmental organization existing apart from the collective member-states—to formulate and execute a common foreign or external policy in economic and commercial areas. For example, Article 3(b) has as an explicit Community goal the "establishment of a . . . common commercial policy toward third countries," and Article 3(k) seeks the "association of overseas countries and territories with the Community with a view to increasing trade." This *economic* external policy has been reasonably successful, and in many areas the EC has negotiated as a single entity and been able to coordinate and harmonize positions: the common external tariff has been in place for quite some time and the EC has concluded several trade/commercial agreements with other countries or with groups of countries (e.g., Lomé, Arusha, Yaoundé).

But the EC Treaty is relatively silent about the Community's ability to formulate and execute a common *political* foreign policy or to coordinate external political positions. The only (implicit) mention of "political" cooperation and integration found in the Treaty is in the preamble—more a statement of hope than an explicit requirement: "DETERMINED to establish the foundations of an ever closer union among the European peoples and DECIDED to insure the . . . progress of their countries by common action in eliminating the barriers which divide Europe."

The EC member-states have recognized, however, that "economic" or "commercial" external policy cannot be separated totally from "political" policy, and some efforts, with varying levels of success, have been made to achieve some kind of cooperation and common positions on external political issues. This chapter discusses two areas within this general scope of "political" integration: (1) European Political Cooperation (EPC), and (2) EC policy toward Eastern Europe.

EUROPEAN POLITICAL COOPERATION

The Evolution of European Political Cooperation

European Political Cooperation (EPC) evolved slowly from two related developments that eventually intersected. The first was the slow realization among the members of the European Community that commercial/economic external policy could not be separated from political issues—the EC decision, for example, to extend preferential access to EC markets for Israeli citrus products was most definitely *not* devoid of political considerations. The second development concerned the increasing desire of the EC to "speak with one voice"—this, it was hoped, would give Europe an equal voice in world affairs and counterbalance the two superpowers.

The origins of the EPC framework can be traced to the Fourchet Plans of 1961 and 1962. These plans were formulated by a committee of EC diplomats chaired by Christian Fourchet, then the French ambassador to Denmark. As Werner J. Feld describes the Fourchet Plans (there were two slightly different reports issued by the Fourchet Committee), the main idea was to create a European Council—a meeting of the EC heads of state or government—that would meet approximately three times a year.[1] This council, acting unanimously, would coordinate foreign and defense policies. The Fourchet Plans also envisaged an intergovernmental European Political Commission, having a permanent secretariat and, not surprisingly, a Paris location. This "commission" would be composed of senior officials in the national foreign ministries and would assist the European Council by preparing policy proposals. The proposals offered by the Fourchet Committee, however, were largely ignored for most of the 1960s. The idea of a European Council was eventually instituted—the EC heads of state or government began to have regularly scheduled meetings—but the idea of real political coordination through a "commission" lay dormant.

It was not until the European Council met at The Hague (1–5 December 1969) that the idea of EPC was taken up again in a serious manner. One section of the Final Communiqué of The Hague Summit instructed the EC foreign affairs ministers (as foreign affairs ministers and *not* as the EC Council of Ministers) to recommend ways of achieving progress in "political unification and cooperation."

This European Council directive from The Hague Summit led to the Davignon Report, the real basis for EPC. The Davignon Report, eventually adopted by the EC foreign ministers (but not acting as the EC Council of Ministers) on 27 October 1970, was the result of the deliberations of the Davignon Committee. This committee was composed of senior officials of the national foreign ministries, chaired by Vicomte Etienne Davignon of Belgium. The Davignon Report stated at the outset that a united Europe—whatever its final form may be—had to be "based on a common heritage of respect for the liberty and rights of man and bring together democratic States with freely elected Parliaments.'' The more important proposals made by the Davignon Report included the following:

1. Foreign Ministers should meet at least once every six months;
2. Conferences of Heads of State or Government should be held when deemed desirable but in the event of a serious crisis or special urgency, there should be extraordinary consultation between the Member-States' Governments;
3. The meetings of the foreign ministers should be prepared by a Political Committee; and
4. The European Council's President-in-Office should, once a year, provide the European Parliament with a progress report.[2]

The 1970 Davignon Report established the basic framework of EPC, and it played a large role in the gradual acceptance by national officials of the need to think ''European'' and create a Europe capable of speaking ''with one voice.'' The EPC mechanism—parallel to but separate from the EC mechanism—involves consultation and coordination in those areas of external policy not covered by the Rome Treaties. The EPC mechanism rests upon regularly scheduled meetings of the European Council (heads of state or government), the EC foreign ministers, and the political directors of the national foreign affairs ministries (the Political Committee or the Davignon Committee).

Subsequent meetings of the European Council have refined the basic contents of the Davignon Report. At the Paris Summit of 19–20 October 1972, the EC heads of state or government, including those from the soon to be new members (Denmark, Ireland, and the United Kingdom), announced that the EC foreign ministers would meet four times a year under EPC, instead of only twice, and made more explicit the relationship of the Political Committee to the EC framework. Also, the Luxembourg (1970) and Copenhagen (1973) Reports of the EC foreign ministers made the aims of EPC more precise:

1. To ensure a better mutual understanding of the great international problems; and
2. To strengthen the solidarity of the EC member-states by promoting the harmonization of their views, the coordination of their positions, and, where it appears possible, to engage in common actions.[3]

The European Political Cooperation Process

The EPC process (it is, unfortunately, still more a *process* for multilateral consultation than an avenue for achieving common actions) is a mechanism and structure parallel to the European Community's framework—EPC is theoretically and legally distinct from the EC. But since EPC and the EC rely upon the identical individuals and groups for most of the process (they just wear different labels), and, since, obviously, the members of EPC are identical to the EC

Figure 8.1
European Political Cooperation

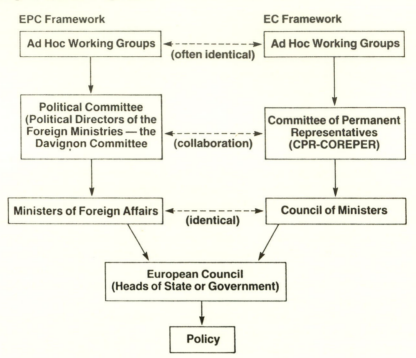

membership, there is no real difficulty in practice in achieving coordination
between the two. But to be precise, EPC is outside the EC framework and it
does not legally represent the European Community as an intergovernmental
organization.

This parallel but almost identical structure is illustrated in Figure 8.1. In both
frameworks, ad hoc working groups within each EC member-state's national
ministries provide information and policy proposals to the next level in the
decision-making/policy-formulation process. These national ad hoc working
groups are frequently identical, depending upon the substance of the specific
issue under consideration. The only real divergence between EPC and the EC
process occurs at the level subsequent to the ad hoc national working groups.
In EPC, the ad hoc groups report to the Political Committee, a group of 12
senior officials (the political directors) of the EC member-states' national foreign
affairs ministries. The Political Committee is frequently referred to as "the
Davignon Committee." In the EC process, the ad hoc working groups report to
the Committee of Permanent Representatives (CPR/COREPER). This latter committee (12 members also) is composed of each EC member-state's ambassador
to the EC at Brussels. These two groups—the Political Committee and CO-

REPER—are separate, with different personnel and different meeting places (COREPER is in Brussels, attached to the EC Council of Ministers, while the Political Committee rotates among the 12 EC capitals), but there is close co-operation, coordination, and consensus formation between the two. The Political Committee–Davignon Committee are very senior personnel (i.e, the political directors) in each EC member-state's foreign affairs ministry, and COREPER members (having full ambassadorial status) are their colleagues.

The subsequent level is identical in both the EC and EPC, although each process/framework assigns a different label to the group and each derives its authority from a different legal text. In the EPC framework, it is the EC foreign ministers who are advised by the Political Committee; in the EC framework, it is the Council of Ministers who are advised by the Committee of Permanent Representatives. These two groups have the *identical* composition—the foreign ministers of the 12 EC countries—but they maintain the fiction of separate and distinct committees. The foreign ministers—whether as the EC Council of Ministers or whether as the EPC's foreign ministers—then provide policy alternatives to the European Council (the heads of state or government of the European Community). The European Council does not bother to maintain the fiction of the legal difference between the EC and EPC, and the Council, in their Final Communiqués, will deal with both EPC and EC matters as a unified whole.

The decision-making process is parallel and although the lines of demarcation are often blurred, the attempt is made to keep the two distinct. Some countries—especially France and the United Kingdom—want to keep political cooperation ("high" politics) separate from Community business ("low" politics). This insistence upon the symbolic distinctiveness of EPC and the EC has, however, led to some illogical consequences. For example, France had insisted that if the Political Committee were to become a permanent institution with its own office space and secretariat, it should not be located in Brussels where COREPER already was housed (the French preferred Paris). This problem was resolved by rotating the place of the Political Committee's meetings among the EC capital cities. Another example is cited by Hugh Arbuthnott and Geoffrey Edwards: "The division between the two [the EPC's foreign ministers and the EC's Council of Ministers] reached its most extreme form in a midday flight from Copenhagen, where Foreign Ministers had met to discuss political cooperation, to Brussels, where they met in the afternoon as the Council of Ministers."[4]

This rigid separation has, however, become blurred in recent years. The foreign ministers now discuss Community affairs in the same room as EPC matters, but not under identical mandates. Rather than flying from one city to another, the foreign ministers simply adjourn their meeting as the Council of Ministers under the EC and then reconvene as the EPC's foreign ministers. But the legal and theoretical demarcation still exists, despite attempts to fuse the two. In December 1975, Leo Tindemans, at that time the Belgian prime minister, issued a report (the Tindemans Report) to the European Union. Tindemans recommended that the facade of separateness between the EPC's foreign ministers and the EC's

Council of Ministers be done away with and that the two be fused by giving the Council of Ministers the competence to act with EPC matters. Tindemans also recommended, however, that the EPC's Political Committee remain distinct from the EC's COREPER.

Tindemans's modest proposal was not accepted by most EC governments. To fuse EPC into the EC at the Council of Ministers level would have meant that the supranational decision-making powers of the EC—limited primarily to economic and commercial matters—would be expanded to include the whole range of political (and perhaps defense) foreign policy questions. The EC member-governments are quite willing to transfer national sovereignty to the EC in limited areas such as commercial trading agreements, but they are not willing to do the same in external political affairs. One of the main reasons for this hesitation is that the governments are still free agents in EPC—the countries will adopt common positions and common actions when it is possible; if it is not possible, each country is free to determine its own position. Within the EC, on the other hand, unanimity is not required for all decisions, and some countries may have to implement a policy that is not supported. Thus European Political Cooperation remains theoretically distinct from EC procedures although, in practical terms, coordination between EPC and the EC is satisfactory more often than not.

The Political Committee

The Political Committee within the EPC framework is composed of the political directors of the 12 foreign ministries of the EC member-states.[5] Reporting to this committee are various ad hoc working groups of experts; these latter groups investigate particular problems and recommend possible solutions. The Political Committee's meeting place is rotated among each member-country in accordance with whichever country is then chairing the EC's Council of Ministers (the chair rotates every six months). The chair of the Political Committee also rotates, changing every six months.

The EC member-governments can request the Political Committee to consider a wide range of policy issues. These issues are not limited to general foreign-policy questions, but can also include matters that would appear suited for EC-COREPER deliberations. When the Political Committee discusses EC matters, the EC Commission is then invited to submit its own position paper and is often invited to send a representative to the meeting. As discussed below in this chapter, it was felt that the Political Committee's discussions regarding the Conference on Security and Cooperation in Europe (the 1974 Helsinki Agreement) was likely to deal with matters within the competence of the EC in the international trade area. Thus an EC Commission representative was invited, and Franco Malfatti, then president of the commission, participated in some of the meetings.

Although the member-states of the European Community have not been able to achieve total position coordination or common actions in all areas, the Political

Committee has been reasonably successful in establishing a coordination *process* (but not its *substance*). Some of these activities include the following:

1. An average of some 100 communications transmitted every week over a common telex system called COREU.
2. More than 100 sessions of common working-groups composed of national diplomats to analyze important international problems.
3. Political Committee meetings are held twice a month to exchange information about the work and operations of the various foreign ministries that are relevant to EPC. A "crisis procedure" is in the planning stage that will assure meetings of the Committee within 48 hours.
4. Representation of the EC members at international conferences and in IGOs is carried out by *one* delegation.
5. Consultation among diplomatic missions of the EC countries has been placed on an institutionalized basis in various third-country capitals to coordinate positions and actions.[6]

European Political Cooperation Outputs

The rate of success of the EPC process has been mixed. The mechanism has been involved in a number of issues over the years, but real accomplishments have been quite limited. This section discusses some of these issues: (1) the Conference on Security and Cooperation in Europe; (2) the Euro-Arab Dialogue; and (3) cooperation in the area of military defense policies.

The Conference on Security and Cooperation in Europe

One of the more successful results (successful in terms of the process; not, however, in terms of objective behavior change by the Soviet Union) of European Political Cooperation can be seen in the multilateral Conference on Security and Cooperation in Europe (CSCE or, as it is more popularly known, the 1974 Helsinki Agreement). The CSCE was both a contributor to, and a consequence of, the process of East-West détente begun with the Nixon administration, but which has been rather moribund in the last few years since the Reagan administration. The agreement was intended to decrease tension in a divided Europe and extend the policy of détente and cooperation into military, economic, political, and scientific affairs. It was also designed, at least from the West's viewpoint, to strengthen and protect individual human rights in the Eastern bloc. The CSCE's final act was signed after lengthy negotiations in Helsinki in 1974, and important follow-up meetings were held in Belgrade (1977–1978) and Madrid (1980–1981), with continuing meetings held in various European cities (the most recent being Vienna in November 1986).

Three major chapters or "baskets" make up the CSCE agreement. The first "basket" of the Final Helsinki Act is titled "Questions Relating to Security in Europe," and it includes a section on "Declaration on Principles Guiding Relations Between Participating States.'' Basket one also includes a document on military confidence-building measures and certain aspects of security and disarmament. The 10 principles of basket one express the basic precepts of international behavior that have traditionally been accepted in the conduct of international relations. Some of these principles concern the peaceful settlement of disputes, nonintervention in internal affairs, and the recognition of human rights and fundamental freedoms. The sections on confidence-building measures and certain aspects of security and disarmament also call for more cooperation and tension-lessening activities. The signatory states are expected to give each other prior notification of major (more than 25,000 troops) military maneuvers, smaller-scale military maneuvers, and major military movements. The increased exchange of observers and military visits are also included in basket one.

Basket two is titled, ''Cooperation in the Fields of Economics, of Science and Technology, and of the Environment.'' The 35 signatory states are expected to improve the quantity and quality of useful, published economic and commercial information—output statistics, export-import figures, trade laws, foreign trading organizations, etc. Scientific exchanges and joint research efforts were to be encouraged and high-level multinational meetings were envisaged to deal with transnational air pollution.

Basket three of the Final Helsinki Act contains a wide range of provisions with a common objective—the freer flow of peoples, ideas, and information. It is this particular basket that relates to the lives of private individuals and seeks to resolve the humanitarian problems arising from a divided Europe. Specific provisions relate to the reunification of families and contacts and regular visits on the basis of family ties; marriage between citizens of different countries; travel for personal or professional reasons; religious contacts; cultural exchanges; and the dissemination of information (journalists, book publishing, journals, films, and broadcasting).

Even though principle six of basket one (''non-intervention in internal affairs'') is cited by the Soviet Union and other Warsaw Pact countries in the attempt to stifle Western insistence upon full implementation of all provisions (especially those in basket three), the West maintains that principle six does not release countries from fully implementing the human rights provisions. The US position at the Belgrade meeting—joined in its entirety by the European Community—can be summarized as follows:

The full implementation of all provisions of the Helsinki Final Act is essential to the successful development of detente and of security and cooperation in Europe; Human rights and humanitarian issues are a major, integral aspect of the CSCE process as well as of detente; Individual states will be held accountable for their implementation failures, both at future CSCE meetings and in the eyes of world opinion; The United States and other CSCE states [the EC] will not hesitate, and indeed consider it important, to point out specific examples of implementation failures which threaten the health and credibility of the CSCE process; [and] Efforts to mask implementation shortcomings with the cloak of nonintervention in internal affairs will not deflect legitimate criticism of a country's implementation record.[7]

The CSCE may not have been very successful, but the EPC process was a remarkable achievement. The EPC framework coordinated the EC's position, first among itself and then with the United States, both for the negotiations at Helsinki and for the various follow-up meetings. And, as mentioned above, the EC Commission actively participated in the EPC process, with former EC Commission president, Franco Malfatti, being invited into the EPC deliberations. The CSCE was an excellent example of European Political Cooperation and coordination with the EC process.

The Euro-Arab Dialogue

The Euro-Arab Dialogue (EAD) was a consequence of the 1973 Yom Kippur War and the resulting Arab oil policy. Here, the EPC mechanism was used in conjunction with the EC's external trade and commercial policy. The EAD is basically a mechanism to seek greater cooperation between the EC and its member-states on the one side, and the members of the Arab League on the other side. Established in Cairo in 1975, the organizations of the EAD are as follows:

1. The general committee (ambassadorial level), which establishes general guidelines for the Dialogue, meets about twice a year, mainly in restricted sessions (without minutes). Chairmanship is held jointly by the heads of the Arab and European delegations; and

2. The working committees (expert level) submits specific proposals and recommendations to the general committee before embarking on their execution. They are equally cochaired by the two sides. Seven have been set up so far: Agriculture and Rural Development; Industrialization; Infrastructure; Financial Cooperation; Culture, Labor, and Social Affairs; Trade; and Scientific and Technological Cooperation. They may meet at any agreed time, alternatively in Europe and in an Arab country. They are entitled to form specialized groups to carry out specific tasks.[8]

The EAD, at least on the European side, is a hybrid. Economic cooperation falls within the EC's competence, but the political cooperation aspect is within the EPC. The dialogue has been reasonably successful in the economic area. The EC has substantial two-way trade with the Arab states: the EC buys approximately 40 to 50 percent of the Arab League's exports (more than the US, the USSR and Eastern Europe, and Japan combined) and the Community supplies about 50 percent of the Arab League's imports (again, more than the US, the USSR and Eastern Europe, and Japan combined). The EAD economic cooperation and development assistance has also been relatively successful, with nine approved projects, including the development of the Juba Valley in Somalia and the establishment of meat production in the Sudan. Financing of these projects is divided on an approximate ratio of five to the Arab League and one to the EC.

But not much real progress has been made within the EAD on "political" issues. Although the EC opposes continued Israeli occupation of the West Bank and has refused to establish its delegation in Jerusalem (thus moving it from Tel Aviv) and repeatedly stated that a solution of the Middle East conflict will be possible only "if the legitimate rights of the Palestinian people to give effective expression to its national identity is translated into fact,"[9] the Arab League believes that these steps do not go far enough. It demands that the European Community suspend totally its economic assistance and tariff preferences now enjoyed by Israel—a demand that every institution within the EC framework has consistently rejected.

The Euro-Arab Dialogue, in reality, follows the fortunes of Arab cooperation itself. After the Camp David Agreement, the EAD was suspended for some time because of severe disagreement within the Arab world over Egypt's treaty with Israel. The shifting alliances concerning the Lebanese Civil War and the war between Iran and Iraq (which began in September 1980) have also limited the EAD's effectiveness. European Political Cooperation is in place with the EAD, but there is yet to evolve a common, unified foreign policy on the Middle East and on the European countries' relations with Israel.

Military Defense Cooperation

The Rome Treaty is totally silent about any type of European Community coordination/cooperation in military defense matters. The EC, as an IGO, does *not* engage in common military defense policy: there is no defense portfolio in the EC Commission and military defense policy is firmly and totally within the national prerogative. An earlier attempt at defense integration—the ill-fated European Defense Community—has not been revived. But these comments do not mean that the EC member-states do not engage in any cooperation or coordination in military defense areas; on the contrary, most EC states are also members of other organizations that do pursue such common actions. NATO is the best known of these parallel organizations, but this section discusses two much lesser known organizations: the EUROGROUP and the Independent European Program Group (IEPG).

EUROGROUP. It was established as an informal grouping of European governments within the framework of NATO.[10] All the members of the EC except France and Ireland are members; the non-EC members are Norway and Turkey. The basic aim of EUROGROUP is to strengthen the Western alliance by ensuring that the European contribution to the common defense is as strong and cohesive as possible. It accomplishes this in two ways: by providing an informal forum in which defense ministers can exchange views on major political and strategic questions and by fostering practical cooperation through the work of specialized subgroups.

EUROGROUP's working arrangements are flexible and pragmatic. Meetings of defense ministers provide the focal point for its work. They meet twice a year, just before the regular ministerial session of NATO's Defense Planning Committee, to discuss important defense issues and consider reports from the specialized subgroups. EUROGROUP's chair rotates each year. Below the ministerial level, work is coordinated and ministerial meetings prepared by an ad hoc committee of EUROGROUP ambassadors at NATO headquarters in Brussels. For day-to-day affairs, the main working body is the Staff Group, composed of officials from the national delegations at NATO. The United Kingdom provides EUROGROUP's Secretariat.

There are various subgroups within EUROGROUP, each with a specific area of activity. These subgroups are as follows:

1. EUROCOM, founded in 1970 under Netherland's chairmanship to deal with the interoperability of tactical communications systems;
2. EUROLOG, established in 1970 under British chairmanship to develop closer cooperation in the logistic field;
3. EUROLONGTERM, established in 1972 under Netherland's chairmanship to prepare joint concepts of operation and outline specifications for equipment;
4. EUROMED, established in 1972 under Belgian chairmanship to increase coordination in the military medical field;
5. EURONAD, in which the national armaments directors of the member-countries meet under Netherlands's chairmanship to encourage closer cooperation in the procurement of defense equipment; and
6. EUROTRAINING, established in 1970 under West German chairmanship to improve and expand existing training facilities and initiate and develop new bi- and multilateral training arrangements among member-nations to the point at which one nation can assume the responsibility for training in specific fields on behalf of all or some of the countries.

Independent European Program Group (IEPG). This is the principal institution through which the European members of NATO (Iceland is *not* a member of the IEPG, but France is) seek greater cooperation in armaments procurement.[11] The IEPG is independent of both NATO and the EUROGROUP. It was established in 1976 and its major objectives are as follows:

1. To permit the most efficient use of funds for research, development, and procurement;
2. To increase standardization and interoperability of equipment;
3. To maintain a healthy European defense industrial and technological base; and
4. To encourage a better balanced two-way street in armaments cooperation between Europe and North America.

The most successful IEPG venture to date has been the collaborative project among West Germany, Italy, and the United Kingdom to develop and produce the Tornado multirole combat aircraft. The IEPG, in face of the overwhelming imbalance of trade in military equipment between the United States and Europe (the United States sells about six to seven times more military equipment to its European partners than the Europeans do to the United States), also lobbies for increased European sales to the United States. The IEPG feels that this is the only way the European countries can maintain a sophisticated defense industry capability.

EUROPEAN COMMUNITY POLICY TOWARD EASTERN EUROPE

There are many areas that could be employed to illustrate European Community political cooperation (or lack thereof) on foreign-policy questions: the Israeli-Arab dispute (Denmark and the Netherlands continue to offer strong support for Israel); the EC response to the United Kingdom's plea for solidarity against Argentina over the Falklands/Malvinas (Ireland and Italy refused Britain's plea);[12] the debate over imposing economic sanctions against South Africa (Margaret Thatcher prefers "constructive diplomacy" over sanctions); or the reaction to the American call for sanctions against Libya (the EC refuses to impose sanctions). Such examples highlight the difficulties in achieving a unified policy position across the EC but, also, they do demonstrate that the European Community has been able to achieve some limited success in certain specific areas.

It is quite difficult, however, to write about European foreign policy toward the East European communist bloc without linking such policies and behavior to EC–US and to US–USSR relations. That there is a triangular relationship here is not disputed; all three sides are interrelated, and the form and substance of one relationship most assuredly affect the other two. That there is a perceived partnership between the United States and the countries of the Community is also not disputed; there are several questions, however, as to the exact nature of this partnership.

Historically, the United States has approached the partnership as being first among equals in a somewhat unequal relationship. Europe was seen as the junior partner, simply expected to follow whatever initiatives the Americans proposed. In exchange, Europe would be protected by the American nuclear shield; the extent to which these American initiatives were congruent only with the American national interest and not the European interest was not seen as a relevant factor. President Carter, although the first US president to recognize the inherent inequities in such a relationship, nonetheless continued to regard the European Community as a junior partner. The Reagan administration, refusing even to recognize the unequal relationship, has attempted several times to force the EC to automatically fall in line behind whatever the current US policy vis-à-vis the Soviet Union happened to be. One such example of the Reagan approach was the president's announcement of the embargo on sales of pipeline technology and equipment to the Soviet Union.

There were two major problems with the American-inspired pipeline embargo: (1) it was directed at legally independent European subsidiaries and licensees of

US firms—a blatant attempt to extend US law to corporations under the jurisdiction and sovereignty of other states; and (2) the embargo was announced
without any prior notification or consultation—it was not discussed at the recently
concluded Versailles Economic Summit Meeting but, rather, President Reagan
simply stated it as policy and expected France, West Germany, and the United
Kingdom to follow suit. Significant segments of European industry were threatened—orders on hand from the Soviet Union totaled about $10 billion—and the
European Community did not perceive the pipeline embargo as furthering its
national interest.

For several years, decades in fact, Europe had acquiesced in serving in this
relatively subservient role. Over the past few years, however, the EC has perceived the US–EC partnership in a different light and begun to strike out on a
more independent path. The European view of the partnership now insists that
differences of opinion must be recognized and tolerated within the partnership.
Fernand Spaak comments on this new approach:

There is nothing necessarily wrong with the fact that Europe and the United States differ
in their perception of an international event or their responses to it. It would be neither
a healthy nor even a credible partnership if we always marched in lock-step. The important
thing is that we both understand the differences of one another's approaches and accept
that these are but minor differences. If, on either side, we choose to systematically treat
any variation in our views or attitudes as major differences, we shall be giving others
the opportunity to drive a wedge between us.[13]

There most certainly are differences in their approaches, and the United States
and the European Community are not marching in lockstep; to call these approaches "minor differences" is an exercise in verbal legerdemain. The focus
of this discussion of a common EC foreign policy is not upon these "minor"
differences; it concerns EC–East European relations although the United States
always remains lurking in the background. The main problem, however, in trying
to discuss EC or "European" relations with Eastern Europe (or with any other
geographical area) is well stated in the quip by Henry Kissinger: "Who do you
call up when you want to talk with Europe?" There are simply too many independent actors, each with their own objectives and constituencies: the 12
sovereign member-state governments of the EC and the various EC institutions
themselves. The 12 members of the Community most certainly do not have a
unified policy position on most external questions, and there have been some
all-too-obvious and all-too-vocal recent antagonisms between the views of the
directly elected European Parliament, on the one side, and the Council of Ministers, on the other, with the EC Commission often caught in the middle. "Europe" may not be in total disarray, but the component parts have engaged in
precious little coordination.

The comments below present a brief overview of some recent developments
in European relations with Eastern Europe: the EC reactions to the December

1979 Soviet invasion of Afghanistan; the American-led boycott of the 1980 Moscow Summer Olympics (repaid in full by the USSR in 1984 at Los Angeles); and some aspects of East-West trade and commercial policy. Some conclusions are then offered on the coordination of the decision-making process within the European Community on foreign-policy questions.

Afghanistan and the Olympics

The Soviet invasion of Afghanistan on 26 December 1979, the subsequent American demands for an embargo on grain and technology exports to the USSR, and President Carter's call for a boycott of the Moscow Olympics severely tested the Atlantic Alliance and its assumed partnership. The invasion also highlighted the increasingly independent stance the European Community had been pursuing with Eastern Europe over the past few years. And, unfortunately, the invasion also highlighted the inability of the EC to coordinate policy positions in several areas.

Afghanistan

The Soviet invasion of Afghanistan clearly brought to light the shortcomings of European political cooperation and foreign-policy coordination. Although there was a formal political cooperation network that linked the members' foreign offices, there were no provisions for ad hoc or emergency meetings and, therefore, Europe's initial collective reaction was rather slow. The immediate result was that the individual governments took the first action. Unfortunately, the three biggest powers—the United Kingdom, France, and West Germany—all had different views of the problem of Afghanistan, as well as of East-West relations in general, and it was not surprising that they reacted in different ways.

The United Kingdom reacted in almost the identical terms as the United States. Prime Minister Thatcher gave almost automatic support to *most* American policies vis-à-vis the Soviet Union. This support did not extend to President Reagan's embargo on pipeline equipment and technology, however. Significant sectors of the British economy were threatened by the pipeline embargo—the John Brown Group of Scotland had 1,700 workers in the depressed Clydebank area dependent on orders for 21 turbines. But British economic interests were not threatened in the Afghan situation, and the United Kingdom quickly echoed President Carter's lead: support the trade embargo and boycott the Olympics as a symbol of Western solidarity in the face of Soviet aggression. The Conservative Thatcher government was very wary about détente long before Afghanistan, and a "get tough with the Russians" policy neatly dovetailed with the prime minister's reputation as the "Iron Lady." The United Kingdom, even after being in the European Community since 1973, has not reduced its acceptance of American hegemony, and it remains the most pro-American country among the members of the EC.

France, compared to the United Kingdom, was at the opposite pole. Ever since Charles de Gaulle, France has evidenced a more independent foreign policy: an independent foreign policy toward the United States, the USSR, the Third World, and even toward her sister Community members. The withdrawal from NATO's integrated military-command structure in 1966 showed that France was convinced that its national interests would be best served by being independent of the superpowers. In addition, France at the time had a significantly greater amount of trade with the USSR than did the United Kingdom, and such trade was increasing at a rather rapid rate. Following an agreement signed in June 1977 between French President Giscard d'Estaing and Leonid Brezhnev to triple trade between the two countries by 1981, the 1979 French exports to the USSR were approximately 40 percent more than in 1978. France was also importing considerable amounts of Soviet energy, and in January 1980—less than one month after the Soviet invasion of Afghanistan—France began to consume Soviet natural gas when a pipeline was completed.[14] Thus France was reluctant to join any kind of trade war or embargo against the Soviet Union. The French of course did not support or even condone the invasion of Afghanistan, but their initial reactions were very tentative—they did not endorse the American embargo or the proposed Olympic boycott, actions that were so warmly endorsed by the British.

The last of the "big" three—West Germany—also had some very hesitant initial reactions. An argument could be made, in fact, that it was the Federal Republic of Germany that began East-West détente in the 1960s with the *Ostpolitik* of Willy Brandt, a policy followed by Helmut Schmidt and not repudiated by Chancellor Kohl. West Germany may be one of the very few countries in the West that has seen some concrete results from the policy of détente, and it was obvious that Chancellor Schmidt did not wish to throw away these benefits. Germany's trade with the Soviet Union was larger than was France's (and, obviously, larger than the United Kingdom's), and its exports to all Eastern European countries were approximately six times larger, as measured as a percentage of gross national product, than America was exporting to the same countries. Relations with the German Democratic Republic were becoming less antagonistic: trade with East Germany was increasing; family reunifications were numerous; some 200,000 ethnic Germans from the Eastern bloc had entered West Germany since the early 1970s; Berlin was no longer a city of tension. Chancellor Schmidt did not want to undercut these benefits of détente, and thus his initial reactions were very similar to those of the French: we cannot condone the invasion but we will not join the trade embargo.

In the first few weeks after the invasion, therefore, "Europe" spoke in many voices from uncertain and tentative governments (except the British). It was not until late January and February 1980 that the EC institutions reacted officially and publicly to the invasion. The EC Council of Ministers verbally attacked the Soviet Union in mid-January by describing the invasion as a "flagrant interference in the internal affairs of a non-aligned country . . . and . . . a threat to peace, security, and stability in the region, including the Indian sub-continent, the Middle East, and the Arab World [and called for] the immediate and uncondi- tional withdrawal of all foreign troops from Afghanistan."[15]

Although not joining the American grain embargo, the Council of Ministers accepted a proposal from the EC Commission to "monitor" (i.e., to receive information only) all Community cereal exports to the Soviet Union in order to (symbolically) prevent European farmers from increasing grain exports to fill the gap brought on by the American embargo. The Council of Ministers also suspended the guaranteed export subsidies, a part of the Common Agricultural Policy, on sales of surplus EC butter to the Soviet Union.

The European Parliament took the strongest stance within the EC institutional framework. A 15 February 1980 EP resolution called upon the governments of the EC countries to boycott the Moscow Summer Olympics as well as for a total embargo on the export of surplus EC agricultural commodities to the Soviet Union. A related EP resolution—an exercise in futile symbolic politics—con- demned the restrictive measures taken against Andrei Sakharov, the Soviet dis- sident. The European Parliament's pleas fell upon deaf ears, both within the EC and in the USSR. At the 19 February 1980 political cooperation meeting in Rome, the EC foreign ministers (acting as the foreign ministers under EPC and *not* as the EC Council of Ministers) ignored the Parliament's resolutions and simply called for a "neutral" Afghanistan.

The Soviet invasion of Afghanistan illustrated two significant issues within European and EC foreign-policy coordination and decision making: The Euro- peans are quite reluctant to forgo détente—they did not "sweep" détente "under the afghan"—and, while paying lip service (especially the French and the Ger- mans) to the United States, Europe is hesitant to take concrete action. The second point is perhaps more significant because the European Community as an insti- tution was slow in reacting and formulating a response. That there was a political crisis was not disputed, but the Community was unable to offer a unified and rapid response. The EC must ensure that in similar future situations there would be an immediate, if not automatic, consultation among the EC foreign ministers. Such immediate and institutionalized consultation would strengthen the political cooperation network and obviously give greater legitimacy to whatever particular policy was agreed upon. Finally, the extreme differences in policy preferences between the European Parliament and the Council of Ministers might lead to future problems, especially if the Parliament ever attempts to implement its resolutions.

The 1980 Moscow Summer Olympics

The problem with the United States–inspired boycott of the Moscow Olympics was that it was tinged with moral trappings and overtones of human rights. If these had not been present, however, the boycott would have had all the char- acteristics of a poorly produced farce. President Carter, displeased with the Soviet refusal to withdraw from Afghanistan, simply announced that the United States was not going to Moscow. The American athletes would not attend the party, and this would punish the Soviet Union, humiliate them, and would dilute the significance of the spectacle. The United States then expected other countries, especially the members of the European Community, to follow suit. The European response to the Olympic boycott was worse than a farce—it was an opera buffo in 21 acts: the European Parliament, the EC Commission, the Council of Ministers, the nine member-goverments, *and* the nine national Olympic committees.

The United States latched on to the Olympic issue as a great moral crusade and employed it as symbolic politics. Participation by American athletes (or, for that matter, by athletes from any other democratic country) would by their very presence in Moscow confer legitimacy on the Soviet Union's actions in Afghanistan and thereby hand a huge propaganda and ideological victory to the Soviet Union. The presence of American athletes in Moscow, but *not* the presence of the American ambassador or businessmen, while the dissidents were being rounded up and locked away, was seen to be against the American national interest. The boycott would demonstrate in clear terms the will of the West in the face of aggression and, by extension, would strengthen the cause of democracy. The president spoke, Congress concurred, the American national Olympic committee obeyed, the athletes stayed home, and NBC was left holding the patriotic bag.

Action by the Community institutions showed a mixed response. In a very surprising show of solidarity with the American posture, the European Parliament, on 15 February 1980, passed a resolution that called upon the EC member-states to boycott the Moscow games. But the Parliament, too, was engaged in symbolic politics—the resolution was only a statement of hope because the Parliament had absolutely no role in any decision concerning the Olympics. The resolution read, in part: "We beseech the nine goverments to show their disapproval in the face of Soviet oppression and aggression in Afghanistan by counseling their national Olumpic committees to ask their teams and their athletes not to participate in the Moscow Olympic Games."[16]

The EC Commission took no "official" position since the Olympics fell beyond the Commission's area of competence (a fact that did not deter the EP). But the Commission's current vice-president, Wilhelm Haferkamp, was present at the Parliament's debate on the boycott, and it was reported that he personally supported the boycott. Haferkamp compared the 1980 Moscow games to those held in Berlin in 1936 and, as those people paid homage to the Nazis and Hitler, such homage and respect should not be accorded to the Soviet Union in 1980.[17]

The EC foreign ministers, at their 19 February 1980 political-cooperation meeting in Rome, ignored the entire issue by rejecting a proposed ministerial statement that would have "favorably noted" the Parliament's resolution. But these activities and statements (or lack thereof) by the Community institutions, while perhaps having some public relations function, were not really relevant. The whole question of the Olympic boycott belonged to the individual member-governments, and attention thus shifted to the nine governments and their national Olympic committees.

The governments' response was at first sympathetic to the proposed boycott, but as time passed—and as the deadline for a final decision approached—the initial support began to falter. At first, some of the governments (the United Kingdom and the Netherlands) agreed to the boycott; others (Belgium, Italy, Luxembourg, and West Germany) said they would support the boycott only if all the other Community members did; still others (France) came out flatly against the boycott. All left the formal decision to their own national Olympic committee: some governments (the United Kingdom and West German, in particular) attempted to influence their committees; other governments did not intervene. Chancellor Schmidt favored the boycott, and he was able to sway the German national Olympic committee not to send the German athletes to Moscow. West Germany was, however, the only country of the Nine that stayed away; the remaining eight went to Moscow. The American-inspired boycott was not a total failure, however, because the US was able to pick up some support. About 60 countries stayed away, the most notable (other than the Federal Republic of Germany) being Canada, Japan, Israel, Norway, and Egypt.

The most comical act in this opera buffo was played out in London. Prime Minister Thatcher promptly and heartily endorsed President Carter's call for the boycott, and, in fact, she even outdid the president in elevating the issue to the level of high-state politics and in presenting the moral arguments. The script of this particular act in the United Kingdom presents a good illustration of the United Kingdom's view of the Soviet Union and of their perception of the Olympic Games in the aftermath of the Soviet invasion of Afghanistan.

In an editorial titled "Piling on the Pressure," the *London Times* went to the heart of the matter. The British athletes were put in the firing line because they were about to join, at least according to the official view, an event out of which the Soviet Union would reap huge propaganda benefits. Perhaps the Olympics would collapse, and this hoped-for situation would be a slap in the Soviet face for all the world to see. The *Times* recognized that the participation of the athletes would not imply an endorsement of Soviet policy, but this was dismissed as irrelevant; also irrelevant was the fact that the athletes were being singled out to carry the message (diplomatic contacts and trade were countinuing as usual). Rather, the *Times* wrote: "The Government is undeniably putting strong and increasing pressure on athletes and their representatives to conform to its wishes. It has lifted the question of attendance at the Moscow games to the level of a matter of state. It has indicated where the national interest lies, and it expects responsible citizens to act accordingly."[18]

On 17 March 1980, Prime Minister Thatcher brought the boycott issue to the floor at Westminster. Although the issue was portrayed as a matter of state, the vote itself was a vote of conscience (a free vote in which each individual MP was given the rare opportunity to vote on personal rather than party lines). The Conservative government scored a morale-boosting victory in the Commons when its motion—criticizing the Soviet invasion of Afghanistan and urging that the United Kingdom should not take part in the Olympic Games in Moscow— was supported by 315 votes to 147, a majority of 168. A second motion that urged that the British athletes be allowed to make up their own minds about going to Moscow was defeated 305 votes to 188, a majority of 117 for Prime Minister Thatcher.

The floor debate prior to the 17 March 1980 votes showed the extent to which 315 MPs saw the Olympic boycott as an effective and significant response to Soviet aggression. The following statements were quite representative of the feelings within the Commons:

The Russians regard the Olympics as a political orgy in glorification of Soviet foreign and domestic policies. Those who go in quest of devalued gold in Moscow will be paying tribute to the guardians of the world's greatest concentration camp. [Winston Churchill, Conservative]

To go . . . would give the appearance of condoning a naked act of aggression of a most brutal nature and would be wrong in the national interest and in the interest of the free world. The feelings of the athletes are perfectly understandable although they were mistaken and thoughtless. The athletes are entitled to guidance from their administrators. [Geoffrey Ripon, Labor]

The Government believes that non-participation . . . offers Western countries the single most effective way of bringing home to the Soviet regime and the Russian people our refusal to accept their occupation of Afghanistan. [Sir Ian Gilmour, Lord Privy Seal][19]

Armed with this symbolic vote in Parliament, the British government then began to apply the not-so-subtle pressure on its national Olympic committee. A whole series of ministerial speeches, laden with moral arguments, were directed at the athletes and their organizations to join the boycott. One of the more representative moral arguments was offered by Norman St. John-Stevas, leader of the Commons and chancellor of the duchy of Lancaster. St. John-Stevas was able to link together in five short sentences the 1936 Olympics, Nazi aggression, the domino theory, Soviet aggression in Afghanistan, the Moscow Olympics, *and* probable future Soviet aggression.

In 1936, the participation by most of the independent countries of the world at the Berlin Olympics was, without doubt, a big propaganda boost for the Hitler-Nazi regime. It greatly disillusioned those opponents of Nazism who were already being persecuted. Less than two years after those Olympic Games the Germans were invading Austria and Czechoslovakia. The parallel is too strong to be ignored by those responsible in Britain for taking these decisions. Britain's athletes should not go to Moscow.[20]

Even Prince Philip, the Duke of Edinburgh, entered the fray, but to the extreme embarrassment of Prime Minister Thatcher. The duke had been attending a meeting of several international sports federations in Lausanne in his private capacity as president of the International Equestrian Federation. The Lausanne meeting unanimously, thereby including the duke, came out against the boycott. The Lausanne statement read that a boycott of a sporting event was an "improper method to use in trying to obtain a political end," and the sports federations protested the pressure put on national Olympic committees to boycott the games—such measures "could have disastrous consequences for the future of world sport." Buckingham Palace denied a charge that it was the duke himself who motivated the statement, but it could not explain away the fact that it was passed unanimously.

After the arguments died down, however, the British Olympic Committee ignored the government's pressure and authorized the British athletes to go to Moscow (Prince Philip had enough political sense to stay home). The symbolism reached all the way to Moscow, however, because some lip service was paid to Prime Minister Thatcher: the British team marched under the Olympic flag, not under the Union Jack, and the Olympic anthem was played to celebrate British victories instead of "God Save the Queen." The opera buffo was well played in London.

The Olympic boycott clearly showed that the European Community believed that there were more important, useful, and significant ways to influence Soviet behavior and voice displeasure over the invasion of Afghanistan than preventing athletes from going to Moscow. As a response, collective or singly, to Soviet behavior, the Olympic Games were for the Community—except for the West German government and athletes and the British government—a nonresponse. It was not that European political cooperation failed in this situation; the EPC mechanism was not even activated, and each country followed its own self-identified national interest.

East-West Trade

The American Approach

The issue of East-West trade is a growing element in the triangular relationship among the United States, the Soviet Union, and the European Community (and its still-sovereign member states). Traditionally, the United States has viewed such trade as an important political and diplomatic tool and not as an economic process. The United States would punish the Soviet Union for "bad" behavior by withholding trade; "good" behavior would be rewarded by consenting to engage in trade. The Nixon-Kissinger policy of détente, followed by President Carter until Afghanistan, clearly evidenced this approach; now that the Soviet Union was on good behavior, the Americans would reward them by allowing trade. This trade, however, basically was a one-way flow because the United States exported far more to the USSR than it imported.

The American perception of employing trade with the USSR in a reward-punishment framework continued with the embargo on grain and technology exports in the aftermath of Afghanistan. The US grain embargo, however, was neither effective nor total. Other grain-exporting countries, especially Argentina, easily made up the shortfall and even the United States continued to sell grain to the Soviet Union. In July 1980, the US Department of Agriculture announced that the Soviet Union had bought some 200,000 metric tons of US grain under the terms of an agreement signed before the embargo was imposed. Presidential candidate Reagan stated his opposition to the grain embargo, and, as president, Reagan ended it. Apparently more concerned with the economic situation (and potential voting patterns) of American farmers than with the 1,700 workers in Clydebank (who do not vote in American elections), President Reagan followed through with the promise made in his nomination-acceptance speech that he would end the grain embargo forthwith: ''Why should the American farmer suffer—no one else is.''

Recently, in November 1985, some of the largest American banks (First National of Chicago, Morgan Guaranty, Bankers Trust, and Irving Trust) quietly and without public ceremony started to lend money to the soviet Union again.[21] About $400 million was lent at unusually low interest rates in order to allow the USSR to buy American and Canadian grain (a Canadian bank was also involved with the loans). The American government's public stance may be against trade with the Soviet Union, but, underneath it all, it's business as usual. The European Community is well aware that American public rhetoric is far different than American actions.

Although President Reagan ended the grain embargo, the United States still perceives trade with the Soviet Union in a reward-punishment framework. This approach is not limited to national policymakers: the governor of Ohio banned the sale for several months of Soviet vodka in the state-controlled liquor stores to punish the Soviets for their misdeeds. An excellent example of this American approach to East-West trade can be seen in the 1975 Trade Reform Act, which is still in force and contains the Jackson-Vanik Amendment.[22] The Jackson-Vanik Amendment linked the granting of most-favored-nation (MFN) status for the Soviet Union to increased levels of emigration from the Soviet Union, especially the emigration of Soviet Jews and other minorities, and in no uncertain terms required ''good'' behavior from the Soviet Union before the United States would condescend to trade with it.

Through a convoluted process involving public and private groups—Jewish and non-Jewish—the US Congress entered the controversy.[23] Led by Charles Vanik in the House and Henry Jackson in the Senate (both non-Jews), both houses showed overwhelming support to employ whatever power and influence they may have had to protect the Soviet Jews from their own government and, at the same time, to emphasize the reward-punishment approach to Soviet trade. The amendment was tacked on to the East-West Trade Bill, a bill describing the conditions of trade between the United States and nonmarket economies (i.e., communist states). The House approved Vanik's amendment by a vote of 319 to 80 in December 1984, and the entire Trade Bill passed 272 to 140. The senate approved Jackson's identical amendment 88 to 0, and the Trade Reform Act passed 77 to 4. The final bill, including the amendment, was signed by President Ford on 3 January 1975.

The Jackson-Vanik Amendment explicitly linked American trade benefits to the emigration policies of nonmarket-economy states. The amendment prohibits the administration from granting MFN status—the conditions of trade (long-term, guaranteed government credits and investment guarantees) will be identical to the country most favored by the United States—to any country that denied their citizens the right to emigrate or charged more than a "normal" fee for an exit visa.

The Soviet reaction was predictable. They rejected the entire concept as blatant and undue interference in a country's internal affairs (proscribed by both the UN Charter and the CSCE) and claimed that the United States had no legitimate right to even attempt to try to influence their domestic policies. The Soviet Union, however, was put in a bind: to receive the needed credits, they would have to allow unhindered (Jewish) emigration, but there would be severe political costs attached to such emigration, any one of which would have been sufficient to limit Jewish and other emigration.

The political costs to the Soviet Union were threefold:

1. Allowing increased emigration would be an obvious admission that the Soviet Union "caved in" to American demands, something the superpowers do not do;
2. Vast numbers of people lined up to leave would call into question the ideological foundations of the Soviet regime; and
3. Soviet relations with the Arab states would be upset if the Soviet Union facilitated a mass Jewish emigration to Israel.

The Soviet Union did *not* allow unhindered emigration, and the number of Jews arriving in Vienna has been reduced to a trickle in recent years. The Soviet Union has yet to receive MFN status and, in America's perception, they are being "punished" for bad behavior.

The European Approach

The Europeans no longer view East-West trade in a manner similar to the United States. For the European Community, trade is no longer a tool of diplomacy or a political lever; it is no longer an instrument of morality or something with which to extract good behavior. Rather, Europe now regards East-West trade as relatively divorced from politics and as straightforward business transactions. One immediate consequence of these differing American-European perceptions is that, even with the American embargo on grain exports (later rescinded by President Reagan) and technology and the pipeline embargo, the economic doors remain open in the European Community. The Community had made efforts to prevent the Soviet Union filling the shortfall in goods and commodities from Europe that were cancelled by the United States (not always successful), but the EC did not cancel any of their existing contracts: the traditional trade patterns are being maintained. These "traditional" trade flows may very well increase in the future since the Soviet Union is likely to turn to Europe rather than risking the very shaky political relations that characterize trade with the United States and since such trade could be shut off at any time.

These differences in political perceptions of the role of trade in international relations help to explain the situation of the United States refusing to deal with the Soviet Union while the EC maintains their usual trading patterns. But there is an economic reason as well: while not dependent on Soviet trade, the EC's trade, when compared to US-USSR levels, is much more a two-way street, and Europe would thus lose far more than the United States in any embargo. Although, as mentioned, the EC is by no means dependent on Soviet trade, as EC-Soviet trade increased during the 1970s and 1980s, mutual expectations and needs developed. For most of the 1970s, the trade was roughly in balance. But the figures shifted in 1979: some $11.5 billion in imports from the USSR compared to some $8.6 billion in EC exports. West Germany, the EC member with the largest amount of trade with the Soviet Union, had over a $1.25 billion swing in 1979 (a 1978 surplus of approximately $480 million to a 1979 deficit of approximately $775 million). The balance of trade again shifted in 1983 in West Germany's favor: approximately $1 billion more in exports to the Soviet Union than imports.[24]

These figures are somewhat misleading, however. They are indeed huge sums, and there is no doubt that some of the larger deals have significance for individual European firms—as was the case with the pipeline turbines—but a sense of proportion is necessary. The overall share of the USSR and other Eastern European countries of the total trade of the EC in the late 1970s was only about 3.8 percent, increasing only slightly in the 1980s. This share cannot be interpreted as establishing any kind of EC "economic dependency" on the Soviet Union. In fact, if there is any dependence at all, the argument should be turned around. As Hannes Adomeit comments, there *are* asymmetries in the significance of East-West trade, but they are more on the Soviet than on the European side.[25] The EC's share of total Soviet foreign trade is much higher than that of the USSR's for the EC (approximately 20 percent of all USSR exports went to the EC, and approximately 12 percent of all Soviet imports came from the EC in 1983).[26] But even this figure must be qualified since the proportion of foreign trade in the Soviet GNP is much lower than it is within the EC. As for oil, the actual volume of Soviet oil imported by the EC is miniscule when compared to total EC consumption. For the USSR to increase European energy dependence, it would be necessary to expand oil exports significantly, an expansion that does not appear possible in the near future. The European Community countries *are* trading with the Soviet Union, but, in relative terms, the trade is neither significant nor makes Western Europe dependent upon the Soviet Union.

Council of Mutual Economic Assistance

The European Community has maintained formal but intermittent contact with the Council of Mutual Economic Assistance (COMECON or CMEA), the Moscow-inspired and Moscow-dominated Eastern European trading organization. Contacts first began in 1973, with several high-level talks taking place since 1976. In late November 1978, there were three days of talks, but the two delegations were unable to resolve their conflicting positions regarding the nature of the proposed relationship (the mutual recognition of the competence of each organization to negotiate). The European Community has insisted since the talks began that COMECON does not have the same full trade-negotiating powers as the EC Commission; COMECON claims that it has only reluctantly accepted the Commission's authority to negotiate on behalf of all the EC members. The 1978 talks primarily were to define the nature of such mutual recognition, but no real progress was made.

Another meeting was held in Moscow (November 1979) after COMECON replied to an earlier EC draft proposal. A revised EC draft for an agreement was then presented to COMECON in Moscow. This latter document went a bit further than previous EC texts in meeting some of COMECON's demands, and it contained a series of detailed proposals on how trade should be handled between the Community and COMECON countries. The EC draft suggested that future bilateral agreements might cover import arrangements, MFN status, safeguard provisions, removal of trade barriers, and efforts toward trade promotion rather than simple trade substitution. It was significant, however, that the EC did not alter its main position: any such agreement(s) would be between the EC and the *individual* COMECON countries and not between the EC and COMECON.

As was the case in 1978, no real progress was achieved at the 1979 Moscow meeting. A subsequent top-level meeting was then scheduled for April 1980, with some preparatory working sessions in Geneva in March 1980. The Geneva sessions were held as scheduled, but, once again, no progress could be seen. The April 1980 meeting was then cancelled by the EC Commission because it saw no prospects of progress in the long-standing negotiations between the two sides. The European Community gave its reasons for unilaterally cancelling the April 1980 meeting in a letter sent on 31 March 1980 by Wilhelm Haferkamp, then EC Commission vice-president and responsible for external affairs, to Nikolai Faddeev, then the secretary-general of COMECON.[27] The letter stated that the meeting planned for April "would only be opportune if it promised substantial progress." After the desultory results in Geneva, the EC judged that "no such progress was likely since COMECON is not prepared to move toward the Commission's compromise proposals of November 1979." This position was apparently cleared with the Community's member-governments because the letter was endorsed by the Committee of Permanent Representatives. Commissioner Haferkamp concluded with the remark that the European Community was prepared to pursue contacts on a technical level, but that a high-level political meeting would be counterproductive.

There is no doubt that the Soviet invasion of Afghanistan, and the deteriorating nature of East-West relations in general, played a role in the Community's cancellation of the April 1980 meeting. But the EC's resistance to a compromise with COMECON predates the invasion: the Community has always been very wary of any agreement that might strengthen or reinforce the Soviet Union's control over the other COMECON countries. The EC also has always employed complex legal arguments to justify its negotiating position that COMECON has no legal institutional framework or mandate similar to the Commission's clear authority to negotiate trade agreements on behalf of its member-states. The Community insists that detailed trade negotiations and agreements must be conducted by the Community with individual COMECON countries and not with COMECON as a separate independent entity. The Soviet Union has usually taken the initiative, arguing for a formal agreement between the EC and CO-MECON. The USSR is no doubt concerned that other COMECON countries might imitate Romania and sign a separate bilateral trade deal with the EC. Such bilateral deals, although obviously not ending Moscow's influence over its East European satellites, would weaken such influence as well as call into question whatever unity COMECON might have.

The formal trading relationship between the European Community and the Council of Mutual Economic Assistance, each as an intergovernmental organization, has been at an impasse since 1980. But, as noted above, some COMECON countries have in their individual capacity as sovereign states begun to consider contacts and limited agreements with the EC. There have been limited negotiations with Poland, Hungary, and even the Soviet Union, but in February 1980 the first agreement between the EC and a COMECON country (Romania) was signed. The EC and Romania agreed to establish a "joint commission" to discuss all aspects of trade and economic relations between them. Significantly, the agreement includes a clause whereby Romania "officially acknowledges and accepts" the legal competence and authority of the Community in certain trade and economic areas—recognition that the European Community will not extend to COMECON.

Negotiations were nonexistent until mid-1985, when efforts were once again revived. On 30 May 1985, Soviet Communist Party Secretary Gorbachev, in a conversation with Bettino Craxi, the Italian prime minister and the current EC Council president, remarked that it was an opportune time to organize economic relations between the EC and COMECON. Two weeks later, COMECON Secretary General Viatcheslav Sytchov proposed a meeting between the two blocs, with the aim of signing a joint declaration, but the EC's response in January 1986 reiterated its long-standing position that any such agreement could not displace any bilateral relations between the EC as an IGO and individual CO-MECON countries.[28] No date has yet been established for a resumption of formal high-level talks.

Yugoslavia

Yugoslavia is not a member of COMECON—it has observer status—and the European Community has maintained cordial relations with this Eastern European country. In the summer of 1979, the EC and Yugoslavia began talks aimed at concluding a new trade and cooperation agreement to replace the one that had expired in 1978 (but extended in the interim). No doubt hastened by Tito's grave illness, the talks were accelerated, and on 2 April 1980, the agreement was signed. The 1980 agreement was designed to help Yugoslav exports to the Community, and it provided EC financial aid to help overcome Yugoslavia's large trade deficit with the EC.

The agreement ran for five years and its major provisions were renewed in 1985. Yugoslavia was provided with free access to the EC market for a whole range of industrial goods, and a framework for increasing agricultural exports was also established. The agreement reduced the Yugoslav trade deficit with the EC—approximately $3 billion in 1979—by some 60 percent, thus reducing Yugoslavia's total trade deficit by about 30 percent. The agreement also improved the status of Yugoslav migrant workers within the Community by providing them with full social security benefits.

The European Community–Yugoslavia agreement confirms the EC's long-standing interest in maintaining and strengthening Yugoslavia's independence and nonalignment. Such independence and stability is doubly crucial in recent years since the Soviet Union has increased its economic pressure after the death of Tito. The European Community hopes that the economic agreement will enable Yugoslavia to continue on its nonaligned path.

EUROPEAN POLITICAL COOPERATION AND EUROPEAN COMMUNITY INTEGRATION

This discussion of European Political Cooperation (EPC) and the EC's relations with Eastern Europe shows that there are obstacles in the path of a unified European foreign policy, let alone coordination with the United States. The idea that European—and then Western—foreign policy should become more of a collective exercise involving all the main partners on a more or less equal footing is tantalizing, but there are serious doubts about its feasibility.

Even if one were to assume that the European Community countries actively desire a common foreign *political* policy—a very tenuous assumption—the constraints posed by a changing international system limit their freedom of movement in achieving harmonization. As discussed in Chapter 1, one result or side effect of growing international interdependence is that governments now control only some of the factors that determine the content of foreign policy decision making. International economic restraints—the need to trade, dependence on foreign energy supplies, fluctuating values of domestic currency—appear to be very important in attempting to explain the lack of a concerted policy by the EC member-governments.

It would, of course, be much easier to coordinate Western policy if "Europe" spoke with one voice. At the present, the slow decision-making process of the Community, with its constant search for unanimity, turns Europe into an impossible partner for the United States. No wonder the Americans act alone and ignore Europe: European "political cooperation" appears more and more to be only an excuse for European inaction. But the European Community is a complicated, multinational, highly politicized society with 12 separate sovereign governments, transnational institutions, diversified interests, and pressure groups. All these are obstacles that must be overcome in order to achieve a genuine "collective" foreign policy. Until then, a unified European foreign policy will remain very far from realization.

NOTES

1. Werner J. Feld, "The Harmonization of the European Community's External Policy," chapter 2 (pp. 25–54) of Leon Hurwitz, ed., *The Harmonization of European Public Policy* (Westport, Conn.: Greenwood Press, 1983), p. 40. For details, see Alessandro Silj, "Europe's Political Puzzle," Occasional Paper No. 17 (Cambridge, Mass.: Harvard University Center for International Affairs, December 1967).

2. Keesing's Research Report, *The European Communities: Establishment and Growth* (New York: Scribner's, 1975), pp. 156–157.

3. See "First Report of the Foreign Ministers to the Heads of State and Government of the Member States of the European Community, 27 October 1970" (Luxembourg Report) and the Copenhagen Report, German Federal Government, Press and Information Office, "European Political Cooperation" (Bonn: 1978).

4. Hugh Arbuthnott and Geoffrey Edwards, eds., *A Common Man's Guide to the Common Market: The European Community* (New York: Macmillan, 1979), p. 169.

5. This section borrows from Feld, "The Harmonization of the European Community's External Policy," pp. 40–44.

6. Ibid., p. 44.

7. Contained in "Fourth Semiannual Report by the President to the Commission on Security and Cooperation in Europe, 1 December 1977–1 June 1978," US Department of State, *Special Report*, no. 45 (June 1978), p. 5.

8. Corrado Pirzio-Biroli, "Foreign Policy Formation within the European Community with Special Regard to the Developing Countries," chapter 11 (pp. 225–254) of Leon Hurwitz, ed., *Contemporary Perspectives on European Integration* (Westport, Conn.: Greenwood Press, 1980), p. 244.

9. *Bulletin of the European Community* (February 1977), 65.

10. The EUROGROUP Secretariat, *Western Defense: The European Role in NATO* (Brussels: n.d.), pp. 17–19.

11. Ibid., pp. 20–22.

12. On 16 April 1982, the EC Council of Ministers adopted Regulation no. 877/82, suspending for a month imports of all products originating in Argentina and recommending the suspension of all EC arms exports to Argentina. *Official Journal of the European Community* (L 102/1 of 16 April 1982). Italy and Ireland agreed not to export arms, but these two countries did not suspend Argentine imports.

13. Fernand Spaak, "Europe and America," 219 *Europe* (May-June 1980), 35.

14. This Franco-Soviet trade must be put into perspective, At the time, the Soviet Union was France's tenth-largest customer, but taking only about 2 percent of France's exports.

15. EC Council of Ministers, as cited in 218 *Europe* (March-April 1980), 9.

16. European Parliament, as reported in ibid.

17. Wilhelm Haferkamp, as reported in ibid.

18. *London Times* (14 March 1980), p. 17.

19. Ibid. (18 March 1980), p. 5.

20. Ibid. (19 April 1980), p. 4.

21. Peter Kilborn, "After 5-Year Halt, Banks in U.S. Set Soviet Loan," *New York Times* (26 November 1985), pp. D1, D7.

22. The discussion of the 1975 Trade Reform Act and the Jackson-Vanik Amendment is from Leon Hurwitz, *The State as Defendant: Governmental Accountability and the Redress of Individual Grievances* (Westport, Conn.: Greenwood Press, 1981), pp. 129–131.

23. For a detailed discussion of the entire process, see William W. Orbach, *The American Movement to Aid Soviet Jews* (Amherst: University of Massachusetts Press, 1979).

24. Michael D. Mosettig, "East-West Trade: Business Arrangements or Political Tool," 220 *Europe* (July-August 1980), 11; *The Europa Yearbook: A World Survey*, Vol. I, Part II (London: Europa Publications, 1985).

25. Hannes Adomeit, "Soviet Policy in Europe: Trends and Issues in the Post-Helsinki Period," 31 *Soviet Studies* (October 1979), 593.

26. *The Europa Yearbook: A World Survey*, Vol. I, Part II (London: Europa Publications, 1985).

27. As reported in the *London Times* (1 April 1980), p. 5.

28. H. Peter Dreyer, "EC-COMECON: A Move at Last?" 256 *Europe* (May 1986), 33.

PART IV

Conclusion

9

The Quality of the European Community: Past, Present, and Future

The creation of the European Community in Rome on 25 March 1957 by France, West Germany, Italy, Belgium, the Netherlands, and Luxembourg—joined subsequently by Denmark, Ireland, and the United Kingdom in 1973, by Greece in 1981, and by Spain and Portugal in 1986—represents a most ambitious experiment in international integration, community building, and the management of international cooperation. Twelve sovereign, independent countries, each with its own separate history, culture, language, values, and traditions—and whose past relations were characterized more by suspicion and warfare than by cooperation and the resolution of conflict by peaceful means—willingly and voluntarily established a supranational organization.

These countries—not just the governments but the general population as well because the relevant treaties, texts, and agreements had to be ratified by each country's parliamentary procedure, usually by referendum—made the conscious choice to transfer some previously national sovereign powers and prerogatives to a supranational organization. This organization, at first by unanimous agreement among the member-states but now (in most situations) by a simple majority vote, has the authority to issue policies in certain areas that are *binding* on the component states and take precedence over any conflicting national legislation. This historic transfer of sovereignty was based on the realization that the future of the individual countries, and thus the future of Western Europe itself, could be secured only by greater international cooperation and integration.

The 12 countries within the European Community have not, however, forgone their own self-defined national interests or political objectives—interests and objectives that are in frequent conflict with other members' perceived national interests—but the phenomenon of the European Community is by itself ample evidence that the individual countries perceive their own national capabilities and resources as insufficient to achieve their national goals. These national goals cover the full range of state interests and objectives: security, economic and social development, political stability, democratic institutions, and technological advancement. It is through the establishment of, and participation in, intergovernmental organizations such as the European Community that the pursuit and attainment of the national interest is enhanced. This international interdependence obviously carries with it constraints on unilateral state behavior, but the EC member-states perceive these interdependence costs to be far less than the benefits received.

This concluding chapter presents a brief overview of the European Community experiment in the management of international cooperation in terms of past developments, present trends, and its future.

PAST DEVELOPMENTS

The European Community has weathered several crises over the past 30 years. At the time, these crises appeared to threaten the continued existence of the Community and most certainly led, at least in the short run, to a much lower level of decision making from the EC institutional framework. But the Community process survived and, in retrospect, emerged stronger and with greater legitimacy.

The entire question of the United Kingdom's relationship to the Community—first as an outside competitor prior to 1 January 1973 and then as a member—represented a continuing crisis that is only now subsiding. The 15-year attempt by the British to reap the benefits of EC membership without being subjected to any of its costs, particularly in relation to the Commonwealth Preference and the EC's common agricultural policy and common external tariff, severely tested the resolve of the original Six. The British suffered two petulant vetoes by French President Charles de Gaulle over their accession demands, and for quite some time, Europe was divided into two competing and rival economic camps (the European Community and the British-inspired and British-led European Free Trade Association). Political compromise, however, eventually took precedence over political rhetoric, but even after the United Kingdom's entry into the EC, there remains a smouldering dispute. The operation and costs of the EC's common agricultural policy most certainly do not advance the British national interest, and this remains an unresolved problem.

The French themselves, however, have not been blameless. In what was perhaps the most severe crisis that the Community weathered—a crisis that at the time threatened to put an abrupt end to the entire EC process—the French boycotted the Council of Ministers for six months in 1965 until a compromise was eventually reached in January 1966. The boycott stemmed from the French refusal to accept majority voting in the Council of Ministers—de Gaulle insisted that, since the EC was a collection of nation-states, each state therefore should have a veto over any proposal—and the entire EC process was at a standstill for six months. This defense of national sovereignty and national prerogatives had a lingering effect on the EC's decision-making process in the sense that it emphasized the importance of the *governments* of the EC members, rather than the EC institutions themselves, and eventually led to the emasculation of the EC process. It is now the Council of Ministers, as the representatives of the national governments and the protector of the national interest, that is the effective decision-making unit within the EC. The Commission has been reduced to implementing Council decisions, and the powers and prerogatives of the democratically elected European Parliament are rendered meaningless by the Council of Ministers.

The 1974 to 1975 OAPEC-induced energy crisis stripped away any pretense the EC might have assumed that full cooperation in the face of a transnational challenge was workable. Each country went its own way, scrambling to ensure its own energy supplies. Not even lip service was paid to the Community's energy policy. The Netherlands was the hardest hit by the OAPEC embargo, but it was not until the Dutch threatened to cut off supplies of its natural gas that other EC members relented and allocated some oil to the Netherlands. Cooperation broke down totally, and it took the EC several years to recover some semblance of mutual trust among the governments.

But the European Community also has had some remarkable successes in international integration, the management of conflict, and in the slow creation of a "European" mind-set in place of a purely national outlook and identity. Many of the traditional barriers that divided Europe in the past are slowly being eroded. The internal market (the customs union) has been in place for years, and there are very few products within the EC that do not enjoy this free trade. The common external tariff (CET) has also been in place for years—the terms of entry for any given product from any given country will be identical across the EC. This CET is a necessary corollary to the free internal market and its operation is no longer an issue of controversy.

The European Community has also been rather successful in negotiating international trade and development cooperation agreements with a number of countries (especially the Lomé, Arusha, and Yaoundé Conventions). The individual EC member-states have transferred to the EC process the ability to negotiate and then to conclude such development-cooperation agreements. This, obviously, reduces the EC countries' freedom of independent action, but the multilateralization of development and cooperation aid has proven advantageous to both the EC and the recipient countries.

Finally, direct elections for the European Parliament in June 1979 and June 1984 marked a *symbolic* milestone in the European integrative process. Over 110 million voters participated across the EC and chose representatives to the first directly elected supranational parliament in history. The members of the EP—from different countries and with different political ideologies—show a remarkable degree of transnational party agreement and a deemphasis of national identity. It just may be that the traditional national mind-sets are breaking down, strengthening the integrative process. These transnational parties may in the future serve as new political forces within the European Community.

PRESENT TRENDS

There are four present trends within the European Community that appear to be quite troublesome: the operation and costs of the common agricultural policy; the unfavorable image of the Eurocrats; the domination of the EC decision-making process by the governments of the member-states through the Council of Ministers; and the inability of the European Parliament to engage in any real meaningful political behavior.

The European Community's common agricultural policy (CAP) was perceived originally to be one of the major cornerstones or building blocks for EC economic (and possible political) integration. The CAP has, however, presented a double-sided result: on the one hand, the CAP has contributed to creating and maintaining a more than sufficient quantity and quality of foodstuffs and commodities in Europe, but, on the other hand, the CAP has also brought high economic and political costs. EC consumers are forced to pay artificially high prices (much higher than the world market price for many commodities); the CAP consumes some 60 to 70 percent of the EC's annual budget; vast surpluses (butter "mountains" and wine and olive oil "lakes" and sugar "lumps") have accumulated; financial fraud and chicanery have been well documented; and intense political friction has developed over the sale of surplus agricultural commodities.

The accession of Greece in January 1981 to the EC and the accession of Spain and Portugal in January 1986 only exacerbate the existing problems. Greece, Spain, and Portugal all have a much higher percentage of farm workers than the other EC countries, and many of the farms are inefficient and in need of extensive modernization. The financial demands on the structural improvement section of the EAGGF are rapidly increasing, and the United Kingdom, after complaining (with some justification) for years that it was subsidizing the French farmer, will now have to subsidize the Spanish and Portuguese farmers as well. In addition, the agricultural sectors of Greece, Spain, and Portugal are competitive rather than complementary to the EC production mode, and this will only add to the already vast surpluses of certain commodities (wine and olive oil, in particular). The CAP will most likely survive although in a modified form. Its real costs—political costs as well as economic—are such that national governments are increasingly ready to consider proposals for reform.

The administrative institutional framework of the Community is another area of concern. A large sector of Community expenditures (approximately $US 1.7 billion) is administrative overhead, and much criticism has been leveled at the EC because of this. It is seen by many to be overstaffed, overpaid, underworked, and fiscally inefficient (if not irresponsible). The traveling road show of the European Parliament, the level of salary paid to chauffeurs, the insistence of translating every piece of paper—even telephone numbers—into all the Community languages are perceived as a vast entitlement program for a very few people. In addition, there exists a severe morale problem within the EC Commission's bureaucratic hierarchy. The practice of hiring senior-level administrators from the outside (i.e., from the national bureaucracies), rather than filling these positions by promotion from within, does not engender collegial relations in the bureaucracy.

A related problem is that of nationality. The EC, as an IGO, attempts to hire and promote the civil service in terms of professional competence *and* equitable geographical distribution (read "national quota system"). The implications of the quota system are far reaching: every country is entitled to its fair share of positions, and quite frequently a vacancy has to be filled by someone of the same nationality of the departing official in order to keep the balance. This policy also does not engender cordial relationships from those passed over because of having the "wrong" nationality. It has also been mentioned that sometimes it is difficult to remove someone unless his or her superior can find a qualified replacement of the same nationality; if not, this too could unbalance the geographical distribution. These are severe problems, and the EC must resolve them in the future.

The power of the Council of Ministers within the EC process is another area of concern for many people (but not for the member-governments). Under the European Coal and Steel Community framework, it was the Community process itself—the High Authority—that was the focal point in the decision-making process, but with the EC, the power has shifted to the Council of Ministers. The Council of Ministers represent the governments and quite explicitly protect national interests first rather than the Community interest. This dominance of the Council can be seen in the development of the process called "European Political Cooperation" (EPC). The formulation and execution of a common EC foreign policy (if able to be achieved at all) is the sole preserve of the foreign ministers acting *outside* the Community framework. Most observers agree that if the Community is to ever move to more integration, decision-making power must be shifted back to the Community framework and the Community institutions.

Finally, the European Parliament is an opera buffo, with over 500 characters (the MEPs), 12 acts (the member-states), seven plots (the transnational party groupings), playing in two theaters (Brussels and Strasbourg). Nine languages are spoken, but none are listened to, and the EP is engaged in the symbolism of politics without its essence. Too many of the EP's resolutions deal with areas far removed from the European Community, let alone the Parliament itself. Resolutions bemoaning the fate of the Indo-Chinese boat people or expressing sorrow over drowned French and German cows do not political influence make. And, when the Parliament does deal with EC matters, its voice is only an opinion without any binding force in Community law.

The very nature of the European Parliament—its lack of any real political power, its atmosphere of a congenial club with much food and drink, the non-binding roll calls, its emphasis upon the symbolism of politics rather than its substance—all these factors combine and detract from the significance of whatever the MEPs do or do not do in Parliament. But after these limiting conditions are recognized, the MEPs do show a remarkable degree of transnational party agreement and a deemphasis of national identity. It just may be that the traditional national mind-sets are breaking down, strengthening the integrative process. The transnational party groups may be able to serve as new political forces in Europe when and if the European Parliament enlarges its power vis-à-vis the Commission and especially vis-à-vis the Council of Ministers. This power enlargement does not appear to be imminent, but the groundwork has been laid.

THE FUTURE OF THE EC

This author is guardedly optimistic about the future of the European Community. After more than three decades, an entire generation of Europeans have become sensitized to the need for greater international cooperation and the harmonization of public policies across national frontiers. The cultural differences within Europe are such that no one is advocating the creation of a homogeneous entity with a veneer of "oneness" superimposed over the Continent. But the need for economic and political integration is recognized as an absolute necessity if Western Europe wishes to maintain its identity in face of the political dominance of the United States and the Soviet Union and in face of the economic dominance of Japan and the United States. There may—or there may not be— an eventual United States of Europe, but the European Community is poised. There exists a legitimate court and judicial function; there exists a reasonably competent bureaucracy; there exists a democratically elected Parliament. What is needed is for the Parliament to seize power from the Council of Ministers and then *act* as a parliament by electing a prime minister and a cabinet (this would also make the Commission superfluous). Such a scenario is not very likely, but after considering the events of the past 30 years, the next 30 years may bring the essence of international integration and the management of international cooperation.

But there are alternative, less optimistic scenarios. The idea of "Europe" is not greater than the sum of its national and subnational component parts. The process of European integration has never been free of controversy, and some of the opposition (Norway's rejection of membership, for example, or Great Britain's continuing tenuous commitment) cannot be dismissed as only minor irritants. The model offered above—an incremental linear model that simply assumes that the next 30 years will enlarge upon past decades—may prove to be false. Rather, perhaps European integration is a curvilinear process, and the next 30 years will witness decay, transformation, or regression.

The European Community as an institution does not involve a high level of mass participation by the European public—it was, and continues to be, a function of elite behavior. There is nothing to prevent future European political elites from exhibiting much lower levels of commitment to the idea of "Europe" than did Jean Monnet, Paul-Henri Spaak, and Robert Schuman. If this were to occur, the EC most assuredly would be on the downward slope of the curvilinear process.

Although a desirable process in and by itself, increased European integration through the European Community's institutional framework may not be the *most* desirable objective. The reemergence of Europe's "regionalism"—its religious, cultural, ethnic, and linguistic groups—may very well require a decentralization of political decision making. Rather than transferring political power and responsibility to Brussels and a remote supranational institution, government may have to be brought closer to the people and closer to where the political problems exist. The rise in subnational loyalties (e.g., the Flemish, the Scots, the Basques), presents a countertrend against the increased internationalization at the European-wide level. These scenarios—the incremental linear process and the curvilinear one leading to decay—as well as an obvious third possibility—total stagnation without any movement in either direction—all have an equal probability. But it would be premature at this time to predict the future of the European Community.

Selected Bibliography

Acheson, Dean. *Present at the Creation*. London: Hamish Hamilton, 1970.

Albrecht-Carrie, René. *One Europe: The Historical Background of European Unity*. New York: Doubleday, 1965.

Alford, Jonathan, ed. *Arms Control and European Security*. New York: St. Martin's Press, 1985.

Allen, David et al. *European Political Cooperation: Towards a Foreign Policy for Western Europe*. Sevenoaks, Kent, UK: Butterworth, 1982.

Alting von Geusau, Frans A. M., ed. *Energy in the European Communities*. Leyden: Sijthoff, 1975.

———. *The External Relations of the European Community*. Aldershot, Hants, UK: Saxon House, 1974.

Antal, K. V. "Harmonisation of Turnover Taxes in the Common Market." 1 *Common Market Law Review* (June 1963), 41–57.

Arkes, Hadley. *Bureaucracy, the Marshall Plan, and the National Interest*. Princeton, N.J.: Princeton University Press, 1972.

Armstrong, Hamilton F. *The Calculated Risk*. New York: Macmillan, 1947.

———. "Postscript to the EDC." 33 *Foreign Affairs* (October 1954), 17–27.

Armstrong, John A. *The European Administrative Elite*. Princeton, N.J.: Princeton University Press, 1973.

Aron, Raymond, and Lerner, Daniel. *France Defeats the EDC*. New York: Praeger, 1957.

Austin, Dennis. *Britain, Commonwealth Africa and the EEC*. New York: Penguin, 1968.

Averyt, William F. *Agropolitics in the European Community*. New York: Praeger, 1977.

———. "Eurogroups, Clientela, and the European Community." 29 *International Organization* (Fall 1975), 949–972.

Bailey, Richard. *The European Connection: Britain's Relationship with the European Community*. Elmsford, N.Y.: Pergamon, 1983.

———. *The European Community in the World*. London: Hutchinson, 1973.

Bailey, Thomas A. *The Marshall Plan Summer*. Stanford, Calif.: Hoover Institution, 1977.

Baklanoff, E. N. *The Economic Transformation of Spain and Portugal.* New York: Praeger, 1978.

Balassa, Bela. *The Theory of Economic Integration.* Homewood, Ill.: Richard Irwin, 1961.

————. "Trade Creation and Trade Diversion in the European Common Market: An Appraisal of the Evidence." 42 *Manchester School of Economic and Social Studies* (June 1974), 93–135.

Balogh, Thomas. "Africa and the Common Market." 1 *Journal of Common Market Studies* (September 1962), 79–112.

Barber, James, and Reed, B. S., eds. *The European Community.* Beckenham, Kent, UK: Croom Helm, 1973.

Barnes, W. G. *Europe and the Developing World.* London: Chatham House, 1967.

Barzanti, Sergio. *Underdeveloped Areas within the Common Market.* Princeton, N.J.: Princeton University Press, 1968.

Bathurst, M. E. et al., eds. *Legal Problems of an Enlarged European Community.* London: Stevens, 1972.

Bebr, Gerhard. *Judicial Control of the European Communities.* New York: Praeger, 1962.

Beever, R. Colin. *European Unity and the Trade Union Movement.* Leyden: Sijthoff, 1960.

Bellamy, C. W., and Child, D. G. *Common Market Law of Competition.* London: Sweet and Maxwell, 1978.

Beloff, Max. *Europe and the Europeans: An International Discussion.* London: Chatto and Windus, 1957.

————. *The United States and the Unity of Europe.* New York: Random House, 1963.

Benoit, Emile. *Europe at Sixes and Sevens: The Common Market, the Free Trade Association, and the United States.* New York: Columbia University Press, 1961.

Berghe, Guido van den. *Political Rights for European Citizens.* Aldershot, Hants, UK: Gower, 1982.

Bertram, Christoph, ed. *Defense and Consensus: Domestic Aspects of Western Security.* New York: St. Martin's Press, 1985.

Bethlen, Steven, and Volgyes, Ivan, eds. *Europe and the Superpowers: Political, Economic, and Military Policies in the 1980s.* Boulder, Colo.: Westview, 1985.

Beugel, Ernst H. van der. *From Marshall Aid to Atlantic Partnership.* New York: Elsevier, 1966.

Birke, Wolfgang. *European Elections by Direct Suffrage.* Leyden: Sijthoff, 1961.

Bliss, Howard. *The Political Development of the European Community: A Documentary Collection.* Waltham, Mass.: Blaisdell, 1970.

Blumler, J. G., ed. *Communicating to Voters: Television in the First European Parliamentary Elections.* Beverly Hills, Calif.: Sage, 1983.

Blumler, J. G., and Fox, A. D. *The European Voter.* London: Policy Studies Institute, 1980.

Boardman, Robert et al., eds. *Europe, Africa and Lomé III.* Halifax, N.S.: Dalhousie University Press, 1985.

Bodenheimer, Susanne J. *Political Union: A Microcosm of European Politics, 1960–1966.* Leyden: Sijthoff, 1967.

Bohning, W. R. *The Migration of Workers in the United Kingdom and the European Community.* New York: Oxford University Press, 1972.

Bok, Derek C. *The First Three Years of the Schuman Plan*. Princeton, N.J.: Princeton University Press, 1955.

Borrmann, Axel; Borrmann, Christine; and Stegger, Manfred. *The European Community's Generalized System of Preferences*. The Hague: Martinus Nijhoff, 1981.

Bowler, Ian R. *Agriculture Under the Common Agricultural Policy*. Manchester, UK: Manchester University Press, 1985.

Bracewell-Milnes, Barry. *Eastern and Western European Economic Integration*. New York: St. Martin's Press, 1976.

Braun, Hans-Gert et al., eds. *The European Economy in the 1980s*. Aldershot, Hants, UK: Gower, 1983.

Brickman, Ronald. "National Science Policy Coordination in the European Community." 31 *International Organization* (Summer 1977), 473–496.

Brinkhorst, L. J., and Mitchell, J. D. B. *European Law and Institutions*. Edinburgh: Edinburgh University Press, 1969.

Brinkhorst, L. J., and Schermers, H. G. *Judicial Remedies in the European Communities*. London: Stevens, 1969.

Brown, L. N; and Jacobs, F. G. *The Court of Justice of the European Communities*. London: Sweet & Maxwell, 1977.

Brunner, Karl, and Meltzer, Allan, eds. *Monetary Institutions and the Policy Process*. Amsterdam: North Holland, 1980.

Buckwell, Allan et al. *The Costs of the Common Agricultural Policy*. Beckenham, Kent, UK: Croom Helm, 1982.

Burrows, Bernard; Denton, Geoffrey; and Edwards, Geoffrey, eds. *Federal Solutions to European Issues*. New York: St. Martin's Press, 1978.

Busch, Peter, and Puchala, Donald J. "Interests, Influence and Integration: Political Structure in the European Communities." 9 *Comparative Political Studies* (October 1976), 235–254.

Butler, David, and Marquand, David. *European Elections and British Politics*. New York: Longman, 1981.

Butterwick, Michael, and Neville-Rolfe, Edmund. *Agricultural Marketing and the EEC*. London: Hutchinson, 1971.

Cairncross, Sir Alec et al. *Economic Policy for the European Community*. New York: Macmillan, 1974.

Camps, Miriam. *Britain and the European Community, 1955–1963*. Princeton, N.J.: Princeton University Press, 1964.

———. *European Unification in the Sixties*. New York: Oxford University Press, 1967.

Caplow, Theodore, and Finsterbusch, Kurt. "France and Other Countries: A Study of International Interaction." 2 *Journal of Conflict Resolution* (March 1968), 1–15.

Caporaso, James. *The Structure and Function of European Integration*. Pacific Palisades, Calif.: Goodyear, 1974.

Caporaso, James, and Pelowski, Alan L. "Economic and Political Integration in Europe: A Time-Series Quasi-Experimental Analysis." 65 *American Political Science Review* (June 1971), 418–433.

Clout, Hugh. *A Rural Policy for the EEC?* New York: Methuen, 1984.

Cocks, Sir Barnett. *The European Parliament: Structure, Procedure and Practice*. London: Her Majesty's Stationery Office, 1973.

Coffey, Peter, and Presley, John R. *European Monetary Integration*. New York: St. Martin's Press, 1971.

Cohen, R. *Europe and the Developing Countries*. Rotterdam: Rotterdam University Press, 1972.

Collins, Doreen. *The Operation of the European Social Fund*. Beckenham, Kent, UK: Croom Helm, 1983.

Cook, C., and Francis, M. *The First European Elections*. New York: Macmillan, 1979.

Coombes, David. *The Future of the European Parliament*. London: Policy Studies Institute, 1979.

————. *Politics and Bureaucracy in the European Community: A Portrait of the Commission of the EEC*. London: Allen & Unwin, 1970.

Coombes, David, and Wiebecke, I. *The Power of the Purse in the European Communities*. London: Chatham House-PEP, 1972.

Cooper, Richard N. "The European Community's System of Generalized Tariff Preferences: A Critique." 8 *Journal of Development Studies* (July 1972), 379–394.

Corbet, Hugh, and Robertson, David, eds. *Europe's Free Trade Area Experiment*. Elmsford, N.Y.: Pergamon, 1970.

Cosgrove, Carol Ann. "The Common Market and Its Colonial Heritage." 4 *Journal of Contemporary History* (January 1969), 73–87.

————. "The Second Yaoundé Convention in Perspective." 3 *International Relations* (May 1970), 679–689.

Cosgrove, Carol Ann, and Twitchett, Kenneth J. *New International Actors: The United Nations and the European Economic Community*. New York: Macmillan, 1970.

Curry, Charles E. et al., eds. *Confrontation or Negotiation: United States Foreign Policy and European Agriculture*. Millwood, N.Y.: Associated Faculty Press, 1985.

Curtis, Michael. *Western European Integration*. New York: Harper and Row, 1965.

Curzon, Victoria et al. *EFTA and the Crisis of European Integration*. London: Michael Joseph, 1968.

Dagtoglu, P. D., ed. *Basic Problems of the European Community*. London: Basil Blackwell, 1975.

De La Mahotière, Stuart. *Towards One Europe*. New York: Penguin, 1970.

Dell, Sidney S. *Trade Blocs and the Common Market*. New York: Knopf, 1963.

Deniau, Jean-François. *The Common Market*. New York: Praeger, 1960.

Denton, G. R. *Economic Integration in Europe*. London: Weidenfeld & Nicolson, 1969.

Deutsch, Karl W. *Political Community in the North Atlantic Area: International Organization in the Light of Historical Experience*. Princeton, N.J.: Princeton University Press, 1957.

Deutsch, Karl W. et al. *France, Germany, and the Western Alliance: A Study of Elite Attitudes on European Integration and World Politics*. New York: Scribner's, 1967.

di Delupis, Ingrid D. *The East African Community and the Common Market*. New York: Longman, 1970.

Diebold, William. *The Schuman Plan: A Study in Economic Cooperation, 1950–1959*. New York: Praeger, 1959.

Dogan, Mattei, ed. *The Mandarins of Western Europe: The Political Role of Civil Servants*. New York: Wiley, 1975.

Druker, Isaac E. *Financing the European Communities*. Leyden: Sijthoff, 1975.

Dyson, Kenneth, ed. *European Détente: Case Studies of the Politics of East-West Relations*. New York: St. Martin's Press, 1986.

Economic and Social Committee of the European Community, General Secretariat. *Eu-*

ropean Interest Groups and Their Relationship to the Economic and Social Com-mittee. Aldershot, Hants, UK: Gower, 1980.

Edwards, G., and Wallace, Helen. *The Council of Ministers of the European Community and the President-in-Office*. London: Federal Trust, 1977.

Einzig, Paul. *The Case Against Joining the Common Market*. New York: St. Martin's Press, 1971.

Elles, James, and Farnell, John. *In Search of a Common Fisheries Policy*. Aldershot, Hants, UK: Gower, 1984.

Erdemenger, Jurgen. *The European Community Transport Policy*. Aldershot, Hants, UK: Gower, 1984.

Etzioni, Amitai. *Political Unification*. New York: Holt, Rinehart & Winston, 1965.

European Parliament. *European Integration and the Future of Parliaments in Europe*. Strasbourg, France: European Parliament, 1975.

Everts, Philip P. *The European Community in the World: The External Relations of the Enlarged European Community*. Rotterdam: Rotterdam University Press, 1972.

Feld, Werner J. "The Association Agreements of the European Communities: A Com-parative Analysis." 19 *International Organization* (Spring 1965), 223–249.

———. *The Court of the European Communities: New Dimension in International Ad-judication*. The Hague: Martinus Nijhoff, 1964.

———. *The European Common Market and the World*. New York: Prentice-Hall, 1967.

———. *The European Community in World Affairs: Economic Power and Political Influence*. Port Washington, N.Y.: Alfred, 1976.

———. *The Foreign Policies of West European Socialist Parties*. New York: Praeger, 1978.

Feld, Werner J.; Jordan, Robert S.; and Hurwitz, Leon. *International Organizations: A Comparative Approach*. New York: Praeger, 1983.

Feld, Werner J., and Wildgen, John K. *Domestic Political Realities and European Unification: A Study of Mass Publics and Elites in the European Community*. Boulder, Colo.: Westview, 1976.

———. "National Administrative Elites and European Integration: Saboteurs at Work?" 13 *Journal of Common Market Studies* (March 1975), 244–265.

Feldstein, Helen S. "A Study of Transaction and Political Integration: Transnational Labour Flow within the European Economic Community." 6 *Journal of Common Market Studies* (September 1967), 24–55.

Fitzmaurice, John. *The European Parliament*. Aldershot, Hants, UK: Saxon House, 1978.

Foxall, Gordon R. *Co-Operative Marketing in European Agriculture*. Aldershot, Hants, UK: Gower, 1982.

Franck, Thomas, and Weisband, Edward, eds. *A Free Trade Association*. New York: New York University Press, 1968.

Frank, Isaiah. *The European Common Market: An Analysis of Commercial Policy*. New York: Praeger, 1961.

Franko, Lawrence. *The European MNs*. New York: Harper and Row, 1976.

Franzmeyer, Fritz. *Approaches to Industrial Policy within the EC and Its Impact on European Integration*. Aldershot, Hants, UK: Gower, 1982.

Freymond, Jacques. *Western Europe Since the War: A Short Political History*. New York: Praeger, 1964.

Fullenbach, Joseph. *European Environmental Policy: East and West*. Sevenoaks, Kent, UK: Butterworth, 1981.

Furmston, M. P.; Kerridge, Roger; and Sufrin, B. E. *The Effect on English Domestic Law of Membership of the European Communities and of Ratification of the European Convention on Human Rights*. The Hague: Martinus Nijhoff, 1983.

Galtung, Johan. *The European Community*. London: Allen & Unwin, 1973.

Gimbel, John. *The Origins of the Marshall Plan*. Stanford, Calif.: Stanford University Press, 1976.

Gladwyn, Lord. *The European Idea*. London: Weidenfeld & Nicolson, 1966.

Gordon, R. L. *The Evolution of Energy Policy in Western Europe: The Reluctant Retreat from Coal*. New York: Praeger, 1970.

Green, A. W. *Political Integration by Jurisprudence*. Leyden: Sijthoff, 1969.

Gregory, F. E. C. *Dilemmas of Government: Britain and the European Community*. London: Martin Robinson, 1983.

Haas, Ernst B. *Beyond the Nation State*. Stanford, Calif.: Stanford University Press, 1964.

———. "International Integration: The European Process and the Universal." 15 *International Organization* (Summer 1961), 366–392.

———. *The Uniting of Europe: Political, Social and Economic Forces, 1950–1957*. Stanford, Calif.: Stanford University Press, 1958.

Hagger, Mark. "Nine Nations Make a Law: A Comparison of the Politics of the Legislative Process for Direct Elections." 15 *Comparative Politics* (October 1982), 1–22.

Haines, C. Grove. *European Integration*. Baltimore, Md.: Johns Hopkins University Press, 1957.

Hallstein, Walter. *Europe in the Making*. New York: W. W. Norton, 1972.

———. *United Europe: Challenge and Opportunity*. Cambridge, Mass.: Harvard University Press, 1962.

Hammar, Thomas, ed. *European Immigration Policy*. Cambridge, UK: Cambridge University Press, 1985.

Harris, Seymour E. *The European Recovery Program*. Cambridge, Mass.: Harvard University Press, 1948.

Harris, Simon et al. *The Food and Farm Policies of the European Community*. New York: Wiley, 1983.

Harrison, R. J. *Europe in Question: Theories of Regional International Integration*. London: Allen & Unwin, 1974.

Hartley, T. C. *The Foundations of European Community Law*. New York: Oxford University Press, 1981.

Hellmann, Rainer. *Gold, the Dollar, and the European Community: The Seven Year Monetary War*. New York: Praeger, 1979.

Henderson, William O. *The Genesis of the Common Market*. New York: Quadrangle Books, 1963.

Henig, Stanley, ed. *Political Parties in the European Community*. London: PEP-Allen & Unwin, 1979.

———. *Power and Decision in Europe: The Political Institutions of the European Community*. London: Europotentials, 1980.

Henig, Stanley, and Pinder, John, eds. *European Political Parties*. London: Allen & Unwin, 1969.

Herman, Valentine. "Is the European Parliament a Parliament?" 6 *European Journal of Political Research* (June 1978), 157–180.

Herman, Valentine, and Lodge, Juliet. *The European Parliament and the European Community.* New York: Macmillan, 1978.

Herman, Valentine, and Schendelen, Rinus van, eds. *The European Parliament and the National Parliaments.* Aldershot, Hants, UK: Saxon House, 1979.

Herzog, Peter E. *Harmonization of Laws in the European Communities.* Charlottesville, Va.: University Press of Virginia, 1983.

Hill, Brian E. *The Common Agricultural Policy: Past, Present and Future.* New York: Methuen, 1984.

Hill, Christopher, ed. *National Foreign Policies and European Political Cooperation.* London: Allen & Unwin, 1983.

Hinshaw, Randall. *The European Community and American Trade.* New York: Praeger, 1964.

Hodges, Michael. *European Integration: Selected Readings.* New York: Penguin, 1972.

Hodges, Michael, and Wallace, William, eds. *Economic Divergence in the European Community.* London: Allen & Unwin, 1981.

Holland, Stuart. *Uncommon Market: Capital, Class, and Power in the European Community.* New York: St. Martin's Press, 1980.

Holm, Hans-Henrik, and Petersen, Nikolaj, eds. *The European Missiles Crisis: Nuclear Weapons and Security Policy.* New York: St. Martin's Press, 1985.

Holt, S. *Six European States.* London: Hamish Hamilton, 1970.

Hu, Yao-so. *Europe Under Stress: Convergence and Divergence in the European Community.* Sevenoaks, Kent, UK: Butterworth, 1981.

Hudson, Ray, and Lewis, Jim, eds. *Uneven Development in Southern Europe.* New York: Methuen, 1985.

Hudson, Ray; Rhind, David; and Mounsey, Helen. *An Atlas of EEC Affairs.* New York: Methuen, 1984.

Hughes, Barry B., and Schwarz, John E. "Dimensions of Political Integration and the Experience of the European Community." 16 *International Studies Quarterly* (September 1972), 263–294.

Hull, Chris. *Inter-Governmental Relations in the European Community.* Aldershot, Hants, UK: Saxon House, 1977.

Humphrey, Don D. *The United States and the Common Market: A Background Study.* New York: Praeger, 1962.

Hurtig, S. *The European Common Market.* New York: Columbia University Press, 1958.

Hurwitz, Leon, ed. *Contemporary Perspectives on European Integration: Attitudes, Non-Governmental Behavior, and Collective Decision-Making.* Westport, Conn.: Greenwood Press, 1980.

————. "The EEC and Decolonization: The Voting Behaviour of the Nine in the UN General Assembly." 24 *Political Studies* (December 1976), 435–447.

————. "The EEC in the United Nations: The Voting Behaviour of Eight Countries, 1948–1973." 13 *Journal of Common Market Studies* (March 1975), 224–243.

————, ed. *The Harmonization of European Public Policy: Regional Responses to Trans-national Challenges.* Westport, Conn.: Greenwood Press, 1983.

Ilgen, Thomas L. *Autonomy and Interdependence: U.S.-Western Europe Monetary and Trade Relations, 1958–1984.* Totowa, N.J.: Rowman and Allenheld, 1985.

Inglehart, Ronald. "Public Opinion and Regional Integration." 24 *International Organization* (Fall 1970), 764–795.

International Political Communities: An Anthology. New York: Doubleday, 1966.

Ionescu, Ghita. *The New Politics of European Integration*. New York: Macmillan, 1972.

Jackson, Robert, and Fitzmaurice, John. *The European Parliament: A Guide to Direct Elections*. New York: Penguin, 1979.

Jacobs, Francis G., ed. *European Law and the Individual*. Amsterdam: North Holland, 1976.

Jensen, Finn B., and Walter, Ingo. *The Common Market: Economic Integration in Europe*. Philadelphia: J. B. Lippincott, 1966.

John, Ievan, ed. *EEC Policy Toward Eastern Europe*. Aldershot, Hants, UK: Saxon House, 1975.

Jordan, Robert S., and Feld, Werner J. *Europe in the Balance*. London: Faber & Faber, 1986.

Keating, Michael, and Jones, Barry, eds. *Regions in the European Community*. Oxford: Clarendon Press, 1985.

Kelleher, Catherine M., and Mattox, Gale A., eds. *Evolving European Defense Policies*. Lexington, Mass.: Lexington Books, 1986.

Kerr, Anthony J. C. *The Common Market and How It Works*. Elmsford, N.Y.: Pergamon, 1983.

Kirchner, Emil J. *The European Parliament: Performance and Prospects*. Aldershot, Hants, UK: Gower, 1984.

———. *Public Service Unions and the European Community*. Aldershot, Hants, UK: Gower, 1983.

———. *Trade Unions as a Pressure Group in the European Community*. Aldershot, Hants, UK: Saxon House, 1977.

Kitzinger, Uwe. *Diplomacy and Persuasion: How Britain Joined the Common Market*. London: Thames & Hudson, 1973.

———. *The Politics and Economics of European Integration: Britain, Europe and the U.S.* New York: Praeger, 1963.

Klaassen, L. H., and Molle, Willem. *Industrial Mobility and Migration in the European Community*. Aldershot, Hants, UK: Gower, 1983.

Knox, Francis. *The Common Market and World Agriculture: Trade Patterns in Temperate-zone Foodstuffs*. New York: Praeger, 1972.

Knudsen, Baard B. *Europe versus America: Foreign Policy in the 1980s*. Totowa, N.J.: Rowman and Allenheld, 1985.

Kohnstamm, Max, and Hager, Wolfgang, eds. *A Nation Writ Large? Foreign Policy Problems Before the European Community*. New York: Wiley, 1973.

Korah, Valentine. *Competition Law of Britain and the Common Market*. The Hague: Martinus Nijhoff, 1982.

Kraft, Joseph. *The Grand Design: From Common Market to Atlantic Partnership*. New York: Harper and Row, 1962.

Krause, Lawrence B. *European Economic Integration and the United States*. Washington, D.C.: Brookings Institution, 1968.

Krauss, M., ed. *The Economics of Integration*. London: Allen & Unwin, 1973.

Kruse, D. C. *Monetary Integration in Western Europe: EMU, EMS and Beyond*. Sevenoaks, Kent, UK: Butterworth, 1980.

Lambert, John. *Britain in a Federal Europe*. London: Chatto and Windus, 1968.

Lambrindis, John S. *The Structure, Function and Law of a Free Trade Area*. London: Stevens, 1965.

Lamfallusy, A. *The United Kingdom and the Six*. Homewood, Ill.: Richard Irwin, 1963.

Lang, J. T. *The Common Market and Common Law*. Chicago: University of Chicago Press, 1966.

Lasok, K. P. E. *The European Court of Justice: Practice and Procedure*. Sevenoaks, Kent, UK: Butterworth, 1984.

Lawrence, R. *Primary Products, Preference and Economic Welfare: The EEC and Africa*. New York: Longman, 1974.

Layton, C. *Cross-Frontier Mergers in Europe*. Bath, UK: Bath University Press, 1971.

———. *European Advanced Technology*. London: Allen & Unwin, 1969.

Leigh, Michael. *European Integration and the Common Fisheries Policy*. Beckenham, Kent, UK: Croom Helm, 1983.

Lerner, Daniel, and Gorden, Morton. *Euratlantica: Changing Perspectives of the European Elite*. Cambridge, Mass.: MIT Press, 1969.

Lewenhak, Sheila. *The Role of the European Investment Bank*. Beckenham, Kent, UK: Croom Helm, 1982.

Lieber, Robert J. *British Politics and European Unity: Parties, Elites and Pressure Groups*. Berkeley, Calif.: University of California Press, 1970.

———. "European Elite Attitudes Revisited: The Future of the European Community and European-American Relations." 5 *British Journal of Political Science* (July 1975), 323–340.

———. *Oil and the Middle East War: Europe in the Energy Crisis*. Cambridge, Mass.: Harvard Center for International Affairs, 1976.

Lijphart, Arend. "Tourist Traffic and Integration Potential." 2 *Journal of Common Market Studies* (March 1964), 251–262.

Lind, Harold, and Flockton, Christopher. *Regional Policy in Britain and the Six*. London: Chatham House-PEP, 1970.

Lindberg, Leon N. *The Political Dynamics of European Economic Integration*. Stanford, Calif.: Stanford University Press, 1963.

———. "Political Integration as a Multidimensional Phenomenon Requiring Multivariate Measurement." 24 *International Organization* (Fall 1970), 649–731.

Lindberg, Leon N., and Scheingold, Stuart A. *Europe's Would-Be Polity: Patterns of Change in the European Community*. New York: Prentice-Hall, 1970.

Lindberg, Leon N., and Scheingold, Stuart A., eds. *Regional Integration: Theory and Research*. Cambridge, Mass.: Harvard University Press, 1971.

Lindsay, Kenneth, ed. *European Assemblies: The Experimental Period, 1949–1959*. London: Stevens, 1960.

Lippmann, Walter. *Western Unity and the Common Market*. Boston: Little, Brown, 1962.

Lipstein, K. *The Law of the European Economic Community*. Sevenoaks, Kent, UK: Butterworth, 1974.

Lister, Louis. *Europe's Coal and Steel Community*. New York: Twentieth Century Fund, 1960.

Lodge, Juliet. *The European Community and New Zealand*. London: Frances Pinter, 1982.

———, ed. *The European Community: Bibliographical Excursions*. London: Frances Pinter, 1983.

———. *The European Policy of the SPD*. Beverly Hills, Calif.: Sage, 1976.

———, ed. *European Union: The European Community in Search of a Future*. New York: St. Martin's Press, 1986.

————, ed. *Institutions and Policies of the European Community*. New York: St. Martin's Press, 1986.

Long, Frank. *The Political Economy of EEC Relations with African, Caribbean and Pacific States*. Elmsford, N.Y.: Pergamon, 1980.

Mackenzie-Stuart, Lord. *The European Communities and the Rule of Law*. London: Stevens, 1977.

Maclachan, D., and Swann, Dennis. *Competition Policy in the European Community*. New York: Oxford University Press, 1967.

Madariaga, S. de. *Portrait of Europe*. London: Hollis & Carter, 1967.

Magnifico, Giovanni. *European Monetary Unification*. New York: Wiley, 1973.

Mally, Gerhard. *The European Community in Perspective: The New Europe, the United States, and the World*. Lexington, Mass.: D. C. Heath, 1973.

Mann, C. J. *The Function of Judicial Decision in European Economic Integration*. The Hague: Martinus Nijhoff, 1972.

Marquand, David. *Parliament for Europe*. London: Jonathan Cape, 1979.

Marsh, John, and Ritson, C. *Agricultural Policy and the Common Market*. London: Chatham House-PEP, 1971.

Marsh, John, and Swanney, Pamela J. *Agriculture and the European Community*. London: Allen & Unwin, 1980.

Maull, Hans. *Europe and World Energy*. Sevenoaks, Kent, UK: Butterworth, 1980.

Mayne, Richard J. *The Community of Europe*. London: Gollancz, 1963.

————. *The Europeans*. London: Weidenfeld & Nicolson, 1970.

————. *The Recovery of Europe*. New York: Harper and Row, 1970.

————. "The Role of Jean Monnet." 2 *Government and Opposition* (April-July 1967), 349–371.

Meade, J. E. *The Theory of Customs Unions*. Amsterdam: North Holland, 1955.

Meade, J. E. et al. *Case Studies in European Economic Union: The Mechanics of Integration*. New York: Oxford University Press, 1962.

Merlini, Cesare, ed. *Economic Summits and Western Decision-Making*. New York: St. Martin's Press, 1984.

Merritt, Robert L., and Puchala, Donald J., eds. *Western European Attitudes on Arms Control, Defense and European Unity, 1952–1963*. New Haven, Conn.: Yale University Press, 1966.

Meyer, F. V. *The European Free Trade Association*. New York: Praeger, 1960.

Michelmann, Hans J. *Organizational Effectiveness in a Multinational Bureaucracy*. Aldershot, Hants, UK: Saxon House, 1978.

Milward, Alan. *The Reconstruction of Western Europe*. New York: Methuen, 1984.

Molle, Willem. *Industrial Location and Regional Development in the European Community: The FLEUR Model*. Aldershot, Hants, UK: Gower, 1983.

Monnet, Jean. *Memoirs*. New York: Doubleday, 1978.

Morgan, A. *From Summit to Council: Evolution in the EEC*. London: Chatham House-PEP, 1976.

Morgan, Roger. *The Shaping of the European Community: West European Politics Since 1945*. London: Batsford, 1972.

Morgan, Roger, and Bray, Caroline, eds. *Partners and Rivals in Western Europe: Britain, France and Germany*. Aldershot, Hants, UK: Gower, 1986.

Mowat, R. C. *Creating the European Community*. Poole, U.K.: Blandford Press, 1973.

Nelson, Charles G. "European Integration: Trade Data and Measurement Problems." 28 *International Organization* (Summer 1974), 399–433.

Newhouse, John. *Collision in Brussels: The Common Market Crisis of 30 June 1965*. New York: W. W. Norton, 1967.

Niblock, Michael. *The European Economic Community: National Parliaments in Community Decision-Making*. London: PEP, 1971.

Nurick, Robert, ed. *Nuclear Weapons and European Security*. New York: St. Martin's Press, 1985.

Nye, Joseph S., Jr. "Comparative Regional Integration: Concept and Measurement." 22 *International Organization* (Fall 1968), 855–880.

Nystrom, Warren J., and Malof, Peter. *The Common Market: European Community in Action*. New York: Van Nostrand, 1962.

O'Keeffe, David, and Schermers, Henry G. *Essays in European Law and Integration*. Dordrecht: Kluwer, 1982.

Okigbo, P. N. C. *Africa and the Common Market*. New York: Longman, 1967.

O'Nuallain, C., ed. *The Presidency of the European Council of Ministers*. Beckenham, Kent, UK: Croom Helm, 1985.

Oudenhove, G. van. *The Political Parties in the European Parliament*. Leyden: Sijthoff, 1965.

Palmer, Michael. *The European Parliament: What It Is, What It Does, and How It Works*. Elmsford, N.Y.: Pergamon, 1981.

Parker, Geoffrey. *A Dictionary of the European Communities*. Sevenoaks, Kent, UK: Butterworth, 1981.

———. *A Political Geography of Community Europe*. Sevenoaks, Kent, UK: Butterworth, 1983.

Parry, A., and Hardy, S. *EEC Law*. London: Sweet & Maxwell, 1973.

Paterson, W. E. *The SPD and European Integration*. Aldershot, Hants, UK: Saxon House, 1974.

Patijn, S., ed. *Landmarks in European Unity: 22 Texts on European Integration*. Leyden: Sijthoff, 1970.

Pegg, Carl H. *Evolution of the European Idea: 1914–1932*. Chapel Hill, N.C.: University of North Carolina Press, 1983.

Pendergast, William R. "Roles and Attitudes of French and Italian Delegates to the European Community." 30 *International Organization* (Fall 1976), 669–677.

Pentland, C. *International Theory and European Integration*. London: Faber & Faber, 1973.

Peterson, R. L. "Personnel Decisions and the Independence of the Commission of the European Communities." 10 *Journal of Common Market Studies* (December 1971), 117–137.

Prewo, Wilfried. "Integration Effects in the EEC: An Attempt at Quantification in a General Equilibrium Framework." 5 *European Economic Review* (1974), 379–405.

Price, Harry B. *The Marshall Plan and Its Meaning*. Ithaca, N.Y.: Cornell University Press, 1955.

Pridham, Geoffrey, and Pridham, Pippa. *Transnational Party Co-operation and European Integration: The Process Toward Direct Elections*. London: Allen & Unwin, 1981.

Pryce, Roy. *The Politics of the European Community*. Totowa, N.J.: Rowman & Littlefield, 1973.

Puchala, Donald J. "The Common Market and Political Federation in Western European Public Opinion." 14 *International Studies Quarterly* (March 1970), 32–59.

———. "Domestic Politics and Regional Harmonization in the European Communities." 27 *World Politics* (July 1975), 496–520.

———. *Fiscal Harmonization in the European Communities: National Politics and International Cooperation.* London: Frances Pinter, 1984.

———. "Integration and Disintegration in Franco-German Relations, 1954–1965." 24 *International Organization* (Spring 1970), 183–208.

———. "Patterns in West European Integration." 9 *Journal of Common Market Studies* (December 1970), 117–142.

Ravenhill, John. *Collective Clientelism: The Lomé Conventions and North-South Relations.* New York: Columbia University Press, 1985.

Reif, Karlheinz, ed. *Ten European Elections.* Aldershot, Hants, UK: Gower, 1985.

Robertson, A. H. *European Institutions: Cooperation, Integration, Unification.* London: Stevens, 1973.

Rogers, Rosemarie, ed. *Guests Come to Stay: The Effects of European Labor Migration on Sending and Receiving Countries.* Boulder, Colo.: Westview, 1985.

Rogers, S. J., and Davey, B. H. *The Common Agricultural Policy and Britain.* Lexington, Mass.: D. C. Heath, 1973.

Rolfe, Edmund N. *The Politics of Agriculture in the EC.* London: PEP, 1984.

Rosenthal, Glenda G. *The Mediterranean Basin: Its Political Economy and Changing International Relations.* Sevenoaks, Kent, UK: Butterworth, 1982.

———. *The Men Behind the Decisions.* Lexington, Mass.: D. C. Heath, 1975.

Rosenthal, Glenda G., and Puchala, Donald J. "Decisional Systems, Adaptiveness, and European Decision-Making." 440 *Annals of the American Academy of Political and Social Science* (November 1978), 54–66.

Rothacher, Albrecht. *Economic Diplomacy Between the European Community and Japan, 1959–1981.* Aldershot, Hants, UK: Gower, 1983.

Rougemont, D. de. *The Idea of Europe.* New York: Macmillan, 1967.

Rybczynski, T. M., ed. *The Value Added Tax: The U.K. Position and the European Experience.* London: Basil Blackwell, 1969.

Sargent, J. R., ed. *Europe and the Dollar in the World-Wide Disequilibrium.* Rockville, Md.: Alphen-Rijn, 1981.

Sasse, Christoph et al. *Decision Making in the European Community.* New York: Praeger, 1977.

Scalingi, Paula. *The European Parliament.* Westport, Conn.: Greenwood Press, 1980.

Schaetzel, R. J. *The Unhinged Alliance: America and the European Community.* New York: Harper and Row, 1975.

Scheingold, Stuart A. *The Rule of Law in European Integration: The Path of the Schuman Plan.* New Haven, Conn.: Yale University Press, 1965.

Schermers, Henry G. *Judicial Protection in the European Communities.* Dordrecht: Kluwer, 1979.

Schmidt, Peter. *Europeanization of Defense: Prospects of Consensus?* Santa Monica, Calif.: Rand, 1985.

Schmitt, Hans. "Capital Markets and the Unification of Europe." 20 *World Politics* (January 1968), 228–244.

———. *The Path to European Union: From the Marshall Plan to the Common Market.* Baton Rouge, La.: Louisiana State University Press, 1962.

Schofield, Norman, ed. *Crisis in Economic Relations Between North and South*. Alder-shot, Hants, UK: Gower, 1984.

Scitovsky, Tibor. *Economic Theory and Western European Integration*. Stanford, Calif.: Stanford University Press, 1958.

Seers, Dudley et al. *Underdeveloped Europe: Studies in Core-Periphery Relationships*. Atlantic Highlands, N.J.: Humanities Press, 1979.

Seers, Dudley; Vaitsos, Constantine; and Kiljunen, Marja-Liisa, eds. *The Second Enlargement of the EEC: The Integration of Unequal Partners*. New York: St. Martin's Press, 1982.

Serfaty, Simon. *France, de Gaulle, and Europe: The Policy of the Fourth and Fifth Republics Toward the Continent*. Baltimore, Md.: Johns Hopkins University Press, 1968.

Shanks, Michael. *European Social Policy: Today and Tomorrow*. Elmsford, N.Y.: Pergamon, 1977.

Shanks, Michael, and Lambert, John. *The Common Market Today—and Tomorrow*. New York: Praeger, 1962.

Shepherd, R. J. *Public Opinion and European Integration*. Aldershot, Hants, UK: Saxon House, 1975.

Shlaim, Avi, and Yannopoulos, G. N., eds. *The EEC and the Mediterranean Countries*. Cambridge, UK: Cambridge University Press, 1976.

Silj, Alessandro. *Europe's Political Puzzle: A Study of the Fourchet Negotiations and the 1963 Veto*. Lanham, Md.: University Press of America, 1984.

Simonian, Haig. *The Privileged Partnership: Franco-German Relations in the European Community, 1969–1982*. Oxford: Clarendon Press, 1985.

Snyder, Francis G. *Law of the Common Agricultural Policy*. London: Sweet and Maxwell, 1985.

Spinelli, Altiero. "Atlantic Pact or European Unity?" 40 *Foreign Affairs* (July 1962), 542–552.

———. *The Eurocrats*. Baltimore, Md.: Johns Hopkins University Press, 1966.

Stordel, Harry. *The Lomé Convention and a New International Economic Order*. Leyden: Sijthoff, 1977.

Sumner, M., and Zis, G., eds. *European Monetary Union: Progress and Prospects*. New York: St. Martin's Press, 1982.

Sumners, Robert E. *Economic Aid to Europe: The Marshall Plan*. New York: H. W. Wilson, 1948.

Swann, Dennis. *Competition and Industrial Policy in the European Community*. New York: Methuen, 1983.

———. *The Economics of the Common Market*. New York: Penguin, 1972.

Sweet & Maxwell's Legal Editorial Staff, eds. *European Community Treaties*, 2nd ed. London: Sweet & Maxwell, 1975.

Talbot, R. F. *The Chicken War: An International Trade Conflict between the United States and the EEC*. Ames, Iowa: Iowa State University Press, 1978.

———. *The European Community's Regional Fund*. Elmsford, N.Y.: Pergamon, 1977.

Taylor, Paul. *The Limits of European Integration*. Beckenham, Kent, UK: Croom Helm, 1983.

Taylor, Trevor. *European Defence Cooperation*. London: Routledge & Kegan Paul, 1985.

Toth, A. *Legal Protection of Individuals in the European Community*. Amsterdam: North Holland, 1978.

Tracy, Michael. *Agriculture and Western Europe: Crisis and Adaptation Since 1880.* London: Jonathan Cape, 1964.

Trezise, Philip H., ed. *The European Monetary System: Promise and Prospects.* Washington, D.C.: Brookings Institution, 1979.

Tsoukalis, Loukas. *The European Community and Its Mediterranean Enlargement.* London: Allen & Unwin, 1981.

———, ed. *Greece and the European Community.* Lexington, Mass.: Lexington Books, 1979.

———. *The Politics and Economics of European Monetary Integration.* London: Allen & Unwin, 1977.

Twitchett, Carol C. *A Framework for Development: The EEC and the ACP.* London: Allen & Unwin, 1981.

Twitchett, Kenneth J., ed. *Europe and the World: The External Relations of the Common Market.* New York: St. Martin's Press, 1976.

Uri, Pierre, ed. *From Commonwealth to Common Market.* New York: St. Martin's Press, 1968.

Usher, John. *European Community Law and National Law.* London: Allen & Unwin, 1981.

Valentine, Alan. "BENELUX: Pilot Plan of Economic Union." 44 *The Yale Review* (September 1954), 23–32.

Valentine, D. G. *The Court of Justice of the European Communities.* London: Stevens, 1965.

Vandamme, Jacques, ed. *New Dimensions in European Social Policy.* Beckenham, Kent, UK: Croom Helm, 1985.

Vaughan, R. *Post-War Integration in Europe.* London: Edward Arnold, 1976.

Viner, J. *The Customs Union Issue.* New York: Carnegie Endowment for International Peace, 1950.

Voelker, E., ed. *Protectionism and the European Community.* Dordrecht: Kluwer, 1983.

Vree, J. K. *Political Integration: The Formation of Theory and Its Problems.* The Hague: Mouton, 1972.

Wall, E. H. *The Court of Justice of the European Communities.* Sevenoaks, Kent, UK: Butterworth, 1966.

Wallace, Helen. *Budgetary Politics: The Finances of the European Communities.* London: Allen & Unwin, 1980.

———. "The Impact of the European Communities on National Policy-Making." 6 *Government and Opposition* (Fall 1971), 520–538.

———. *National Governments and the European Communities.* London: Chatham House-PEP, 1973.

Wallace, Helen; Wallace, William; and Webb, Carole, eds. *Policy-Making in the European Communities.* New York: Wiley, 1977.

Walsh, A. E., and Paxton, John. *Into Europe: The Structure and Development of the Common Market.* London: Hutchinson, 1972.

Walter, Ingo. *The European Common Market: Growth and Patterns of Trade and Production.* New York: Praeger, 1967.

Walton, Clarence C. "Background for the European Defense Community." 68 *Political Science Quarterly* (March 1953), 42–69.

Warnecke, Steven J. *The European Community in the 1970's.* New York: Praeger, 1972.

Wexler, Imanuel. *The Marshall Plan Revisited*. Westport, Conn.: Greenwood Press, 1983.

Williams, Roger. *European Technology: The Politics of Collaboration*. Beckenham, Kent, UK: Croom Helm, 1973.

Willis, F. Roy. *France, Germany and the New Europe: 1945–1967*. New York: Oxford University Press, 1969.

Wise, Mark. *The Common Fisheries Policy of the European Community*. New York: Methuen, 1984.

Woolcock, Stephen et al. *Interdependence in the Post-Multilateral Era: Trends in U.S.-European Trade Relations*. Lanham, Md.: University Press of America, 1985.

Wyatt, D., and Dashwood, A. *The Substantive Law of the EEC*. London: Sweet and Maxwell, 1980.

Young, S. Z. *Terms of Entry: Britain's Negotiations with the European Community, 1970–1972*. London: Heinemann, 1973.

Yuill, Douglas, ed. *Regional Development Agencies in Europe*. Aldershot, Hants, UK: Gower, 1982.

Zartman, William I. *The Politics of Trade Negotiations Between Africa and the European Economic Community: The Weak Confront the Strong*. Princeton, N.J.: Princeton University Press, 1971.

Zurcher, Arnold J. *The Struggle to Unite Europe: 1940–1958*. New York: New York University Press, 1958.

Index

About the Author

LEON HURWITZ is Professor of Political Science at Cleveland State University, Ohio. His earlier works include *Contemporary Approaches to European Integration*, *The State as Defendant*, *The Harmonization of European Public Policy*, and *Historical Dictionary of Censorship in the United States* (Greenwood Press, 1980, 1981, 1983, 1985) as well as *Introduction to Politics* and *International Organizations* (with Werner J. Feld and Robert S. Jordan). He has also published articles in the *Journal of Common Market Studies*, *Comparative Politics*, *Studies in Comparative Communism*, and *Comparative Political Studies*.